KATE MOSS

Laura Collins

KATE MOSS

The Complete Picture

SIDGWICK & JACKSON

First published 2008 by Sidgwick & Jackson
an imprint of Pan Macmillan Ltd
Pan Macmillan, 20 New Wharf Road, London N1 9RR
Basingstoke and Oxford
Associated companies throughout the world
www.panmacmillan.com

ISBN 978-0-283-07063-1 HB
ISBN 978-0-283-07074-7 TPB

Typeset by SetSystems Ltd, Saffron Walden, Essex
Printed in the UK by CPI Mackays, Chatham ME5 8TD

Visit www.panmacmillan.com to read more about all our books
and to buy them. You will also find features, author interviews and
news of any author events, and you can sign up for e-newsletters
so that you're always first to hear about our new releases.

To my husband Steve
with all my love

ACKNOWLEDGEMENTS

There are many people to whom I owe an enormous thank you for their help and advice over the course of writing this book.

My thanks to Ingrid Connell, my commissioning editor at Pan Macmillan – without her enthusiasm and conviction this book could not exist. The same is true of my literary agent, Pat Lomax.

My thanks too to Peter Wright, editor of the *Mail on Sunday* and deputy editor, Eric Bailey, whose support has been tremendous. And to Sian James, assistant editor and doyenne of the *Mail on Sunday* features department – the role she has played and the help she has given is simply too great to quantify or, I fear, ever fully repay.

To Elizabeth Sanderson, Racheline Benveniste, Fiona Cunningham and Fidelma Cook, thank you to each of you for the litres of wine and words of wisdom and for demonstrating such faith in my abilities that I actually began to believe I could do it.

PICTURE ACKNOWLEDGEMENTS

First Section

page 1: *top left* Rex Features, *top right* Rex Features, *bottom* © David Ross, 1998

2: www.celebritypictures.co.uk / Corinne Day

3: *top left* Big Pictures, *top right* Rex Features, *bottom* Corbis

4: PA Photos

5: Rex Features

6: *top* PA Photos, *bottom* Corbis

7: *top* Getty Images, *bottom* Corbis

8: *top left* Big Pictures, *top right* Rex Features, *bottom* Corbis

Second Section

page 1: *top* Rex Features, *bottom* Big Pictures

2: *top* Rex Features, *bottom left* Corbis, *bottom right* Rex Features

3: *top left* Getty Images, *top right* Rex Features, *bottom* Rex Features

4: *top* Corbis, *bottom* Getty Images

5: *top* Rex Features, *bottom* PA Photos

6: *top* Getty Images, *centre left* Big Pictures, *centre right* Getty Images

7: *top* Corbis, *bottom* Big Pictures

8: *top* Getty Images, *bottom* Rex Features

'You're a quaint little determinist,' laughed Anthony. 'It's your world, isn't it?'

'Well—' she said with a quick upward glance, 'isn't it? As long as I'm – young.'

She had paused slightly before the last word and Anthony suspected that she had started to say 'beautiful'. It was undeniably what she had intended.

Her eyes brightened and he waited for her to enlarge on the theme. He had drawn her out, at any rate – he bent forward slightly to catch the words.

But, 'Let's dance!' was all she said.

F. Scott Fitzgerald, *The Beautiful and Damned*

Prologue

On the afternoon of Friday 16 January 2004 I checked into Claridges Hotel in Mayfair. It was Kate Moss's thirtieth birthday and this was where she was staying. It was where she would return after a day and evening of celebrations. And it was where, word had it, her landmark birthday would culminate in the most decadent and intimate party of all, to be held in her seventh-floor penthouse suite.

For any likeminded person of my generation it promised to be the event of the decade. Kate, with all the glamour of wild excess that hung around her, was the party girl of the age. Her theme was *The Beautiful and Damned* – a throwback to a bygone era and the heyday of another hedonistic youth cult for which, it was rumoured, Kate and her friends were more than a match. Entry into the seventh-floor penthouse that night would offer a glimpse into her world. More importantly, it would offer an insight into the woman who, for all the photographs taken and gossip column inches filled, remained enigmatic and dazzling.

I was twenty-eight years old and determined to be there. I was a journalist living and working in London and relishing all the excitement and challenges that brought, and I hadn't checked into one of the most expensive hotels in the world to spend the night getting hit on by businessmen in the bar. I was going to have to steel myself against my natural anxieties and go for it. At least as a guest of the hotel I had a legitimate foot in the door. As the evening wore on, the film crews and reporters who had buzzed around the foyer since late afternoon were politely ejected from its tranquil luxury to join the paparazzi huddling outside in the biting January air.

Then, at 9.30p.m., the lift doors opened and a girlish giggle announced the arrival of the first twinkling figure in the lobby. The chatter of guests, who sipped drinks by the fire or relaxed in the hotel's vast atrium lounge, stilled and the air fizzed with the effort of their unified affectation of indifference. The excitable little crowd of intimate friends who bustled from lift to front door, guided by a deferential member of staff, just happened to include some of the most recognizable faces in the world. Among them was Marianne Faithfull, looking happy, if bemused, and Sadie Frost, giddy in a vermillion-red flapper dress. There was Naomi Campbell, who towered and shimmered like an unearthly bird of paradise; Jefferson Hack looking surprisingly prepossessing in a remorselessly tailored fitted white suit, and behind him, squeezing his hand and giggling, there was Kate – the most recognizable of them all. In life she was more delicate, in motion more graceful and in all much, much more beautiful than any of the many pictures of her ever quite conveyed.

Kate and her friends did come back to Claridges that night arriving, breathlessly, with Rolling Stone Ronnie Wood broadcasting their return by yelling, 'We're in fucking Claridges!' to an audience of night cleaners, impassive marble and me. I did get into Kate's penthouse celebration. There were no more than forty people there and I had slipped in under the radar. As I sucked on a vodka and tonic, I scanned the room and felt a jolt with each famous face I saw. They were unguarded and smiling. I smiled back. It was thrilling. As the hours passed and my fear of discovery subsided, a new and wholly unexpected thought occurred to me. How on earth could it be that in such a supposedly – even notoriously – tight circle of friends, a complete stranger could remain unchallenged?

The next five hours partying – chatting, laughing, smoking and drinking with this exclusive crowd – were both memorable and intriguing, because the Kate who danced across the penthouse suite that night was so far removed from the version of her found in the pages of magazines and newspapers. It was obvious that there was much more to her than the dissolute image offered up for public scrutiny. And after the music had stopped, the party guests had left and the next day's news had been written, read and forgotten, one thought would not leave me: when it came to the outside world's perception of Kate, this generous, isolated, excitable and exciting woman deserved a lot better.

That night in January became the first step of my journey to discover more about Kate, and this book is its culmination. It's a process that has taught me Kate can be petulant and spoilt and quite vicious. But she is also generous and creative, brimming with energy, loyal to her friends and capable of the sort of earnest endeavour, hunger for knowledge and self-betterment that would confound her many critics. Ted Hughes once wrote that we are all still children inside – 'unprotected, incapable, inexperienced. Every single person is vulnerable to unexpected defeat in this inmost emotional self. At every moment, behind the most efficient seeming adult exterior, the whole world of the person's childhood is being carefully held like a glass of water bulging above the rim. And in fact, that child is the only real thing in them.' If that is true of all of us, and I think it is, then it is powerfully so of Kate.

This is an unauthorized biography, but it has involved speaking to Kate's family, friends and business associates, in an effort to illuminate the complexities of the woman and the realities of her world. I am grateful to each and every one who agreed to speak to me, and I hope that they will recognize the portrait of Kate that they have helped me paint.

This is a story of triumph too often treated as failure, of hard graft and pot luck; a fairytale of sorts, a rise and fall and rise again. This is a story of outrageous success. This is the story of Kate Moss.

1

One look at Kate Moss's family tree is enough to dispel the notion that in life there is one true love for each of us.

For Kate, for her parents and for their parents before them, romantic love has proved fallible. It could neither last out life nor face down death, but it could be found and acted upon many times over.

It is an unsettling, if liberating, fact.

However seductive it might be to believe in the existence of 'the one', and however drawn to that thought Kate might once have been, a glance over her slight shoulders would inspire uncertainty in even the most fervent romantic. Kate would not be alive if it weren't possible to find more than one person to share a life with, or at least part of it.

Look back across any family tree and you'll find the mundane rigours of everyday life punctuated by pockets of light and moments of personal tragedy. The geography of relationships and lives are here, stapled to the pages of history with each certificate and official registration of moment. Here are the incidents and accidents that shape lives in the most profound sense: the span of a life distilled down to the space between a birth and death certificate. Hatches, matches, dispatches – it's as simple and as complicated as that.

Kate's maternal grandfather was George Frederick Shepherd, a greengrocer born in 1883 in Croydon. He was married, widowed and ready to marry once more by the age of forty-four. By 1927 George had struck up with the prettily named Emily Louisa Cresswell, a girl from Watford, twenty years his junior and the daughter of a greengrocer. They married on 1 August that year in Croydon Register Office. The groom wore a suit while the bride struggled to conceal her advanced state of pregnancy. Three months later, on 5 November 1927 the first of the couple's seven daughters was born. Twenty years later, on 8 September 1947, their last was born. Kate's mother, Linda Rosina Shepherd.

George was sixty-four by the time Linda arrived, so it was a rather ambitious hope that he would survive to see all of his daughters grown and married. In the event, he lived to see three settled before he succumbed to pneumonia on 6 September 1964 at the age of eighty-one and already having suffered a debilitating stroke. Linda's mother Emily registered his death on 7 September; the following day was Linda's seventeenth birthday.

Barely one mile and a handful of streets away Peter Moss was celebrating his twentieth birthday. It would be seven years before Peter and Linda married, but in the year her father died Linda unwittingly took one step closer to the man who would become her husband, as while she had to reconcile herself with the fact that her birthday would forever be linked to her father's death. Peter had lived his life in the knowledge that his birth had been the last great achievement of his mother's life.

Peter's father, Herbert Edward Moss, was a Post Office engineer and Sergeant with the Royal Signals. The son of a coal merchant's clerk Herbert was born and predominantly bred in

Wandsworth in south London. He fell in love with Queenie Louisa Stanbridge, two years his senior and the daughter of a railway ticket collector, from Camberwell. When they married on 19 December 1927 it was in Wiltshire, at Buckford Camp, where the then twenty-two-year-old Herbert was stationed, in a ceremony witnessed by two of his regiment. Perhaps her parents didn't approve of the match. Perhaps it was his mother – his father was dead by then – who had her reservations. Or perhaps the young couple were simply eager to marry and got carried away by the romantic notion of elopement. Whatever the case, Herbert and Queenie set up home in North Cheam, and within two years of marriage celebrated the birth of their first child, a son, Edward. Ten years later, in 1939, Queenie gave birth to a girl, Janet, and on 31 August 1944 Peter Edward Moss was born. Fourteen months after Peter's birth his mother died of cancer.

Little is known of Queenie, but she was a remarkable woman in the Moss dynasty. There is every probability that the cancer that killed her took hold when she was carrying Kate's father, and if that were so she must have faced an awful choice: undergo treatment and jeopardize the life of her unborn child or make the ultimate sacrifice and risk her own life for that of her baby.

However sentient the sacrifice Queenie made and however heroic the treatment that followed quickly after Peter's birth, one thing is certain: Queenie died just over one year later on 28 October 1945 at the age of forty-three, leaving Herbert, then forty-one, with three children to raise alone. He would not have to do so for long.

On 13 September 1947 Herbert married telephone receptionist Joan Muriel Padden. This time the wedding was not the breathtaking dash of two decades earlier but a ceremony conducted at the couple's parish church of St Mary's in Beddington. Within a year, four-year-old Peter was no longer the baby of the Moss family. Joan and Herbert had two children together, Christine, born the year after their marriage, and Alan, who arrived two years later in 1950.

It cannot have been easy for Joan, thirty years old when she married Herbert, to become an instant mother of three. When she did so, two years after Queenie's death, Herbert's eldest child was eighteen, the little girl just eight and Kate's father, Peter, only one year old, yet there is nothing to suggest that Joan did not love Queenie and Herbert's children as her own. Certainly Peter would grow up to be a man of notable intelligence and charm, suggesting he was secure in the love of the woman who was the only mother he ever knew.

Linda met Peter at a mutual friend's twenty-first birthday party in Croydon. For years they had lived within streets of each other, but finally on that evening they met. They made a handsome couple. Linda had long tawny hair, pale, wide-set eyes and an undeniable sense of style – at the time she was selling hair accessories for Carmen – while Peter was three years her senior, tall, debonair and working as a ticket clerk with American airline Pan Am. It was a job with a certain glamour by proxy, one that seemed to place the world beyond the streets of Croydon within touching distance. When they married it was also at St Mary's Church, Beddington. There is nothing to suggest that either Linda or Peter were particularly religious, but the church had, by then, a place in the Moss family history and its beautiful chapel was made even more so that day by the scent of the spring flowers that filled it.

Peter and Linda married on Saturday 17 April 1971 in a service conducted by the church's affable rector, John Hanson Read. Linda wore a pale dress suit rather than a traditional long white gown and was given away by her uncle, Frederick Cresswell. On the marriage certificate her occupation is given, rather aspirationally, as 'boutique manageress', since by then she was managing a local clothes shop. She was only twenty-three years old, so why should she not aspire to something wonderful?

Peter was twenty-six, good-looking, hard working and loved her just as she loved him. They had grown up so close to each other without ever meeting that it must have seemed kismet that finally they had. And perhaps it was, for a while at least.

Katherine Ann Moss was born three years later on 16 January 1974 at St Mary's Maternity Hospital, Croydon. She weighed 7lb 1oz and her parents were thrilled beyond expression. A few days later Peter took his wife and newborn child back home to the semi-detached house barely five minutes away from the house where Linda had been born and grew up. At times the young mother must surely have wondered how her life could change so wonderfully and irreversibly with the birth of her daughter and yet, geographically, not change at all.

There were, of course, holidays to enjoy. Thanks to Peter's job in the travel industry he and Linda travelled abroad more than their contemporaries and ten months after Kate's birth they took her on her first holiday abroad for some winter sun. It was blissful.

Kate spent much of holiday covered from the sun, a little yellow sunhat plopped like a fabric bucket over the cloud of blonde hair that would darken over the years. Days were spent by the hotel swimming pool, with Linda keeping a careful eye on Kate, holding her steady as she sat by the water's edge and dipped her toes in the warm water. It was a package deal, nothing extravagant or ostentatious, and it was just what the young family needed. That year Christmas was spent back in Croydon. Life was good.

As Kate grew, she showed a streak of what could most flatteringly be described as independence. To a mother at the end of her tether she presented something of a challenge and according to Linda, 'Kate was always her own person with her own mind. She developed her personality quite young. She wasn't one of those children who, if you told her off, would start crying. She was quite defiant.'

In the spring of 1976 Linda learned that she was pregnant once more, and in November Nicholas Peter Moss was born, completing the family. Both Linda and Peter had come from large families – she one of seven, he one of five – but it was not a family tradition they were keen to continue. With a second child the rhythm of the household changed. Kate, a smiling, chubby little girl, may not have been entirely delighted by the attention being given to the new arrival – what two-year-old would be? – and it didn't help that, unlike his sister, Nick howled and cried and was a fractious baby and infant. For Kate's father, Peter, a light sleeper almost to the point of insomnia – a trait his daughter would sometimes share – those early months must have been a trying time since he worked long hours, often returning home after seven o'clock. But it was worth it, wasn't it? They were, after all, a happy and successful family, and they did what happy, successful families do. They looked after their garden, a series of terraces and rockeries sloping steeply up behind the house to woodland beyond, and at the weekend they would bundle the children into the family car and take day trips.

It has been written in newspapers and magazines – always with a heavily judgemental tone – that the young Mrs Moss 'seemed to have a lot of spare time', in contrast to her husband Peter's work schedule, but it's a moot point how much 'spare time' a twenty-nine-year-old full-time mother of two pre-school children can have, and Linda was a devoted mother. When she was old enough Kate spent her mornings at a local playgroup and when she was older still she started school, carrying a home-made shoe-bag and wearing the grey skirt, yellow poloneck sweater, grey cardigan, socks and sensible T-bar shoes that constituted the uniform for Ridgeway Primary School.

On the morning of her first day Kate, like thousands of other five-year-olds across the land, stood in shy excitement at the front gates of the family home while her photograph was taken. By lunchtime she would be home again clutching a piece of artwork and full of chatter about the day's (or rather morning's) events. For the first few weeks school was a part-time affair as she and her classmates were eased into the notion of full-time education, and barely ten years later school returned to a part-time affair for Kate as she, and some of her classmates, eased themselves *out* of the notion of full-time education and discovered the adolescent joys of bunking off.

In January 1980 Kate was just six years old and had completed her first term at school. The most momentous thing that happened to her that year was a family holiday to Disney World in Orlando. Life for a six-year-old lasts forever and passes in a blur. Days flash by and hours stretch out agonizingly as the sun shines beyond the classroom window. A four-year-old brother is a much-loved annoyance. Ailments and upsets can be soothed away with a mother's cuddle and kiss. Weekends consist of Saturday morning ballet lessons and visits to grandparents. Ecstasy is the giddy fun of dressing up in your mother's shoes, trying on her jewellery, thrusting your fingers into her pots of eyeshadow, smearing the powdered colour over your lids and blinking back at the result in the mirror. Special is something you are made to feel by the people who love you, not something that strangers insist you are, as became the case for Kate in later years. News is boring, world events are irrelevant . . . only they're not.

Because as Kate settled into the routine of term times and school holidays, thousands of miles away the opening scenes of an era were being played out, an era that would reach its denouement nearly a decade on and come to a close with the discovery of something new: Kate.

The excesses of the Eighties came hurtling out of the dying days of the Seventies. In 1980 the cultural era to which Kate would provide a startling antidote had begun. *Dallas*, with its self-seeking, avaricious cast of characters and high gloss, high camp, was the most talked-about programme on television. Wealth was pointless unless it was conspicuous. In New York, Donald Trump opened the revamped Commodore Hotel as the Grand Hyatt: 14,000 rooms of luxury sheathed in a smoked-glass skyscraper. And, most relevant and significant for Kate and her own future, American supermodel Gia Carangi was at the peak of success, having featured on the cover *Vogue* that year. She was everything a top-flight model was meant to be at the time – voluptuous in figure and feature, tall, athletic and powerful. This was the image that Eighties consumers wanted.

They neither knew nor, one imagines, wanted to know that the picture-perfect Gia was addicted to heroin. Six years later that unpalatable truth was impossible to ignore. In 1986 Gia gained the unenviable distinction of being one of the first famous women to die of AIDS – or at least the first to be recorded as having done so. She was twenty-six years old.

By the latter half of the Eighties, the decade's lifestyle was seen to be literally killing people. For Kate, it was a development that was both beneficial and detrimental: she gained from the simple fact that she was the physical antithesis of all that had gone before, but she suffered because once the glitzy Eighties had been exposed as tarnished, people saw darkness everywhere. When Kate appeared in *Vogue* in June 1993 modelling underwear in her London flat, critics condemned the images of her as the epitome of 'heroin-chic'. They were not. The real heroin chic had come thirteen years earlier in the buxom, apparently healthy figure of Gia. Had it come in a different guise, however, Kate might never have garnered such favour or hostility.

In 1980, the public simply weren't ready for some things, as designer Calvin Klein was to discover. That year he took a fifteen-year-old ingénue and made her the face of his jeans. The adverts were met with outrage, described as 'kiddie porn', and banned by American network CBS's flagship channel, WCBS. The fifteen-year-old was Brooke Shields and the advert that provoked such good old-fashioned North American moral indignation showed Brooke in cowboy boots, jeans and a chocolate-brown shirt, crouched cat-like in a white studio. Her head is tilted to one side and her glossy hair is so long that it sweeps over one shoulder and falls over the other to the floor. 'You wanna know what comes between me and my Calvins?' she asks. 'Nothing.'

Klein withdrew the campaign, but he didn't abandon his hunger for all things new. He had simply played his hand too soon and with the wrong girl. An ocean, and what might as well have been a lifetime, away the *right* girl was living her life in oblivion . . . well, in South Croydon. She could not imagine the world outside the safe lines within which her life had, so far, been drawn. Nor could she imagine the events that would violently rub them out with more immediacy and potency than anything fame or fashion had to offer.

Kate completed primary school with no particular distinction or shame. She was a sweet little girl whose most daring moment to date was an abortive attempt to pierce her ears with a sewing needle borrowed from the school's needlework room. She acted in school plays but was shy in front of the audience and far happier putting on impromptu shows with her little friends for the benefit of nobody in particular except the general hilarity of all involved.

In 1986 Kate started the local secondary school, Riddlesdown High. She and Helene, with whom she had been firm friends since infancy when their mothers met and chatted in a supermarket aisle, sat side by side in the large school hall as it was decided what form classes the new arrivals would be placed in. Kate was nervous and shy and the girls swore to look after each other. They chatted to another new girl, Claire, and the three would remain friends throughout their school days and, as much as their disparate lives would permit, beyond.

It would be three years before her brother, Nick, followed in Kate's wake and started secondary school. Because of where their birthdays fell in relation to the school calendar the academic gap between them was larger than their age difference, so for a while at least Kate was on her own, a prospect that must have felt like something of a mixed blessing.

Brother and sister had always had what could best be

described as a tempestuous relationship. When he was really little Kate, by virtue of her seniority and comparative size, treated Nick like a plaything, though not always a particularly loved one. He endured the classic sisterly humiliations of being dressed in girls' clothing, pinned down and spat at or tied up and left whining while she went off to play with her friends. In retaliation he would lunge into his sister's bedroom and tear her Blondie posters off the walls. Deborah Harry was Kate's first pop idol and hers was the first album Kate ever bought. Nick's actions would invariably provoke howls of rage from his sister, and on more than one occasion, running 'mousse fights' through the house. Often these ended with both exhausted, giggling and friends again. For all the sibling rivalry and irritation that passed between them they loved each other dearly and Nick has recalled Kate as a 'protective big sister'.

At school Kate's favourite subjects were English and Drama – not because she particularly loved them, but because they were subjects in which, by her estimation, 'you never had to do anything'. She was pretty, though not stunning by the standards of most teenage boys. She was flat chested and incredibly skinny and was known as 'Stick' though it was 'Mosschops' or 'Katie Mosschops' that really stuck as an affectionate playground nickname.

Kate's recollections of those early high school days are of having her period every week to skip games, of smoking – cigarettes and pot – and drinking cans of Super Tennants or bottles of cider. 'We used to go to people's houses and steal their mum's booze. On the way to school. Anytime. Some bloke would have brought it in a bag from his dad's stash. We used to go to Tesco and nick things – well, I never would do it but my friends used to and I'd stand there and watch.'

'Literally,' she once admitted years later with the hint of a teenage boast, 'my parents let us do what we wanted. I was smoking when I was thirteen in front of my parents and drinking. I'd have parties when I'd come in at three in the morning because someone chucked me out then. It's actually worked to my benefit, because you end up thinking for yourself because you know you're not rebelling against anything.'

Or, if you are, then nobody – not your parents nor your teachers – seems to be paying the slightest bit of attention. In later years Kate was forced to reflect on those adolescent indulgences with cigarettes and alcohol and perhaps rue her bullish refusal to countenance the notion that either might ever prove a problem.

'I was smoking pot then too,' she admitted. 'It's south London innit? I remember everyone at school going, "Oh God, she's a junkie." And I was just, "They don't even know what they're talking about." I suppose I was quite blasé about everything. I thought everyone was just making a fuss about nothing.'

Perhaps, more pertinently, Kate was simply postponing the moment when she, along with the rest of her family, would have to confront an unpalatable truth. After all, drink and drugs can soften reality to a background buzz; they can even erase it entirely for a time. Years later, Kate would admit, 'You stop growing when you start doing (drugs and drink) . . . because you don't deal with pain and stuff, you just go and turn to drink, so you don't grow.' Back then, perhaps, that – and suffering through classes with a thumping hangover – seemed a small price to pay for the blissful abandonment of the previous day and night. For by 1987, as Kate and her pals drank their cans of illicit booze, smoked their cigarettes and whooped, hollered and danced the school nights away, Linda and Peter were facing up to the pressing and painful reality that their marriage was at an end.

For Kate, Nick and their parents the day trips, Christmases and New Years welcomed in with the neighbours and being one big happy family were all but over, and the new reality ushered in with its demise would be a lot more complicated. It was a realization first acknowledged and, it seems, initially most powerfully felt by Linda. Perhaps as a result it is Linda who, publicly at least, seems to have shouldered the blame for the marriage's demise, though it was not as black and white as all that. It was Linda who met somebody else and asked for a trial separation, and she who would find herself the subject of disapproving gossip, rumour and speculation. In later years, the family events of 1987–88 as the Moss household imploded, would be offered up as explanation for any scrape, difficulty or upset in Kate's adult life. Linda is well aware that the implication in many a newspaper report and magazine feature has always been that she, as Kate's mother, is the reason Kate is the way she is. The tone is inescapably negative in spite of Kate's considerable success and achievements and such an attribution of guilt is very unfair.

It is worth noting that Kate's parents were married for seventeen years, and that this was no fickle fad or phase in either of their lives. When they married, Linda was twenty-three and working in a boutique. More than a decade on, Peter had done well in his chosen career and was working as a travel consultant. Linda's life, on the other hand, was less satisfying. She was a mother but found no great satisfaction in being a housewife and was never, by any stretch of the imagination, an 'earth mother'. She loved her husband and children, but life was too safe, mundane and frankly a little boring. She craved excitement. She was, after all, still in her thirties, though only just.

When Kate was approaching secondary school and Nick was happily settled, Linda took a job as a barmaid and waitress in a local brasserie. It was something to do, something to be interested in, a way out of the confines of a life that, to an observer, might seem perfectly blessed.

It is remarkable how swiftly a long-drawn-out dissatisfaction can be brought to a resolution. In taking that job Linda took a path that would lead to Geoffrey Collman and the end of her marriage – or at least to a palpable reason for it. It would be hard to imagine a man more different to her 'safe' husband. One of his long-term acquaintances recalls fondly, 'Geoff is like a white-collar Del Boy Trotter, only he drives a Porsche, not a Robin Reliant.' Geoff was good-looking, racy, a bit outrageous and able to turn a phrase as quickly as he could turn a pound.

Linda had not gone looking for love. She had, if anything, gone looking for something that might stem her boredom and save the marriage she must have known was disintegrating around her. It was not something that either she, or Peter, let go of easily, but there was a lot of emotional upheaval in Linda's life at the time. On 2 January 1988 her mother died, having been ill with cancer for some time. Grief and relief at an end to her suffering would have been a natural response; so too would an intense realization of life's brevity.

Linda asked Peter for a trial separation to 'give each other space and time'. Peter thought his wife was simply bored and dissatisfied. But the separation solved nothing and probably brought out into the open insecurities, dissatisfaction and pent-up frustrations harboured for years. It was over. There was no going forwards or back.

So began the process of dismantling a life, a family and, for Kate and Nick, a world. The family home was put up for sale. Peter found a home in nearby Purley, Linda a maisonette in

Forestdale, a 1960s Croydon suburb of cul-de-sacs and neigh-bourhoods, where Geoffrey joined her. But before the family home was divided up and packed away, the business of custody had to be agreed. Neither Linda nor Peter wanted their children to suffer any more than was inevitable, but it is clear that they could not come to an amicable decision on their own, as Kate recalls: 'A man came round and asked us which of them I wanted to live with. I said me mum and my brother said me dad.'

Kate was fourteen years old. Her brother was not yet twelve.

2

Linda has always maintained that Kate took her parents' separation and subsequent divorce very well. There is no reason to doubt her veracity or the sincerity with which her assertion is made, but Kate was thirteen years old when the difficulties between her parents came to the surface and fourteen when it finally ended. However coolly Kate absorbed and lived with the news there is no way that the events of that time could be considered anything other than cataclysmic to the teenager or her brother, not least because the separation meant the division of the Moss household in the most profound sense: wife from husband and sibling from sibling.

In fact the living arrangements were rather more fluid than Kate's straightforward, 'I said me mum, my brother said me dad,' recollection of the custody arrangements might suggest. Nick often stayed at his mother's and Kate was no stranger to her father's new home. In the months following her parents' separation Kate's relationship with her father was warm and contact with his daughter was frequent. It was not without its strains, however, and at times Kate struggled not to apportion blame for the unhappiness her mother had felt but concealed in the months before the marriage ended. Before and after his split from the children's mother, Peter made a concerted effort to be involved in their lives, attending school concerts, parent/ teacher evenings and so on, but it cannot have been an easy time for any of them.

Decades on, there are many who see in Kate a neediness that characterizes the children of broken marriages. On her own, it seems, Kate feels off-balance and uncomfortable – being Kate Moss is neither easy nor always enough; she always seems to need to be with someone, and in that she is not alone.

In the weeks and months after her parents' separation Kate's interest in school dwindled. She bunked off whenever the mood took her or the moment allowed. And when she *was* there she was happy to be a back-of-the-class sort of girl, more into boys, gossips and her friends than schoolwork. She wore short skirts and heavy black kohl eyeliner, and to this day it's the one item of make-up she claims she couldn't live without.

Kate aged fourteen was fun, quirky, cute and feisty. She was a rebel, but never a malevolent one, never a bully or cruel, just bored, restless and disinterested in what academia had to offer. She wanted to have fun. When she was eleven her father bought her a David Bowie poster of Bowie in his Aladdin Sane phase. She loved the look but didn't discover the music until a few years later. When she listened to 'Life on Mars?' she heard the lyrics, 'And her mummy is yelling no', linked to the reference to 'the girl with the mousey hair', and thought he was singing about her. 'Life on Mars?' along with 'Rock 'n' Roll Suicide' and 'Golden Years' became her favourite Bowie tracks. It summed up so much of what she felt; an adolescent confusion of aspirations and bleak recklessness. She didn't seem scared or bothered by anything much, apparently including the loss of her virginity.

It was this year that she lost her virginity. She was fourteen, early by some standards perhaps. Kate has said that the moment came while on holiday with her brother and father in the Bahamas, a significant holiday for other reasons too as it would turn out. According to her maybe rose-tinted version, the object of her desire was a handsome young American with whom she enjoyed a brief and passionate holiday romance until one day they consummated the fling on the Bahamian sand. The deed done with Mills & Boon aplomb, this young stud seems to have exited Kate's life stage left. Any young girl, however self-consciously 'street', would have cherished the heart-fluttering thrill of a holiday romance: brief, unexpected, exotic.

But if Kate really viewed her virginity as 'just something to lose', – and she has described it as such – then it's surprising that she should feel the need to tell the world the details of its abandonment. Perhaps the specifics seemed more significant with hindsight than they did at the time. After all, it happened in quite remarkable year.

1988 proved a turbulent twelve months for the Moss family and for Kate in particular. For her it was the year that one era fell away and another began. It started with the funeral of her maternal grandmother and drew to a close with the promise of new and entirely unexpected opportunity. In between lay months of upheaval.

On 28 June 1988 Peter Moss filed for divorce naming Linda's lover, Geoffrey William Collman, as co-respondent. Two months later, in an understandable effort to draw the family together in the midst of a crisis, Peter took Kate and her brother on holiday. Her father had planned a two-week break to the Bahamas and it was a great success, but once over there, there was an urgency about the return trip. Peter's mother Joan, by now a widow for ten years, was getting married and he,

Kate and Nick needed to be back in Croydon for the ceremony. Instead on 26 August 1988, barely twenty-four hours from the wedding date, the trio found themselves stranded at JFK airport in New York. Peter did his best to pull some strings since he specialized in US travel, but even he feared he was out of luck when an airline representative apologetically informed him that they would be there for the night. Peter explained his family's predicament. Sucking air through her teeth and turning once more to the computer monitor, the airline check-in clerk said she would see if there was any space on the last flight out. It was doubtful. They would have to go on standby. Kate recalls closing her eyes and silently offering up the prayer, 'Please let us get on that plane.'

In later years Nick has commented with an element of wistful longing that of all of their family Kate was the only one who really managed to 'escape'. There were three seats left on that flight from JFK to London: one in economy, one in business class and one in first class. Peter Moss took them without hesitation and in doing so, though none of them could have known it, he handed his daughter her ticket out of Croydon.

For as Kate, her brother and her father idled away their time between check-in and boarding, across the airport concourse another weary traveller was organizing her own small party for the transatlantic trip ahead. Sarah Doukas was travelling with her then six-year-old daughter, Noelle (now a successful model turned scout like her mother), and her brother, Simon Chambers. She was exhausted, disheartened and desperate to get back to London and back to the offices of her fledgling business, Storm model agency. Sarah was thirty-five years old and less than twelve months into the start of her own agency. She had plenty of experience in the field having worked for

Laraine Ashton, founder of IMG Models, for six years, starting as a junior assistant and progressing to the dizzy heights of general manager. But however senior the role sounded, to Sarah the job was mundane and unsatisfying requiring her to act as little more than a glorified gofer, collecting her boss's dry-cleaning and running basic errands. So she did the gutsy thing and struck out alone.

Like the girl who would be her making, Sarah's interest in schoolwork had been most notable by its absence, though unlike Kate she had parents who expected a level of academic excellence, or at least effort. Her father was a naval lieutenant surgeon, and her mother was, in Sarah's own words, 'very eccentric . . . a pharmacist and the model doctor's wife. At sixty-five she became a pig farmer.' Medicine and law were the only real routes to success as far as the Doukas family were concerned – or at least the only guaranteed path to stability and security and all the things to which the teenage Sarah did not aspire. When it came to her A levels she completed one and walked out of the others. Her father was incandescent with fury and according to Sarah he didn't speak to her for two years.

That failure, however, led directly to Sarah's greatest success. Her outraged father sent his far from humbled daughter to an expensive boarding school to retake her exams, and there she shared a dormitory and became firm friends with Lindy Branson. It was Lindy who, fifteen years later, spoke to her brother Richard about the business Sarah was starting up. Richard Branson's Virgin empire was by then well and truly underway. Virgin Records had begun with the signing of Mike Oldfield and the release of *Tubular Bells* in 1973, and he'd gone on to sign the Sex Pistols and launch Virgin Atlantic Airways, showing that he was not a man afraid of risk. In fact, it thrilled him as much as the notion of helping somebody out.

In 1987 he lent Sarah £250,000 on a three-year, no interest basis. Better still he lent, and subsequently gave, her a town-house in Kensington to use as offices – it was a building he said he had been planning to sell. She looked him straight in the eye and told him, 'Don't expect to make any money.'

Twelve months on, queuing at JFK's crowded check-in desks, those pessimistic words seemed horribly prophetic. Sarah was not, it should be pointed out, totally without suc-cess. Rachel Hunter, a sixteen-year-old Australian, was a recent signing and already an established model in the southern hemisphere, but it would be another five years before her mar-riage to Rod Stewart saw her cause any ripples in the northern hemisphere and put her name in the public consciousness. And besides, you could hardly expect to build an empire on one girl . . . could you? Establishing her own agency was prov-ing a tough, tiring, thankless task. After weeks in America on a talent scouting trip, moving between the spirit-sapping August heat and the bone-chilling blast of air-con, Sarah was begin-ning to wonder what the hell she'd been thinking of in going it alone.

'I was in such a bad mood,' she has since admitted. 'I was razzled and desperate to get home and the last thing I said to my brother before I went to sort out a cab to pick us up from the airport was, "I never want to see another model again."'

Then she saw that face. And she was captivated. The skin was translucent, the whole impression ethereal, hung on phenomenal bone structure. Sarah saw her and thought her unutterably beautiful. It is not a description of Kate with which everybody would agree. Even Linda admits that her daughter is not, and never has been, 'traditionally beautiful'. But Sarah was captivated. Finally after wasted weeks she felt the flicker of excitement that told her she had found somebody. Then Kate disappeared from view.

'I was on the phone,' Sarah later remembered. 'I saw this wonderful face in a sea of other faces. I saw those wonderful cheekbones. Then she disappeared. I knew she had to be on our flight because she was at the same check-in desk and, as I was in the departure lounge, I was searching for her. We got on the plane and the engines revved up and I thought I'd lost her. Then I saw her getting on with her father. They were the very last two people on the plane.'

Sarah was jammed at the window end of a row of seats, so once the seat-belt signs were no longer illuminated and the flight was underway, she sent her brother to find out where Kate was sitting in economy and broach the subject of modelling. The meal had been served and Kate was fiddling with her Walkman when he smilingly made his introduction and explained that his sister ran an agency – she was just over there, he nodded, gesturing across the rows of passengers, and she'd like to talk to Kate. 'Have you ever considered modelling?' he asked.

Kate's response was a look of sheer incredulity and the words, 'No! I'm too small.' At just over 5ft 6in it was a perfectly reasonable objection. No doubt she believed she was pointing out a fatal flaw that would soon come to light and snuff out any further interest from this well-spoken stranger. But height made no difference to Sarah. Her modus operandi was even then to follow her instinct and go with what she felt. Kate, to her, looked like the sort of girl who could transcend the trends of modelling because of an indefinable 'something'. Her brother once tried to articulate it: 'With all of these girls you get the feeling that when they walked across the playground, their friends went, "Where are you going?" They have a charisma about them.'

Simon handed Kate the Storm business card. It was over to her now.

Perhaps it is surprising that Kate didn't immediately make her way up to first class where her father sat, or even to business where her brother had bagged a seat. For the hours between Simon's approach and the flight landing in Gatwick the knowledge was hers alone, a secret thrill to toy with and disbelieve by turn. When she eventually told her father and brother, all three of them laughed. It seemed so unlikely.

Kate told her mother too, of course, once her father had returned her to the Forestdale home they shared. She told her as if it was an afterthought, 'Oh, Mum, this lady saw me and wants me to be a model.' The revelation was met with natural scepticism. The offer, such as it was, wasn't really considered – not that evening anyway. But however fantastic that mid-air encounter must have seemed and however foolish the notion that Kate, a shade under 5ft 7in, could occupy space alongside the Amazonian models of the late Eighties – girls like Christie Brinkley, Cindy Crawford, Yasmin Le Bon and Tatjana Patitz – Kate still held on to the businesscard handed to her by Simon somewhere over the Atlantic. While dismissing the very idea of modelling as preposterous, she slipped the card quietly into her pocket.

A few days later, over dinner at the kitchen table, it was Kate who raised the matter again. How, after all, could a girl ignore such a possibility? Linda tried to play it down, worried that Kate was setting herself up for disappointment. She could not, truth be told, quite see how her daughter – however lovely she was – could make it in modelling. Certainly it wasn't something that had ever been considered within the family. Why would it? Kate was too small and she wasn't beautiful enough. Neither mother nor daughter thought she was even terribly photogenic. Yes she had been spotted, but it was probably a scam that relied on the seemingly universal ambition of being a model to separate teenage girls, or rather their parents, from their money. Linda worried that if they were to call the number on the business card it would lead to an expensive photography session on the pretext of putting together a professional portfolio – something that would cost thousands and go no further than the agency filing cabinet.

Then again, what if this lady, Sarah Doukas, *was* genuine? Was she being overly cynical and cautious? Kate seemed excited and intrigued, but her persistence was playful rather than desperate, and that was reassuring. It would be 'a laugh' according to Kate. Couldn't they just 'have a go and see?' Linda smiled at her tanned daughter, her face sprinkled with the freckles that always bloomed when she spent hours in the sun. 'OK,' she conceded, 'I'll come up to London with you.'

The telephone call was made to Storm the very next day. Sarah was understandably thrilled – however many girls one approached, the time between handing over a card and receiving that tentative call could feel like a lifetime.

Linda and Kate took the train to Storm's Kensington offices a few days later, neither knowing what to expect nor anticipating the long day that would unfurl before them. Sarah must have cut a pleasingly unthreatening figure: 5ft 2in tall, with blue eyes and blonde hair cut to her shoulders and tousled in a way that suggested a great deal of activity and an absence of vanity.

More importantly Sarah knew what she was talking about. She knew that Kate thought she was too small and she had a ready tale to counter any reluctance that mother or daughter might have that day. Sarah had been a model herself in the early Seventies. A photographer friend sent some pictures of her to an agency and she was called in as a result. When she showed up she was met with the words, 'Christ, you're far too small.' 'I know,' she replied. 'I don't know why I'm here.' Admittedly her career, in keeping with her physique, did not reach dizzying heights, but she stayed on their books – and working – for seven years. She did facial and body work, commercials for Harmony hairspray, shoe modelling because of her size four feet and car modelling because the daintier the model the roomier the vehicle appeared.

At Storm the niceties were interspersed with necessities. Kate's measurements were taken: not quite 5ft 7in tall (but at fourteen there was every possibility that she would grow a bit at least) a shade under 32 inches at the bust, waist 23, hips 33, shoe size 6½. Her colouring was noted: eyes hazel, hair brown. Part of the allure of her youth was her fresh, dewy skin. The freckles were endearing but, Sarah cautioned, from now on Kate would have to take good care of her complexion – sun damage is never a good look. A couple of Polaroid shots were taken and Sarah explained that there were several castings she wanted to send her new signing to that very day. It all seemed so unreal, so big, to Kate. The offices, in truth uncomfortably cramped for their purposes even then, seemed huge and buzzing and filled with people who inhabited a strange and glamorous world that Kate couldn't believe she would ever be part of, though already she felt hope prick in her heart. Later she reflected, 'I just kind of took my chances really.' And why not?

So mother and daughter set out on an afternoon of 'traipsing' (Linda's word) around London. Back home that evening, exhausted and with precious little to show for their efforts, Linda was clear: the lady at Storm seemed nice but travelling all over London only to sit and wait and come away with nothing was no way to spend a day. Sarah had gone some way towards outlining the nature of the business and the fact that there would be rejections and that, in the beginning at least, the effort involved in travelling to 'go-see' after 'go-see,' would outweigh the glamour, but this was Kate's thing not her mother's. If Kate seriously wanted to pursue this modelling lark then Linda would not stand in her way, but when it came to hauling herself all over town for castings she was on her own.

To Kate, intrigued and buoyed up by Sarah's infectious energy, it was a daunting but thrilling prospect. Of course Kate had been nervous during that first day – incredibly so. The people, the buzz, the machine that she had just witnessed – one that moved and functioned while barely acknowledging her existence as she and her mother sat waiting for their appointment with Sarah, was phenomenally intimidating. She was a fourteen-year-old with no knowledge of that world and, until then, no particular interest in it.

Once, on holiday, Kate had got chatting to a girl her age whose ambition it was to be a model. It was an admission that the pubescent Kate found incredible, arrogant perhaps, vain certainly. So to find herself now admitting in action, if not in words, that she too wanted such a thing . . . well, it would take some getting used to.

Yet the incredulity that accompanied Kate's first tentative steps on a career path she had never dreamed of was met in equal share by a straightforward sense of, 'Why the hell not?' 'It', whatever 'it' was, did not feel beyond Kate's reach, even at the very beginning. And so when, soon after her signing, Storm arranged for some professional shots to kick-start Kate's portfolio and send out to prospective clients, she noted the time and the address and went alone.

Kate may have affected a degree of adolescent nonchalance, a teenage shrug of 'whatever', but her first session with a professional photographer was a big deal. In that, she was no different from any other young model, or, indeed, any other fourteen-year-old girl. Her measurements had been taken and she had posed for her Polaroid in the offices of Storm, but *this* was where it all began.

Well, not quite. When Kate arrived at the door of Apartment 3, Langham Mansions – a redbrick block in London's Earls Court Square – she did not receive the welcome she had hoped for.

It was to photographer David Ross's apartment that Sarah Doukas sent her new discovery for her first professional shots. It was Tuesday 25 October, less than two months after Sarah had spotted Kate at JFK and within days of Kate and her mother visiting Storm's London offices for her official 'signing'. Ross was just twenty-two years old and, like Sarah, was trying to establish himself as a force to be reckoned with on the fashion scene. He went on to work for *Vogue*, but on the October day that Kate pitched up at his flat, his motivation was twofold: filling his portfolio with images that would impress magazine editors and cementing the rapport that had sparked between him and Doukas when they'd met some months earlier. At the time they had struck a deal: he would photograph new girls for Sarah, helping to build up their books and shape their image, and in return she would give him the girls that he wanted to work with to build up his own portfolio.

It was a rather haphazard arrangement, but it worked. Ross lived only ten minutes from the Storm offices in Marloes Road, Kensington, and he quickly became used to receiving last-minute telephone calls from Sarah, checking that he was in and asking if she could send a girl round. Sometimes she called days ahead of time, sometimes she didn't. Sometimes the girl arrived, sometimes she didn't. Sometimes he scribbled the appointment in his diary, sometimes he didn't.

Ross cannot remember whether Sarah called him the day or the week before Kate's appointment. But however advanced the warning the one thing he knows is that he neither wrote Kate's name in his diary nor heard the entryphone buzzer when it was pushed. Instead it was the caretaker who came to Ross's door and told him there was a girl waiting to see him. Ross assumed a model must have left something after a previous shoot and told her to come on up. When he answered the knock at his door that swiftly followed, Ross was momentarily confused.

'I opened the door to see this scrawny little child,' he recalls. 'I thought it was some girl who had pressed the wrong buzzer and her mum was obviously in the building and she was trying to find her. I didn't think this was the girl who had come to see me.'

Still expecting a model to arrive at any moment Ross admits, 'I didn't look twice at her beyond that. I was expecting her to say, "Can you tell me where flat so and so is?" Or, "Is my mum in here?" Or something like that.'

Instead she said, 'I'm Kate.' Suddenly it dawned on Ross that this was one of Sarah's girls and he was covered in confusion.

She was so young, so scrawny and so obviously unaccompanied. Ross was not so insensitive as to ask a fourteen-year-old where her mother was, though that was the question he bit back. Instead he asked where she had come from.

'Croydon,' came the reply. 'What? You came all the way up here by train from Croydon yourself?' he continued.

'Yeah,' she said.

It was a long journey and it was one that, Ross was about to inform Kate, had been wasted. He was very sorry, he explained, he wasn't going to be able to take her pictures today.

'Why not?' came Kate's understandably peeved demand. Because she was so young, he said. Because she was on her own. As he explained himself, Ross was as bemused by the fact that this rather miffed child at his door could be one of Sarah's new girls as he was by the knowledge that she had travelled and turned up unchaperoned.

He told her to come back tomorrow and to bring, if not her mum, then a friend. He said he'd put it in his diary and wrote it in there and then. Seeing she seemed less than mollified he pointed to the newly made appointment and assured her of his serious intent with the words, 'Kate Moss – OK?'

She rolled her eyes and turned on her heel. Ross closed the door, doubtful he'd ever see her again. Still, he checked his photographic stock and above Kate's name, hastily written in his diary, he scrawled in large letters, 'BUY FILM!!'

If the little girl *did* come back, he wanted to make sure he was ready.

On Wednesday 26 October 1988 Kate Moss got her second chance at her first shot at modelling. It was far from glamorous and, as far as the photographer was concerned, the resultant shots were neither particularly remarkable nor desperately promising. She didn't bring her mother but a friend – small, blonde and a bit dumpy. Kate also brought with her a couple of changes of outfits: a white jumper with a leaf motif stitched in black around the wide neckline, a black coat and black felt boater hat, black tapered trousers, neat plain pumps and a scrunchy to tie back her unkempt hair.

'She was a fourteen-year-old schoolgirl,' Ross recalls with some affection. 'She was trying, God bless her, but she didn't have a clue.'

Years later Kate would say that on meeting Sarah and sitting in the Storm offices she had felt that 'anything was possible'. No doubt that was true, but on that second day that she arrived at Ross's flat she couldn't have had any true sense of just what that 'anything' might be. She could not have known that she was edging into an industry in a state of flux, or just how much that flux would work in her favour. She had no insight above and beyond that of any teenage girl flicking idly through the pages of *Just 17* or *Mizz*. There was nothing in her demeanour – or indeed in the clothes she brought with her – to suggest a burning interest in fashion or the supposedly innate sense of style that would later earn her plaudits and wealth. She had no point of reference other than a fond imagining of what it might be like – *must* be like – to be photographed, adored and looked upon again and again. The very thought of it made her crinkle her nose and giggle.

It was a bright, blustery October day, and while Kate and her friend whispered together and Kate's friend helped her apply a little mascara and lip balm, Ross thought about how he could make something out of this child.

This, it should be remembered, was a time of power dressing, shoulder pads and thick, glossy make-up. It was 1988 and the overblown excess, glamour and sheen of the Eighties had yet to implode. In Britain, Chancellor Nigel Lawson's promise of an 'economic miracle' seemed within touching distance after a stock market crash the previous year. It was a time of fevered and unsustainable economic growth. The fashion pages of *Vogue* and *Marie Claire* and *Tatler* were still bullishly peddling the dream that the salad days of the beginning of the decade were far from over: the girls were tall and their features voluptuous – heels, hair and, for the time being, City slickers were high.

Of course it couldn't last, but in October 1988 the day when Kate would represent something even vaguely commercial was a long way off. She wasn't particularly tall. Her features were not voluptuous. She lacked the 'toothpaste' smile of some young girls and had, instead, crooked teeth. Her lips were rosebud-like but pursed, not generous. Her complexion was youthful but not flawless and her bone structure pretty enough but, however much it has been admired in the intervening years, on that day it seemed to Ross no more remarkable than that of countless other far prettier girls who had stepped into his studio. Her eyes were interesting – arresting even – but not truly astonishing.

This was the young photographer's honest assessment. Kate was, by virtue of her very make-up, a physical rebellion against the style, look and fashion of the time. Neither Kate nor Ross was to know that it was this entirely accidental rebellion on Kate's part that would prove her fortune. Instead, keen to boost his portfolio, Ross viewed this smiling, sweet and eager little girl from Croydon and saw a far from ideal subject. This, as far as he was concerned, would most likely be a day of wasted film, useful only for the good will it would bring from Sarah

Doukas. Still, Ross had a job to do and, frankly, he was impressed by the fact that Kate had turned up after the previous day's debacle.

From the roof of his Earls Court block there was a panoramic view across south-west London. Most of the time it was hazy and reminded Ross, somewhat nostalgically, of the Los Angeles skyline visible from the Griffin Observatory. The sun was bright and strong in the autumn sky – too strong, as it turned out, for the purposes of the pictures. As Kate's friend helped her apply her make-up, Ross determined to take Kate up onto the roof for some warm-up shots. It was hardly the sort of west London roof terrace to which Kate would, in later years, become accustomed as a familiar extension of the countless penthouse apartments to which she would be a guest. Instead it was a grimy awkward network of pipes, bricks and felting, onto which Ross and Kate scrambled after gaining permission from the building's caretaker.

Kate was nervous and understandably so. She did not, after all, know what was expected of her. She had no stock of familiar poses, no sense of what might and what might not work for the lens. She must have felt awkward, but she was, quite clearly, keen to learn and follow direction – keen to do anything that might prevent her from looking, or feeling, foolish.

She perched on one of the strips of low bricking that crisscrossed the roof. The wind buffeted her hair, blowing it across her face and into her eyes, necessitating frequent stops and adjustment. Every now and then the photographer's reflector slipped as she strained to hold it in front of her, out of shot, angled so that it would bounce the sunlight against which she sat, back into her face just enough to bring her eyes to life as bright pools of light.

She began to relax and enjoy what, even then, must have

seemed a vaguely ridiculous exercise. After half and hour or so on the roof Ross decided to take his young subject back downstairs to photograph her in the leafy private gardens at the centre of Earls Court Square.

Or at least that had been the plan until Ross realized that his flatmate had the keys to the square's secluded patch of green. Instead, they trudged down the stairs and across the road, where Kate posed on the pavement in front of some wrought-iron railings and overhanging leaves. She had changed from her dark top and hat into the white jumper and had pulled her hair back into a demure ponytail at the nape of her neck. Standing on the pavement doing her best to follow directions, relaxing into this odd new pastime, she drew barely a second glance from the occasional passer-by. For Kate, the whole afternoon seemed, according to Ross, 'a bit of a lark'.

'She was appeasing people I think,' Ross recalls. 'Sarah [Doukas] is a very powerful personality. [Like] a lot of people who are posh, who don't necessarily have money but are from good backgrounds . . . she could either be very, very cold and you would be cut off because you don't speak like us and you're not from us and you're not part of the old boys' network, or else she could be very overpoweringly warm and "Oh you're just marvellous, darling." It wasn't in a "fashion" type way where it was just very camp and gay, she was just really like that, as those people often are.

'You would feel slightly intimidated on one hand and slightly excited on the other that [she] would want you to be part of their world. Kate may well have been affected by that big personality in the same way. Kate would have just gone along with it. I don't get the idea that she had any preconceived ideas about being a star or a model by any means.'

On that day in October 1988 Kate, with her two changes of

clothes, her unkempt hair and her slightly dumpy friend, was, Ross remembers, 'trying so hard I wanted it to work for her. She was really very sweet.' The purpose of the afternoon's shoot was to sell nothing but Kate. The resulting shots would be sent out to potential clients and shown to magazine editors looking for young girls for make-up and fashion spreads. Photographic retouching was a prohibitively expensive process in those days and one so fledgling that few were expert at it. As a result, the only commercially viable, guaranteed way to get shots of the sort of youthful, dewy skin that sold cosmetics was to use extremely young models, girls of fourteen . . . or younger.

In lieu of artistry and glamour were the nuts and bolts of the modelling business. Colour shots were taken to show that Kate's hair was naturally brown, that her eyes were hazel with a hint of green, her skin prone to freckles but her complexion clear. Black and white shots were also taken to enhance her bone structure and to make up for the lack of variety in her outfits.

The following day Ross took his transparencies into the Storm offices. These days even test shot Polaroids of Kate, taken on set to test lighting and colour, are fallen upon hungrily and praised to the high heavens. Back then, however thrilled and excited Sarah Doukas professed to be with her new discovery, the cargo of transparencies that Ross carried with him was not so tantalizing that it caused anybody to break off from their telephone calls or bring any meetings to a halt. He sat and waited in the uncomfortably busy offices of Sarah's fledgling empire until, an hour later, a member of staff called him through to lay out the shots on a light box. The images were scanned through with a loop and a couple were chosen and sent off to print.

It was close to five years before Ross gave the scrawny little kid from Croydon another thought. By then he had lived in Australia, travelled the world plying his trade as a photographer and, by his own admission, spent most of his money in the process. The money that during the mid-Eighties came thick and fast had dried up, leaving many heavily in debt.

Ross was back in London, broke and trying to re-establish some of the connections he had let slip over the intervening years. He called Sarah Doukas offering his services once more – they had always got on and he liked and admired her. It was 1992 and negotiations with Calvin Klein had just been concluded for what was at the time Kate's biggest deal, one that would later be recognized as her breakthrough moment.

'Did you hear about Kate?' Sarah asked.

'Kate who?' came his response.

3

The thin drizzling rain was sharpened by the briney spray that whipped off the sea and up towards the dunes of the Camber Sands, East Sussex. It was the tail end of 1989 and the air was brisk and wintery. Little wonder that the request to take her clothes off was met with a moan of 'I don't want to,' from a tearful Kate. The fact that the occasional passer-by, walking a dog or simply taking in the air, was bundled up in a coat, scarf and boots only added to her embarrassment and discomfort at the prospect. Kate must have been shy, self-conscious, horribly aware that it all felt . . . well, a bit silly. She was fifteen years old and conscious of every awkward contour of her slight body, from the flat chest to the prominent moles that flecked her skin. But she trusted the photographer as much as she resented the requests for semi-nudity. She wanted the day to work, as she had wanted each of the many days, even weeks, that they had already spent together to work. She liked the woman who held the camera and cajoled and giggled and seemed, more than anything, to want Kate simply to be Kate, albeit in a state of undress on a bitter stretch of English beach.

So she took off her clothes, clutched a battered straw hat to preserve her modesty and got on with it. Her hair was tangled and blustered about her face and her nose crinkled with the sort of natural, laughing smile that's usually confined to the pages of a family album. It was that natural, laughing smile that changed the course of fashion history.

It was several months before the pictures that photographer Corinne Day took of Kate that day were published. When they were, in *The Face* magazine's July edition, however excited and confident the magazine's editorial team were that they had found a true gem in this gawky teenager, none of them could know how significant those pictures would be, both for Kate and the fashion industry.

The iconic status they acquired in later years was such that it led Corinne to exhibit some of the shots and contact sheets from that period in the Gimpel Fils gallery near New Bond Street in a collection called simply '15' – the age Kate was when Corinne first met and photographed her. As for Kate, the importance of those pictures and of that photographer and her particular vision cannot be overestimated.

Instead of the saturated colours, high gloss and artifice that had characterized the fashion photography of the Eighties, Corinne wanted something that appeared real, gritty . . . even bleak. Instead of the toned, Amazonian models of that dead decade, girls styled, photographed and viewed through the prism of an altogether more masculine notion of beauty, Corinne wanted her models to be beautiful in their imperfections – pale, skinny, vulnerable and spirited. Corinne wanted Kate, and between 1989 and 1990, she played a key role in convincing others in the industry that they did too.

None of the jobs that Kate had won in the first months of 1989 could be described or regarded as particularly glamorous, even with the heavy rose tint of nostalgia and the benefit of hindsight, knowing that she got there in the end. But for Kate, newly fifteen, even the drudgery of the castings that had her trudging around London was thrilling because of the promise each one held. In her very first week of castings the previous year she had struck lucky and been signed up for a beauty scrub editorial by teen magazine *Mizz*. It was a title she was familiar with, being more Kate's speed back then than *Vogue*, *Tatler* or *Marie Claire*. When she arrived at the studio there was already another young model there having her make-up applied and her hair teased into a style that, to Kate, looked ludicrous. The thought, Oh my God, what are they doing to her? flitted through Kate's mind, but she pushed it to one side and submitted herself to a similar styling. She was paid £150 and it seemed like a fortune. It was something to tell her friends back at school and something that, following on so swiftly from her signing seemed to excite Sarah Doukas far more than it did Kate.

Kate had never been terribly interested in school, and what little hold it had on her slackened in the months that followed as she went to casting after casting. She would skip out of school, change from her school uniform on the train and find her way to the office, flat, hall or studio in which the first casting of the day was being held. Sometimes there would be half a dozen or more such cattle calls to get to, and often she would be appraised, found wanting and let go. At fifteen, she did a shoot for *Brides* magazine, something she would cringe over later but at the time it allowed her the tiniest taste of her teenage fantasy of marriage, children and a house in the country – dressing up is a childlike pastime Kate would never grow out of. By her own admission, however, there were times when she simply thought, Fuck this. I want to go home, and few would have blamed her.

Kate's career certainly didn't lurch from that mythical moment at JFK to the supermodel stature she would come to enjoy and endure. In later years, once her success was secure, that is how Kate's rapid rise was often presented in the newspapers and magazines, but her mother has pointed out that it didn't 'just happen', and that Kate worked hard and went around 'for years and years', before she got a break. Peter, too, a man who bursts with paternal pride at his daughter's achievement, dismisses the notion that 'overnight success' is something that exists in any walk of life, particularly in the competitive and fickle world in which his daughter has excelled.

It is a natural instinct. After all, so great is the part played by luck in that concept that it leaves no space for genuine achievement or talent. It closes down the possibility of having 'earned' anything and leaves wide open the almost inevitable envy of others that must surely follow on. Little wonder then that both Linda and Peter take pains to defend their daughter.

And it is true, in part. Because Kate *did* work hard, showing an enthusiasm and energy without which she wouldn't have gone on to achieve the success she did. She made herself popular and bookable by being fun on set, chattering to everybody from the make-up artist to the lighting assistant, turning the music up and, from very early on, demonstrating the knack of 'getting' whatever it was the photographer needed from her. In that very first year as a model Kate *did* also get a break. In fact, she got several, although they wouldn't come to fruition straight away.

Most importantly, she met some of the people who would be the making of her and she did so within a remarkably brief time frame. Success wasn't handed to her on a platter – her involvement in her career was always far more proactive than such trite assessments suggest – but the opportunities *were* presented to her, thanks in no small part to the ferocious energies of Sarah Doukas. And when these opportunities were offered to her, Kate took them with a gusto that wowed those who had taken the risk by offering. Towards the end of the year Kate got her first photographic break in the form of her meeting with Corinne Day. It would prove so significant that, in time, everything that came before it would fade out of Kate's history. But there were other crucial encounters that year, and one in particular sparked another remarkable and enduring professional relationship.

In 1989 John Galliano put Kate on the London catwalk for the first time. Today, Galliano is a lauded and established designer, a former creative director of Christian Dior in Paris, a label worn by some of the most beautiful and extravagantly wealthy women in the world. But back in 1989 he was more successful at making ripples in the fashion scene than at making money. Galliano had graduated from St Martin's College of Art and Design with a first class honours degree six years earlier. His graduation collection had been inspired by the French Revolution and entitled, 'Les Incroyables' – The Incredibles/Unbelievables. This fantastical group, and not the more dowdy and predictable 'Miserables' of that era, was where Galliano's imagination found focus. The collection had been bought in its entirety by Joan Burnstein who put it in the window of her clothes boutique, Browns, in London's South Molton Street during London fashion week. The French designer Joseph had also been there and placed several orders with the twenty-three-year-old Galliano. One year later Galliano launched his own label and took another step towards establishing himself as a designer of talent and note, combining exquisite tailoring with outrageous flights of fancy, punk and irreverence.

In 1987 he was named British Designer of the Year. He was

wild, he was likeable and, by 1989, he was practically broke. He was dependant not on the kindness of strangers, but on that of friends and associates within the fashion scene who shared not only in his desire to shake things up but his sense that change was not only inevitable, it was vital. His work was spectacular in the truest sense and, notably, the historic eras that inspired him most were pivotal moments of high drama and revolution. It somehow seemed to fit with the level of excitement at which his designs 'lived'. He was hot, if barely solvent, and willing to push boundaries and take artistic risks with his designs and the models he used. That year he was casting for what would be his last show as a London-based designer. In 1990 he decamped and headed to Paris to join the host of international designers seeking their fortune in the French capital's *prêt-à-porter* ranges. But before he left British shores there was one final casting and, among the many girls he saw, there was Kate.

Kate was too small really for the runway, a good four inches shorter than most of the other girls with whom she would share it, but Galliano, like Sarah Doukas and like Corinne Day, had a feeling – a hunch – and he followed it. No doubt it helped that Kate, hard-working unknown that she was, was prepared to work for little more than her train fare and a shot at something more exciting than another day in Croydon.

Galliano had to adjust his clothes for Kate – everything had to be pinned and tucked around her delicate frame as it was too big, too long, too much. Backstage, the other models looked askance at this chirpy catwalk novice. Where they carried Chanel bags and wore Alaia bandage dresses, Kate wore jeans and a vest top. Her boots were clumpy and her hair unstyled. No doubt for the more established girls – and thanks to his talent Galliano could call upon the likes of Linda

Evangelista, Christy Turlington and Naomi Campbell – Kate's presence just didn't make sense. Yet she was irresistibly endearing in her nervous, chattering state, and when she set foot on the runway she carried it off . . . and how.

Dressed in outrageous outfits bearing the Union Jack emblem, complete with extravagant hats and precarious heels, she was a revelation. When Galliano staged his first show in Paris in March the following year there was no doubt in his mind, Kate Moss would be there. There was something in the energy Kate effervesced that made her, in spite of her lack of stature, the only girl on that catwalk that anybody noticed, looked at or wanted to look at. Kate in motion was compelling. It was extraordinary.

Corinne Day caught a glimpse of that energy – and something of the motion too as the shot was blurred – in the Polaroid she took from Storm when she began casting for a shoot for *The Face* magazine towards the end of 1989. Like Galliano she was interested in revolution, though it was not so much the upheavals of the past that fascinated Corinne and seeped into her work as those of the present and the future. She was new to photography and perhaps that helped as she wasn't mired in the traditions of the Eighties and, as far as she was concerned, she was *making* the ropes not *learning* them.

Like the girl who would be her most famous subject, Corinne grew up on the edges of London, in Ickenham, Middlesex, and she had rather more street cred than the lower-middle-class Kate could ever lay claim to. For all her schoolgirl rebelliousness and fondness for pot, Kate had present, if liberal, loving parents from hard-working backgrounds. Corinne's father divorced her mother when she was five. She and her brother, Matthew, moved in with their paternal grandparents and somehow ended up staying there.

Corinne herself had worked as a model for a while and was signed by Premier when she was sixteen. Later she would admit that there was perhaps more than a hint of narcissism in her fascination with Kate. It was a straightforward statement of truth rather than an attempt to vainly compare herself to the more physically admired of the two. Corinne was twenty-four when she and Kate met, yet she was as slight as the teenage model. She wore her brown hair long and unstyled, in keeping with a look that was defiantly counter-culture and grunge. Her eyes were round, doll-like and deep set, and her pale complexion was clear. But where Kate's face was arresting, Corinne's slimness seemed pinched and sparse. She didn't have great cheekbones like Kate. She was pretty rather than compelling, and had always felt during her modelling days that she was 'quite plain looking' for that particular line of business. Her greatest signing was for Guess Jeans' Japanese advertising campaign but her modelling had been confined predominantly to catalogue work. Barely 5ft 6in, she was on the short side for any high-flight or catwalk work. Besides she never really found life on that side of the camera terribly fulfilling and her face didn't look particularly good plastered in the heavy make-up of the Eighties. It was just something to do for a while and the money, though not great, wasn't bad.

Photography was something Corinne fell into thanks to an above-average set of holiday snaps taken in South-East Asia and an encouraging partner, New Zealand film and documentary maker Mark Szaszy. He showed her how to use a camera and urged her to show the results to Phil Bicker, then art director of *The Face* magazine. The pictures were enough to pique Bicker's interest and start her photographic career. The meeting fell at a time when the editorial team at *The Face* were, in the words of Sheryl Garratt, the publication's newly instated editor, 'dying to do something new'. They wanted to reinvent the magazine and the time felt right to do it.

The strong colours and flashiness of the Eighties were no longer in step with what seemed, to them at least, to be going on in the world. Everywhere things were changing. The sickly-sweet, highly synthesized pop acts of the decade had fallen away in favour of grungy, earthy rebellion in the form of Nirvana or the new hedonism and drug-fuelled relief offered by the Happy Mondays, Inspiral Carpets and The Stone Roses. The bands and the Ecstasy culture in which they grew had been around for some time, the whole Madchester scene – a mix of indie and dance music – had, after all, begun in the mid-Eighties. But it was the spring of 1989 that saw The Stone Roses release their first commercially successful album and break through from the Northern Indie scene to something with a larger fanbase and wider influence.

Kate was a fan. She loved the music that had begun life as something niche and underground and now starting to reach a more mainstream audience. It was the same audience who had grown up with, and tired of, Thatcherism; the same audience who no longer believed in the 'greed is good' mantra that had, as far as they were concerned, characterized and sullied the decade. Besides, many who had benefited from that were no longer counting their riches but the cost, as recession followed boom as surely as night follows day. The scent of change and revolution was everywhere. In November the Velvet Revolution in Prague began the bloodless end of Communism in Czecho-slovakia. That same month the checkpoints opened and the Berlin Wall fell.

To anyone who sees fashion merely as assembled frippery, drawing these events and movements together may sound absurd, even irreverent. But to those who see it as an integral part of our lives and culture, and who view photography, styling and the clothes we put in our magazines and on our backs as a statement as political as any party broadcast, then to consider fashion in isolation is the absurdity.

Perhaps the team at *The Face* took it rather too seriously – the magazine, now defunct, was so street and counter-culture that within a matter of years it was forced to face facts and Day's commissions dried up as sales flagged and the realization hit home that the commercial imperative cannot be entirely ignored. Towards the end of 1989, though, the hunger was for change, for something fresh, pared down and different. Corinne's holiday snaps struck a chord; she was commissioned to do a shoot for the magazine and began casting. One day she brought in a Polaroid of a girl she thought exciting. The picture was blurred but, egged on by Corinne's enthusiasm, Phil Bicker and Sheryl Garratt agreed. By the end of the meeting they did more than agree, they shared a conviction that they had found the 'gem' they had been looking for. It was the perfect moment for change as a new generation of stylists and photographers were emerging, and they had been talking for some time about 'launching' a new model as the face of, well, *The Face*. Kate didn't know it but, in Day, Bicker and Garratt, she got lucky breaks three, four and five.

Kate made her debut in *The Face* in March 1990. She and Corinne had been working together for months; they got on as Kate reminded Corinne of her younger self. She was cheeky, cocky and brimmed with a gutsy personality that belied her years and which was unusual in an industry where girls are often so willing to please and desperate to work that their characters come off with their make-up. The first photographs Corinne took of Kate were in her grandmother's front garden, where they ate sandwiches and drank tea. Corinne took Kate to a park where she and her brother had hung out for years. The pictures she took were, in her own words, 'snapshots of nothing more than us hanging out in the suburbs where I grew up'. Kate wore a V-neck jumper, Kickers and, coincidentally, a bias-cut John Galliano maxi skirt from Browns, the London clothes shop that stocked Galliano's first ever collection. Corinne worked in black and white, partly because she had little experience of handling the more complicated technical requirements of colour. She showed six pictures to Bicker who published one – not a particular favourite of Corinne's as it turned out.

At the beginning of that same month, Kate was called upon by Galliano once more. This time it was for his Paris debut, which was Kate's Paris debut, too, and an experience she would never forget. She found herself sharing the runway with girls who were already at the top of their game: Linda Evangelista, Christy Turlington and Naomi Campbell, the Streatham girl who would become Kate's great ally and friend, sometimes nagging her, sometimes goading and, in those very early days, showing her, through her own remarkable poise and confidence, how to *really* 'walk'.

Galliano had cast Kate as his Lolita though, confusingly, the inspiration for that particular show was, in part, Anastasia Romanov, the so-called last Grand Duchess of Russia. Anastasia's supposed escape from the Bolsheviks who slaughtered her father, Tsar Nicholas II, and the rest of the Russian royal family was one of the great romantic mysteries of the last century. There was, in the years following that horror, more than one pretender to her title claiming to be the seventeen-year-old girl who 'died' along with her family in Yekaterinburg in July 1918 before a Bolshevik firing squad. The desperate tale and the faint hope that some link to an age so savagely concluded might have survived in the figure of Anya, or Anna, as she became known in her Western incarnations, was captivating and inspirational: films were made, diaries discovered, genetic tests conducted, musicals scored and fashion collections designed.

Before Galliano sent her down the runway – a stretch that in Kate's nervous estimation seemed to go on forever – he told an understandably jittery Kate who she would be. She would be Anastasia, frightened, hounded, running for her life and chased by wolves. He must have made a convincing case, because when the lights fell on Kate as she stepped out onto the runway, her hair dusted with talc, her dress an extravagant, fantastical blue crinoline, she went, he recalls, 'all guts out for it'. With Galliano's yells of, 'Go Kate! Go!' echoing in her ears she started pelting down the catwalk.

The audience actually stood up in amazement. Nobody had ever seen crinoline flying on the catwalk like that. It was breathtaking; this tiny blur of energy, talc and crinoline. It was brilliant. *She* was brilliant. She was Lolita and Anastasia all rolled into one, a fizzing blend of romance and energy. Sarah Doukas was in the audience that day and described it as 'a moment of magic'. The show was a phenomenal success. The sixteen-year-old Kate should have been at school, but what teenager, never mind aspiring model, would pass up on such an opportunity in favour of the fag-end of another school week? The show was on Wednesday 14 March. Kate, her booker assured her mother, would be back in the classroom – or in the country at least – on Monday.

Only it didn't quite work out that way. Kate's last appearance on the catwalk had introduced her to the champagne culture that saw most models drink a flute before setting foot on the runway, whether it was ten o'clock in the morning or ten o'clock at night. It was just part of the lifestyle, part of being – and more importantly believing – you were fabulous. Naturally it followed that, after a successful show, the drink flowed freely.

Buzzing from the applause that greeted the show, Kate, Galliano, the rest of the girls and an assortment of stylists, dressers, hairdressers and make-up artists, went back to Galliano's Parisian office to play back the video of the show and savour once more their mutual success. Somebody had taken the champagne Galliano had intended to celebrate with, leaving only harder stuff – whisky to be precise. Kate and another girl polished off a bottle between them before dinner, at which Kate promptly passed out. She may have been proud of her capacity for drink but she had been so taut with nerves before the late-afternoon runway appearance that she'd been unable to eat all day. Now, filled with excitement and topped up with whisky it was all too much. She was violently sick all through the night and the following day. When her mother arrived at the airport in London to pick her up and take her home there was no sign of Kate. She had missed her flight and was still being sick in a Parisian hotel. She didn't make it home until Wednesday, but a hangover and alcohol poisoning in Paris beat a hangover and school in Croydon any day.

Back in Britain Kate's attention and time was commandeered once more by *The Face*, and in May she appeared for the first time on the magazine's cover. Coming only two months after her debut in its pages it was quite a coup, but one that was quickly usurped and lately forgotten. The Football World Cup was one month away and would be held in Italy, so, in a nod to the sport and the excitement that such an event inevitably generated, Kate was photographed by Marc Lebon, clutching a football, swathed in a football scarf and looking rather fed up with the whole affair. Corinne Day informed Phil Bicker that his publication was in danger of looking like a *Boy's Own* annual. They should use Kate more, she said, and they should use her better.

A few weeks later, Bicker commissioned Corinne to photograph eight pages of fashion. She wanted to use Kate and he agreed. That same week Corinne was walking down Old Compton Street in Soho with a friend. She told her about a stylist called Melanie Ward who, she explained, shared Corinne's fondness for second-hand clothes. That day they saw her on the street and invited her for coffee. Over coffee, Corinne invited Melanie to work with her on *The Face* photoshoot that she had just been offered and was planning to do with Kate. It's strange, sometimes, how the world conspires to place people in the right place at the right time. Together Corinne and Melanie set about working out what and whom the eight-page shoot should be about. They went to Portobello and Camden markets, picking up the sort of items of clothing they would wear, sharing the cost as both were on the dole. Corinne had the advantage of already knowing and having worked with Kate, so she knew that they both liked Nirvana, The Stone Roses and the Happy Mondays. They would provide the soundtrack, in terms of inspiration at least, for the photoshoot that followed and which would appear in *The Face* under the title 'The Third Summer of Love.'

The pictures that Corinne took, many of them on a day trip to Camber Sands, look carefree and natural, as if she simply stood back and let Kate frolic freely while she snapped away. The fact that the two had hit it off so well certainly added an intimacy to the pictures, which look like the result of two girls just mucking about, having a fag and a drink. As Kate put it, that time was all about people wanting to 'get off their tits' and have fun.

The photos Corinne shot looked almost artless in their candour, which was precisely the effect Corinne and Melanie and, in the hours and weeks she put into the shoot for a grand sum of £50 a day, Kate worked so hard to achieve. Corinne didn't give Kate direction; she wanted to photograph Kate as herself – the antithesis of the shoulder pads and blush of the 1980s. She wanted to reverse that notion of beauty and style of photography and make it all about the model, and in that her success was complete. Everything that, in his brief interlude with her on a windswept rooftop in west London and the empty pavement below, photographer David Ross had initially seen as wrong or problematic about Kate, Corinne recognized as absolutely right and seething with potential.

In the time that the two – three counting Melanie Ward – spent together, Corinne photographed Kate constantly. Years later the result of that incessant exposure to the camera at such an early stage in her modelling career can be seen in Kate's peculiar rapport with the lens. Very few girls, regardless of their experience and talent, have her ability to provide the perfect canvas for the photographer's vision without allowing their own character to disappear entirely. Being utterly used to being photographed has a lot to do with that knack. But back then Kate wasn't always happy about it. Who would be? At times Kate and Corinne fought, bitterly and furiously, screaming at each other in their tight whispery south London voices: petulant, demanding scrappy little pieces of girls, who were downright fed up with the whole thing and yet far too engaged in it all to ever make good on, or even mean, their threats to jack it all in. At times Kate cried. She didn't want to take her clothes off; she was embarrassed and uncomfortable, in every sense of the word, and she was tired. But still they carried on.

Bit by bit Kate was becoming more professional and experiencing more of a world she'd been oblivious to eighteen months earlier. It wasn't exactly glamorous yet – a school friend came with Kate to the Camber Sands shoot and they stayed at Butlins, giving the whole experience a slightly budget-holiday feel. But with each day that Kate lived this particular and remarkable existence, the real world dropped further from view. Many of the Corinne Day pictures, destined to be trimmed down to the eight-page editorial commissioned by *The Face*, were taken during Kate's school holidays, but not all.

In later years, Kate would point out wryly that when she was slogging away for her daily rate, a sandwich and a cup of tea on a far from glamorous shoot – half the time shivering in a hotch-potch ensemble of her own thrift-shop finds or those gathered by Melanie and Corinne – she could have been bunking off school with the rest of her friends. At different times she has recalled the 'Third Summer of Love' shoot, occurring when she was still at school and after she left. Her brother, Nick, most certainly *was* still at school and on the receiving end of a thorough ribbing when the pictures were published that July. After all, Kate Mosschops, thirteen-year-old Nick's skinny big sister, was suddenly visible in print, topless, naked even, save for a battered straw hat, posing about in an achingly cool, über-trendy magazine. There must have been the odd smart remark at the gates of Riddlesdown High School, the occasional brash adolescent announcement of, 'Oi, I've seen your sister's tits.' Girls too could be cruel and there was more than a touch of jealousy about in Croydon in the aftermath of Kate's appearance in *The Face*. According to Linda, there were 'some problems at school', in that respect, but nothing enduring or, she is certain, scarring.

In light of all this, Kate's confusion as to whether she was or wasn't at school is in itself revealing. Technically she was at school when she first appeared in *The Face*. Technically she was about to sit her GCSEs and technically she was about to scrape through a couple of them. By the time the 'Third Summer of Love' came out she had left, though school had, in any real sense, long since ceased to be anything but a social hub for Kate.

By this stage Kate had her first serious boyfriend, in the form of Clark Gregory. They went out in Croydon and nearby Purley. He was a good-looking boy and had more disposable income than she, thanks to his job as a sales assistant at the local branch of Next. He got her earrings for her sixteenth birthday and it was, according to Linda, 'a real love job'. Kate was far from ready to settle down with Clark – as her mother has pointed out, if she had been she'd still be in Croydon – but they were intimate and she shared her teenage insecurities with him as she did with her real and enduringly close friends.

Today Kate's figure may be one that many young, and not so young, girls aspire to, but few women, never mind teenagers, are truly comfortable in their own skin, and at a time when every anxiety and uncertainty was heightened, Kate's body, face and appeal was being scrutinized at every casting she attended and, it naturally followed, rejected with every job she didn't get. She may have been drafted in as the poster girl for a sort of 'street' revolution, but the physique Kate aspired to then was rather more fulsome than the one nature had provided.

In one of Corinne's most famous images of the teenage

Kate in that 'Third Summer of Love' collection she is wearing a feather headdress. A thin strand of beads hangs around her neck and sits against her ribs in the curve beneath one breast. She wears a tiny little skirt which rests snug to her hips, its waistline several inches beneath her own delicately indented form. Her shoulders, sparse but strong, seem somehow pinned back against the sea breeze blowing in her face, causing her eyes to crinkle as she smiles and drawing her long hair together in salty strands. It's an arrestingly beautiful image. Kate's response? 'I was like, "Corinne, how could you give them that picture of me looking so gross with my flat tits?"'

But however much Kate hated her 'flat tits' and rolled her eyes at the pictures Corinne had taken of her and which, she would later reflect, focused on all the things she hated about herself at that age – 'my bow legs, the mole on my breast, the way I laughed' – they were the images that would carry her face and name, with a ripple of excitement, across the Atlantic.

4

It must be difficult, with the benefit of hindsight, for Kate not to feel a certain vengeful glee when she thinks back to the agents, publishers and editors who rejected her in her earliest days. But if she does feel the warming touch of smugness these days, she is too professional and too well attuned to the fickleness of the fashion business, which can knock even the most glorious creature off her perch, to allow herself any delicious indiscretions. The same is true of Sarah Doukas and Corinne Day, both of whom also endured knock-back after knock-back.

In the months following Kate's first appearances in *The Face* Corinne, who was, after all, trying to establish herself in the notoriously male field of fashion photography, took her burgeoning book of pictures to the art directors of every glossy magazine that would see her. Again and again she was told that her work showed promise, it was interesting, they liked it but they didn't like the girl.

Sarah also endured her fair share of set-backs while promoting the girl she remained convinced Storm would be the making of, and vice versa. Sarah was nothing if not alive to commercial opportunities. Storm was the first agency to employ their own in-house public relations officer, primarily with a view to promoting the agency's profile, and that of its models, to prospective clients. It was an astute investment that would pay dividends for the agency and for Kate in particular. Doukas had an insight into the world of fashion and magazines, gleaned from years spent working for Laraine Ashton, one of the industry's biggest agents. She knew that to really make it big a girl had to sell in America. Kate was working hard but she wasn't earning big money. She was winning a fair number of editorial jobs and her popularity with the team at *The Face* seemed likely to guarantee her continued appearances there should she want them. A 'good' job might pay her several hundred pounds, maybe a couple of thousand, but *The Face* had more street-cred than cash. Sarah set her sights on America, deciding Kate needed a break there. To do that, she needed an American agent, but convincing one to see her wasn't going to be easy. In 1991 Sarah sent Kate to the door of one of New York's most prestigious agents. He took one look at her vital statistics and on hearing her height refused even to see her, saying she simply wasn't tall enough to be a model. As Sarah accurately points out, 'He must be kicking himself now!'

At the time, however, it was a blow to both Sarah and Kate, but the extent to which Kate could deal with these blows was, according to those who knew her then, quite remarkable. Kate had left school and become, to all intents and purposes, a jobbing model. She had never had any great plans or ambitions to be or do anything else. She had only ever thought of leaving Croydon. Then she had been 'discovered' and the means of escape were, to some extent at least, presented to her. She had never had to think about what she wanted and besides, now that she was a model – however awkward that sounded to her when she said it – she was finding the world into which she was edging absorbing and exciting. 'Home' was still very much

Croydon, though she was spending more and more time with Corinne Day in London – she pretty much lived with her between the ages of fifteen and seventeen – hanging out, dressing up, talking about and listening to music, visiting clubs and bars and going to parties unlike any she'd ever known.

Corinne had become her best friend as well as an ad-hoc documentary-maker of her life. And when Corinne wasn't taking photographs, and sometimes even when she was, her boyfriend Mark Szaszy was filming the young Kate and Corinne in Super 8mm footage. Kate and Corinne enjoyed the sort of intense friendship that seems peculiar to women – a flurry of revelations, intimacies and sharing that borders on a crush, a flirtation even. If they were going out they might spend the entire evening going through their wardrobe, pulling together the elements of outfits they would wear only for an hour before coming home. On meeting Corinne, Kate's fondness for jumble sales and 50-pence bin-liners full of random clothes gave way to rummaging through the markets of Portobello and Camden.

Still Kate would often find herself sitting on the train to or from Croydon, and still, though she had been lauded by some of the fashion industries' most luminous talents, she was chatty, unaffected Kate, open to meeting people and forging new friendships. It's how she got to know James Brown, the hairdresser five years her senior who has been one of her closest friends and most trusted confidant since they met and started chatting one day on the Croydon train. They knew each other by sight. James's sister had been in Kate's year at school, and even though he was older and, according to schoolyard rules, should therefore have been more savvy and hip than Kate, James had always been struck by the extent to which this particular girl seemed to set the temperature when it came to cool.

It is testament to their shared passion for clothes and style that Brown remembers what Kate was wearing on the day they had their first proper chat: she wore red lipstick, jeans and a white vest, black Katharine Hamnett boots with thick heels and a goose-down leather jacket from New York (having a father who specialized in transatlantic travel was not without its benefits). That jacket was, he recalls, 'the thing everybody wanted', though looking back he doubts that she knew that – she just liked it, had it and wore it. Brown spoke about fashion and music and it chimed with all the things Kate was into back then, all the things she's still into in fact. Having fun was also high on his list of priorities, and so was making it.

Brown was working as an apprentice hairdresser in a local salon at first, and in those very early days of friendship Kate would bunk off school and hang out with him. When business was slow, Kate would sit on the washing machine at the back of the salon, chattering away, and they would while away hours drinking coffee and smoking cigarettes. When he moved to London to continue his apprenticeship at the fashionable Zoo salon in Covent Garden and then on to Brinks and Huck, Kate continued to visit him there. Increasingly it was life as a session stylist that held a greater appeal for Brown and which would ultimately bring him acclaim. Sometimes Brown would do Kate's hair and sometimes he would go to castings with her. The extent to which she allowed nothing to discourage her was, he recalls, breathtaking. In Paris he witnessed a photographer telling Kate that she was 'just another common bitch', and that she would never make it. History does not record what provoked such a comment but Kate just laughed; she creased up and giggled till tears streamed down her face.

That streak of resilience would stand her in good stead, as would her sense of fun. She was working hard at making it work, but in spite of her popularity with *The Face* there was little in her early jobs to suggest the extent to which she would set the fashion world alight, nor how imminent that moment was. In 1991 she was busy but had yet to land a seriously lucrative contract or career-making cover. Typical of the sort of editorial slots she was winning was an appearance in trendy music and fashion publications like *Sky* Magazine and featuring in *Rowland Knitting Book, Number 10*. It was a job that Kate enjoyed, however daft she may have felt clad in knickers, a thick-knit sweater and a bobble hat. The stylist, Karen Harrison, had been inspired by Arthur Ransome's 1930s children's story *Swallows and Amazons*. It may not have been cool, but it was whimsical, childlike and fun; three traits that were, and continue to be, forceful elements of Kate's character and appeal. Kate was evidently popular on the shoot and with the client, because when it came to selecting the cover image for the book of patterns it was a picture of Kate that made the cut.

It was all very comforting but not massively encouraging in the grand scheme of things. During this period at the beginning of the 1990s, though Kate might not have known it at the time, the foundations were being laid and the characters cast for an altogether new, and ultimately powerful, fashion scene. Corinne Day and James Brown, stylist Melanie Ward, Sarah Doukas and of course Kate were at the beginning of something new. Towards the end of 1990 Italian American Mario Sorrenti arrived on the scene when he came to London and into Kate's life, both personal and professional. In Kate's world, perhaps more than many, the lines between these two areas have often been rather blurred, and it is both her strength and deepest flaw.

Sorrenti was incredibly good looking. Born in Naples in 1971 his family moved to New York when he was ten years old and he had lived there with his mother, Francesca, his brother Davide and sister Vanya ever since. His face, and for that matter his body, would already have been familiar to Kate when they met through Corinne, since by then Mario had appeared on British television screens in an advert for Levi's jeans, slamming ball after ball into the pockets of a pool table in a steamy roughneck bar. But it was really an interest in photography that led to Mario's flirtation with modelling.

At eighteen he had enrolled in the prestigious School of Visual Arts in Manhattan; he lasted eight months before dropping out. Structured learning and classes of the sort on offer were not, it seemed, for him. And besides, the contacts he had made and what he *had* learned in that space of time had caused life to take over from lectures. Established photographers Bruce Weber and Steven Meisel spotted Mario. At the time, Meisel in particular had a reputation for being able to make or break careers. In 1992 Meisel shored up his influence by gaining the dubious distinction of having helped conceive and execute a work described as arguably the most obscene coffee-table book in history: Madonna's *SEX*. At first these kingmakers in their field saw Mario's potential in front of the lens, not behind it, and they used him as a model and he, in turn, used their example as his guide. He learned not from books but from the masters, assisting on shoots where he could and honing his skills.

When he was nineteen he came to London and quickly fell into the excitement of a new scene visible, for the most part, in the pages of *The Face* and *iD* magazines but, which was beginning to seep into the consciousness of the fashion editors and art directors of more mainstream publications. It was in the more underground magazines, the ones pushing the new edgy London sensibility that would bloom into Cool Britannia, that Corinne's pictures were published alongside shots by Juergen Teller, Marc Lebon and David Sims. New talents were being nurtured, if not highly paid. Established professionals were pushing themselves and their readers towards something new. Rising stars were getting breaks. In the July edition of *The Face*, in which Kate appears, the 'Third Summer of Love' fashion spread precedes an interview with American filmmaker and writer John Waters, talking about his forthcoming film *Cry-Baby*. With a budget of $3million it was the most expensive production he had ever made, and in the midst of pictures of Waters and the cast there is one of a youthful and relatively unknown Johnny Depp. He was, the British readership was informed, a 'US TV heart-throb', for whom the film constituted his first big-screen break. He was also, it noted, the first 'conventionally handsome' hero to be cast by Waters. But it was not Johnny Depp that Mario noticed, it was Kate, and when he eventually met her through Corinne he was enchanted by the south London chatterbox, though it would be months before anything romantic happened between them.

Clark Gregory, Kate's Croydon boyfriend for more than a year, was still around, and however thrilling Kate found her new friends and the lifestyle they lived, she still had strong and genuine feelings for him. Looking back she would realize that this was not, in fact, love, or at least not the grand passion that her sixteen-year-old self had believed it to be, but it was the closest approximation she had experienced to that point and it still tugged her back to Croydon – and doubtless it hurt when, in May 1991, she faced up to the fact that the relationship and life that went with it were already things of the past.

She cried hot tears of disappointment and regret as she and Clark sat in his car outside the White Bear Pub in Warlingham, Surrey, and ended their youthful romance. They had been arguing all the time and no longer brought out the best in each other. They told each other they would get back together one day when their lives weren't pulling so strongly in opposite directions, but deep down they must have know that such a reunion was never going to happen. Then Clark drove Kate home. She had to pack as she was flying out of Britain to a photoshoot the next day. Clark fought back tears as they parted.

Over the next months Kate continued to press the flesh, travel to castings, spend more and more time in London and, in her attitude and sheer charisma, she unwittingly impressed each photographer she worked with. Sarah Doukas and Kate's booker at Storm, Jessica Hallett, were similarly impressed by their find's apparently indefatigable nature. She was relentlessly keen and quick – even hungry – to learn. She had never been this way at school but now that she was out exploring something that really caught her interest, she devoured it all: music, books, styles. These energies and appetites would prove both blessing and a curse as her career was about to take off, threatening to swamp her in the process.

This was the year that Corinne's photographs – those grimy images from *The Face* – made their way onto the desk of Fabien Baron, then creative director for *Harper's Bazaar*. Towards the end of 1991 Baron had been tasked with working on a relaunch of *Harper's Bazaar*. The magazine was looking tired, staid and horribly conventional; something more sassy and edgy was required. He looked to England for inspiration, tuning into what was happening around the edges of London's mainstream magazine culture, and there he saw Corinne's pictures and Kate. His reaction was immediate: 'I remember thinking, "Wow. That girl's different from anyone else!"' he recalled. He wanted to see her.

Meanwhile Sarah Doukas was still trying to get Kate onto the radar of agents and bookers in America. Her first unsuccessful attempts had not deterred her, she just needed to find the right person, the one willing to take a risk and represent Kate in the tough, and lucrative, American market. Sarah was a professional powerhouse, but she knew her limitations – she could not do it all single-handed – so she introduced Kate to New Yorker Paul Rowland. Paul was a former model who had become an agent and a man with a mission. More importantly, he was a man with an agency and no models. Paul was established – when Sarah and Kate met with Rowland in late 1991 he was already successfully running Men Management – but he knew that the real money lay in women, so he'd set up Women Management. Rowland was a risk-taker who was, at that golden moment, in the blissful position of having absolutely nothing to lose. He also didn't particularly care for going with the majority view. Popularity did not hold him in thrall. He was charming and had a punchy business sense, and he liked Kate and agreed to take her on. For Kate, New York, and America, was about to open for business.

By this time Mario and Kate had become an item, and a passionate, glamorous one at that. For the first, but far from the last, time Kate was one half of a fashionable 'power' couple. Admittedly the circumstances in which they lived during their early relationship didn't live up to the label. For many months Mario and Kate lived in Croydon with her mother, Linda, and Geoff Collman. As far as Linda was concerned Kate liked Mario and so did she. She had never been a conventional mother and was under no illusion that her daughter was chaste. Why on earth should she be, as long as she was safe, happy and loved? Kate was almost eighteen years old when she asked Linda if Mario could stay with them for a while. He had been sleeping on friends' sofas in London – a far from ideal scenario – and Linda didn't hesitate in agreeing. They did their thing and she and Geoff did theirs. It was only ever going to be a temporary arrangement, though it offered a surprising side effect in the form of a brief foray into modelling for Kate's then fourteen-year-old brother Nick.

Sorrenti met Nick when Kate introduced him to her mother. It was early 1992 and Sorrenti felt that there was something about Nick's unconventional looks: his wide-set eyes, long, rather crooked nose – the legacy of four breaks – and his pony-tailed hair. The Croydon teenager could hardly be accused of having an overworked look – he played football well, but that was pretty much where his exercise regime began and ended. No one could have blamed Nick for feeling flattered by Sorrenti's suggestion that he too could model. Sorrenti took pictures of Nick and Kate together and showed them to Storm, and within weeks Nick Moss was on Sarah's books, too.

After that early flurry, Sorrenti's involvement in Nick's fledgling career fell away; it wasn't a lack of interest so much as a matter of logistics. From early in their relationship Kate and Mario spent an increasing amount of time travelling. Within six months of them embarking on what would be a great romance and a pivotal relationship for both of them, professionally and personally, they were in New York. Mario had gone from next to nothing to having a contract with *Harper's Bazaar* and working for Calvin Klein, and so had Kate.

1992 was the year that Kate suddenly found herself living the model life and doing her first runway season. Still a rather gawky addition to the Amazonian tribe that included Christy Turlington, Naomi Campbell, Helena Christensen and Linda Evangelista, Kate was nevertheless there, making an impression and forging friendships as she went. For Kate it was still all fabulously exciting. She was in demand for Paris fashion week, walking the runway for Karl Lagerfeld, Azzedine Alaia, Versace, Galliano . . . the lot and living between Christy and Naomi's rooms in the Ritz. She drank champagne before and after every show, whether turning up for fittings and rehearsals at six in the morning or six in the evening. She went to dinners and parties. She discovered what would become her favourite bar, The Hemingway, and her favourite cocktail – a blend of gin, lemon, sugar and, of course, champagne. *This* was what it was all about.

All the time she was meeting and mingling with exciting and inspirational people, like DJ Jeremy Healy, who provided the soundtrack for Galliano's shows and who became a close friend to Kate, along with his one-time partner and business manager Fran Cutler. Fran, a well-connected party organizer and music manager, has remained a confidante of Kate's for close to two decades.

Sorrenti was still doing a bit of modelling during this time, but increasingly he began devoting his time to photography and, of course, to photographing Kate. They travelled together in the early months of 1992 to Milan, Paris, New York and Berlin. It was, Kate once recalled, 'a full-on' time, 'twenty-four-hours-a-day'. Since her days travelling from casting to casting across London, suddenly she was working all the time, shooting pictures or doing shows. And afterwards there was always a party or a dinner to go to, people to hang out, smoke pot and have a laugh with. For a while – close to two years – she later reflected, 'it all just kind of rolled together in a great way'.

Kate went to New York with Sorrenti. She didn't know quite where she wanted to be; she just knew that she was happy with him at the time. She was welcomed into Mario's mother's home, as he had been into Linda's, and Francesca Sorrenti and

Mario's siblings, Davide and Vanya, became a second family to Kate.

That summer Kate was invited to the offices of *Harper's Bazaar*. Years later the late Liz Tilberis, then editor-in-chief of the magazine, remembered the air of scepticism with which she, model editor Sara Foley and fashion director Paul Cavaco anticipated Kate's arrival in the office. They knew that she had worked mostly for *The Face* and therefore mostly for a fashionable but uncommercial audience, and they had heard that she was little, but as Tilberis recorded, 'The second she walked into our office, Sara Foley and Paul Cavaco knew they were looking at a true beauty: someone whose face and attitude were a personification of the time. There was just one problem: Kate was small. When she stood up against our office wall, she measured a shade less than 5ft 7in.'

But the key to Kate's success then – and arguably today – was that having met her, however briefly, Foley, Cavaco and Tilberus *wanted* to work with her. They talked away the obvious and unchangeable height problem: small models, they reasoned, *had* made it in the past – Twiggy for one, who in many ways wasn't dissimilar to the girl now standing smilingly before them. The truth was that on meeting Kate the staff fell in love with her. They wanted fashion to be more pared down and accessible and less complicated. Tilberus summed it up thus: 'This girl was so mesmerizing she was worth a try.' The result was a nine-page story in the magazine's relaunch issue of September 1992. Kate appeared in a series of photographs taken by Patrick Demarchelier. Dressed in outré designs and jewel-coloured velvets, in some Kate wears a blonde curling wig, piled high and flowing long; in others she sports a distinctly synthetic brunette crop. Alongside the images runs the legend, 'Wild: remember a time when genders were bent, rules broken, inhibitions shed and all the best girls were pretty wild?' It was, in the grand scheme of Kate's career, rather prophetic. This was the big time.

That same month Kate appeared in *Vogue* for the first time, modelling for Dolce & Gabbana. Croydon pal Brown styled her hair and became, in the process, the youngest hairstylist to work on a *Vogue* shoot. Both he and Kate were struck by the unreality of it all; they just couldn't quite believe it was happening.

Back in America, Fabien Baron was understandably excited about Kate's successful début in *Harper's Bazaar*, and she was featured again the very next month. Coincidentally, at the time that Baron was involved with reinvigorating *Harper's*, he was also working with Calvin Klein. He knew that Klein was looking for a new girl and was impatient, having been frustrated already in his quest. However, although Kate may have been Baron's first choice, she was not Klein's. How could she be? Klein had never heard of the little girl from Croydon until Baron placed her under his nose. His original interest had been in a French girl, two years Kate's senior, called Vanessa Paradis. Paradis had already established herself in her home country as a singer and actress of note. 'Joe le Taxi' may have been as irritating as it was successful – in 1987 it topped the French charts for fourteen weeks – but it was undeniably a hit. In 1991 Paradis appeared in adverts for Coco Chanel, dressed in black feathers, whistling and swinging prettily on a swing like an exotic bird in a gilded cage. Little wonder then that Klein saw great potential in her. The feeling, however, was not mutual. Paradis turned down his offer to appear in adverts for his range. Baron suggested an alternative.

An afternoon appointment was set up with Kate, Baron and Klein in his New York offices. Baron asked Kate to put on a pair of jeans and Calvin 'fell in love right away'. In that New York minute Kate became the ultimate CK girl. Earlier that year Klein had signed Mark Wahlberg. Today Wahlberg is known for his acting career, having starred in a string of films such as *The Perfect Storm*, *Three Kings* and *The Italian Job* and having been nominated for an Academy Award and a Golden Globe for his performance in *The Departed* in 2006, but when Klein signed him he had an altogether more dangerous reputation, in America at least.

Wahlberg called himself Marky Mark, and while his older brother Donnie had carved out a mainstream pop career with *New Kids on the Block*, Marky Mark opted for the more edgy existence of a rap star. He had, in fact, been part of the original band line-up but quit, preferring his Marky Mark persona to the clean-cut pop-idol mould into which he'd be forced in a boy band. He had a history of violence and had been jailed for assault as a teenager. This tough-nut image was epitomized by a six-pack to die for and a fondness for grabbing his crotch and showing off his boxers on stage. Klein signed him for $1million, and before 1992 was out, Kate and Mark would appear in a series of advertisements on billboards and bus shelters, in magazines and on television on both sides of the Atlantic.

It has been said that the Calvin Klein contract Kate signed that year – initially earning her £75,000, increasing to £2 million when she signed a five-year-deal, committing to work for Klein for 100 days over that time frame and to advertise for him exclusively – made her, but it could equally be argued that she made Klein. The designer's business sense and advertising awareness was phenomenal, but it had also got him into trouble before now. His decision to use young, non-professional models had seen his adverts branded 'kiddie porn'. Consequently he needed to appeal to the mass market and that meant not alienating the conservative elements of the American public. There was only so far they could be pushed.

On set there was no sexual chemistry between Kate and Mark – he liked his women more chunky, she liked her men less commercial and self-consciously honed – but the images were hot enough without it. The pictures of Marky Mark, with his torso stripped bare to reveal taut muscles and his jeans low slung to expose the CK waistband of his boxers, and Kate, thin, innocent and curving her naked torso towards him, certainly provoked a reaction. But it was a 'safe' enough outcry. Just enough to make sure people looked and wanted to see what all the fuss was about, but not so much that self-appointed moral guardians would kick up a real stink.

Back in Croydon, Linda saw the pictures and thought them beautiful. She viewed pictures of Kate in outré designer clothing – particularly the outlandish designs of Galliano – with a certain wry disbelief. To her Kate's hair often looked a bit of mess, the outfits were mismatched and as for the individual items, never mind the overall look, well, would anyone ever really wear such outfits in Croydon? So when it came to the pared-down Calvin Klein pictures, their simplicity must have held a certain appeal. After all, Kate's hair was glossy and simply styled and she was wearing very little make-up . . . she was wearing very little of anything.

People asked Linda how she felt viewing such images. Friends and journalists asked her if it felt strange viewing images of her semi-nude daughter posing provocatively with a scantily clad man. She replied that it did not, because the pictures that she saw did not really seem like Kate. It was a sense of dislocation Kate herself experienced in later years, as her fame spread and her image was projected around the globe. 'The more visible they make me,' she would explain, 'the less visible I become.' She would smilingly acknowledge that this was a quotation from Cocteau, describing the turn of phrase as one 'too clever' for her, but the sentiment was hers all the same. It was an observation riddled with ambivalence, a disappearing act that could, at any given time, be considered a boon or the price that Kate would pay for her success. Equally, Kate's arrival in terms of mainstream, high-rolling fashion was, for her, made difficult by all the leaving it necessitated.

Sorrenti travelled with her whenever he could and they flew first class and had a ball. But the reality was that whenever Kate arrived somewhere and got comfortable, decking out her hotel room with the candles, throws and little touches of home she liked to bring with her, she had to scoop them all back into her travel bag and leave. Of course it was fabulous that wherever she landed she was in such demand, but sometimes, just sometimes, it must have crossed her mind that it would be nice to stay in one place for a little while longer and luxuriate in the riches that were newly hers to enjoy.

From appearing predominantly in trendy youth titles such as *iD* and *The Face*, Kate emerged into the American market and made regular appearances in *Harper's Bazaar* and *Vogue*, where she worked with photographers at the absolute top of their game. It was a thrilling, if exhausting, time and Kate wasn't looking back. From travelling round the world to shoots and shows, her life fell into a hectic pattern of bouncing back and forth across the Atlantic, predominantly between New York and London, a phase she once summed up as, 'Working, working, working, working.'

Her brother Nick also found that life since signing with Storm had become surprisingly hectic and successful. Perhaps it's churlish to suggest that the 'Kate factor' was the only reason Nick won bookings and shows – certainly it was something about which Nick was understandably defensive – but it's impossible to completely ignore the part that Kate's success, and the new wave of fashion she heralded in, played in her brother's career. He was, after all, spotted in his own home by his sister's boyfriend and not across a packed airport. Nick would come to feel, in a way that Kate never would, the stinging unfairness of the fashion world, one populated by fluttering acolytes who would laud you one day then drop you without a backward glance in order to snare the next new thing. It would only be natural if Nick watched Kate's career with a tinge of envy, something that must have added another layer to the always complex relations between brother and sister.

For Nick, it was fun while it lasted. Within six months of being signed to Storm he had been called to New York to be photographed by Richard Avedon alongside Linda Evangelista, Naomi Campbell, Christy Turlington and, of course, Kate for that season's Versace catalogue. He worked for Levi and he took to the catwalk in Paris that autumn. He flung himself into the après-runway lifestyle on the very first night, rolling back to his hotel at eight in the morning with just two hours to spare before the first job of the following day. It was, he later reflected, 'just stupid to go so crazy when I was working early the next day'. But part of the reason, part of his need to let off steam had, it seems, been more than a simple what-the-hell approach to life.

When Nick landed in Paris and discovered that no one spoke English he was blindsided. He had been given an address in Paris – his first show of the week – so he got himself there and found himself handed four different outfits and manhandled into line. When he staggered out onto the runway he was faced with a daunting bank of photographers. It was overwhelming. Little wonder then that later that night, when he met up with Kate, whose confidence and ease must have seemed reassuring and awe-inducing, he kicked back. Kate disappeared back to her hotel after a couple of hours, but Nick continued partying into the night.

For Kate there would be many more seasons, shows and shoots, but not for Nick. Yet the year closed on a high for Nick, and in December 1992 he appeared alongside Kate in *Harper's Bazaar* in a photoshoot taken by Sorrenti. Nick's brief modelling career is typical of the vast majority of young models' experience of the business. In the shoots he secured and bookings he received he was rather *more* successful than many.

When asked eighteen months after his signing what he would choose for his epitaph he said simply, 'I am my own man – not my sister's brother.' If this was a bid to be taken on the same level as her, either by the business in which his sister was causing such excitement or, as that excitement spilled over into the public consciousness, by a wider audience, it was mired in folly. It was like Nadia Comaneci's little sister doing a handstand in the back garden and shouting, 'Look, a handstand!' In all likelihood, Nick was well aware that his own modelling career would never be viewed in isolation from or without comparison to that of his sister. He may have wanted the world to know that he was more than just Kate's brother but modelling was never going to be the way to prove it.

Certainly it did little to change his material existence in any lasting way. In later years Nick and Kate's complex relationship must have been made even more difficult by their mutual awareness of just how much she had in comparison to him.

When she was generous towards him materially, she could run the risk of being accused of high-handedness, or even being patronizing. If she kept what was hers to herself it could be viewed as mean-spirited. During his early modelling career Nick's father expressed a wish that he would focus, instead, on honing his talents on the football pitch. Linda, meanwhile, was an unflappable presence who remained more concerned with hectoring her teenage son into tidying his room than swooning over another of her offspring's forays onto the international fashion stage.

Towards the close of 1992 Kate and Sorrenti managed to have some much-needed time to themselves, taking a blissful break in the Virgin Islands. They rented a villa and Sorrenti took photograph after photograph of Kate, with almost obsessive fascination. Kate was only a few months short of her nineteenth birthday when Sorrenti showed the pictures to Calvin Klein. He loved them. It was clear to Klein just how much Sorrenti worshipped Kate, and as he looked at the artful studies, with Kate stripped of clothing and make-up, he saw the potential of this sort of arrestingly intimate portrait. He already had Kate lined up to advertise his new perfume, Obsession. Now he knew exactly who would shoot the campaign. He told Kate and Sorrenti to 'go off again and do something for the perfume'.

5

The island of Jost van Dyke is just four miles long. Its main street is a stretch of beach. It is a laid-back and remote spit of land in the British Virgin Islands, known by locals as 'barefoot island' because that is how its inhabitants spend most of their days. Shoes are just something that sand gets into.

If location was anything to go by, Kate and Sorrenti's shoot for Obsession should have been blissful, yet it was anything but. Looking back, Kate recognized that in deciding to use Sorrenti as the photographer, Klein had been 'very clever'. He could see, she felt, the intensity between the lovers and how it would burn on the page and screen. He was not to know that that same passionate intensity would also make it almost impossible for the couple to work together. Had he known, would it have changed his decision? After all, commercially the resulting campaign was sublime. The reality of the shoot, however, was somewhat different, being marred by bickering and squabbling as Mario became engrossed in the shoot.

She has recalled how, on one occasion, she heard Sorrenti working on the footage he had shot of her. 'I remember hearing Mario's voice in the other room going, "I love you, Kate. I love you, Kate." And I was like, "What is that?!" He was like, "Well, it's true man! It's true!" and I was like, "You're mad!"'

It was an appropriate enough state of mind for the campaign with a tagline, 'Between love and madness lies obsession.'

The couple rented a house on the beach and had, in Kate's words, 'the worst time', but for all that they were still in love with each other, and still Kate's presence in front of the camera and on film was mesmerizing. After six days, understandably anxious at Klein's decision to go with a relatively untried photographer and place two young lovers in seclusion on an idyllic island, Neil Kraft, Senior Vice President of Advertising at Calvin Klein, flew out to join the couple and oversee the shoot. Always with an eye on the end product, he insisted on lining up a professional director and hair and make-up people for the final two days of filming, but when it came to it, none of their services was needed. Kate and Sorrenti had turned their obsession with each other into advertising gold.

Looking back at that period in Kate's career, Sarah Doukas admits that Kate's work schedule was phenomenal. By her own admission the team at Storm were 'real slave drivers'. In one week Kate ping-ponged across the Atlantic six times for three different shoots, a physically exhausting feat that was beginning to take its toll. All her 'working, working, working, working' meant that Kate barely saw her friends, and she struggled to keep in touch with family and home life. There was, for the time that she lived with Sorrenti's family in New York, a certain security, but even that would have to be jettisoned in pursuit of ever-greater exposure and currency. As is so often the case in life, Kate was to discover that as her professional life took flight, so her personal happiness began to founder.

In the midst of a period that was frantic and in many ways exhilarating, Kate found herself flying all over the world and, so it seemed for a while, crying all the time. Suddenly her career had gone stratospheric and the speed with which it was all happening was understandably difficult to handle. She was living fast and hard and starting to earn serious money. Kate prided herself on being a girl who never said no to anything, be it work or play. Her mother once cautioned her that she couldn't have fun all the time, no matter how nice that might be. Kate's response was typically bold and hard to counter: 'Why the fuck not? Why the fuck can't I have fun all the time?' But as would happen more than once in her life, the very time when it should have been 'fun all the time', it just wasn't. Instead it was quite overwhelming. Kate was in New York at Francesca Sorrenti's home when suddenly she felt quite ill and couldn't get out of bed. She didn't know what was wrong, and it must have been a frightening and isolating sensation.

An appointment was made with a local doctor who informed her there was 'nothing wrong' and proceeded to prescribe her Valium. Francesca Sorrenti was horrified. She took Kate's prescription and informed her there was no way she was going to allow this healthy young girl to start popping pills in order to blot out whatever stress and anxieties she was experiencing and instead gave Kate a fraction of what she had been prescribed. The only purpose Valium could have served would have been to mask the very human anxieties Kate must have been experiencing. She was away from home all the time and being continually judged. It was a lifestyle practically designed to breed self-consciousness, even fear, and for a brief time those feelings seemed crippling.

The beginning of 1993 was a whirl of photoshoots and magazine appearances. In January Kate appeared in German

Vogue on a photoshoot in Marrakesh. That same month, for her nineteenth birthday, Calvin Klein gave her a slinky black evening dress. Kate wore it with trainers and, back in Croydon, Linda rolled her eyes at the pictures and wondered what on earth Mr Klein would think. She had a gift for Kate, too, a beautiful ring, but with her daughter's busy schedule it would be months before Linda saw her eldest child to give it to her. By now, Kate and Sorrenti had moved into a maisonette in London's Notting Hill. It was more fashionable than lavish, but they rarely got a chance to spend any time together there anyway.

From week to week and even day to day, Kate was on flights to shoots and runway shows all over the world. When she and Sorrenti managed to catch a few days together at home, they played at being the sort of conventional couple. He cooked and she cleaned. He teased her that they should have a baby. She laughed and told him he only wanted her to have a baby so she couldn't run away from him, and in that jovial notion they both may have recognized that they were slipping apart. After all, Kate was well and truly financially independent, and had used some of her wealth to rent a flat in the Pigalle district of Paris.

It was a fashionable choice and demonstrates the sort of bohemian decadence to which Kate was drawn even then. It was a seedy, funky place and all around her were the influences that would inspire her style in years to come; the Belle Epoque design of the French Metropole, the sangfroid of Parisian chic and the tug of the underworld, sex shops and sexual experimentation for which the city's red light district was well known. How it all must have appealed to the young model's open mind and sense of adventure.

In purely pragmatic terms, the property abroad provided a

neat way of avoiding paying a hefty tax bill on her increasingly large earnings. By the age of twenty, Kate was commanding fees of between £1,000 an hour and £15,000 for a day's work. She had become a tax exile, juggling jobs all over the world, travelling constantly and finding, in this breathless, rootless existence, that she would, literally, run out of time – ninety days in Britain, a similarly strict count in America.

In all of this it was to her father and Sarah's brother, Simon Chambers, that Kate turned for advice. And in February 1993 Kate Moss, model, became SKATE Enterprises, a limited company with her father and Simon Chambers as directors. Kate did not become a director herself until 2001. It is worth noting that, when it came to handling the now blossoming business side of her life, it was to her father, not Linda, that Kate turned. Linda has never pretended to be business savvy, and when asked what traits he would wish to have inherited from his parents, Nick admitted to desiring his father's cleverness and his mother's personality. It's a revealing choice. As for the choice of company name, 'Skate' was the nickname Sorrenti coined for Kate, and when the moment came to name her business, it simply seemed the best fit.

One month after SKATE Enterprises came into being, the movement Kate had been a trailblazer for found official recognition – and a nametag – in the March edition of *Vogue*. The phenomenon in question was termed 'London Girl' style, and suddenly the focus of the fashion world turned upon the British capital and its pale laconic girls with their jutting cheekbones, scrawny physiques and hair the colour of weak tea. For Kate, Corinne Day, Melanie Ward and Sarah Doukas, it was a moment of united and unifying glory. The look, of which Kate was unquestionably queen, and which, at it most extreme became 'waif' which Corinne, Melanie and Sarah had spotted, identified and nurtured as something new in true fashion-forward style, was being hailed by that arbiter of international style, *Vogue*.

Kate appeared on the front cover in a picture by Corinne looking like Penelope Tree. The Sixties model and contemporary of Twiggy – less commercially successful, but still a muse to David Bailey – was spotted at the age of thirteen by renowned photographer Diane Arbus and photographed by Richard Avedon four years later. The whole 'London Girl' style, identified in that month's *Vogue* as 'fashion's new spirit', owed much to the Sixties and the original London girls, not all of whom, as it happened, hailed from the city, but whom, for the sake of editorial, were deemed to embody the spirit most closely associated with it. Among them, rather prophetically, was Marianne Faithfull, a woman who would become a dear, close and enduring friend to Kate, and French model, Lucie de la Falaise. Parisienne Lucie went on to marry Marlon Richards, Keith Richard's son by Anita Pallenberg.

It was Anita who introduced Kate to Marianne, a kind and intelligent woman with first-hand experience of a world that, with all its music and indulgences, Kate found fascinating and compelling. So it was through honorary London girl Lucie that Kate gained an entry into the wonderful, chaotic and rock'n'roll world of the Rolling Stones, their children, wives and lovers, past and present. It was a scene she adored and which, for the most part, adored her right back.

'London Style . . . London Girls – fashion's new spirit', was writ large across the image of Kate on the cover of that March edition of *Vogue*. Inside, the fashion editorial welcomed a 'refreshing style that's half feminine, half tomboy and wholly pretty'. The clothes that, the reader was informed, they would – or should – all be wearing that season were 'intoxicating' for their 'sense of freedom ... These clothes are as far from uptight, power dressing as it's possible to get.' After years of having the 'international beauty standard set by glowing super-women, of trying to match the tans, the curves and the hairdos of Cindy Crawford and Claudia Schiffer, London Girl has come into her own.' Sighs of relief all round then.

The essentially aristocratic taste for 'the old and tatty – two qualities that are integral to London Girl's style', had made a resurgence with this new spirit. Somehow the wild child attitude of the Sixties and the eccentricities of aristocratic trendsetters such as Lady Birley, coincidentally grandmother of Lucie de la Falaise, who was praised for her beauty and extraordinary dress and habits – she fed lobster thermidore to her roses – collided and evolved into this new look.

It was, essentially, an 'elegantly wasted' look, one with more than a hint of drug-induced nonchalance, which would see the London Girl give way to the waif, a development that would hurtle into controversy more rapidly than anyone involved in the *Vogue* editorial that spring could possibly have imagined.

Corinne's discoveries were heavily represented – Rosemary Ferguson, a former Tesco check-out girl, was there and Sarah Murray, who worked at a chip shop and, briefly, at a go-kart track. There was no place for the likes of that other famous London Girl, Streatham-born Naomi. She was something else, part of the supermodel elite, an untouchable, extraordinary creature known, even then, for her diva-like tendencies. Naomi never seemed anything but aware of her own beauty, and that awareness was as inherent to her appeal as its absence was to Kate's, Rosemary's, Lucie's and Sarah's. These girls not only looked like they didn't try, they took it one step further. They looked amazing because, if anything, they were determined to underplay their looks. John Galliano, an integral part of the scene, saw it in the models he used on his runway and in shoots. Referring to 'London Girl style,' he summed it up: 'Supreme messiness combined with some of the best complexions in the world. It's an art-school sensibility.' That 'sensibility' might owe much to the reality of the life of an art-school student which left them looking as undernourished and broke as they were. This is not to suggest that the look as it appeared in the pages of *Vogue* that month was accidental or artless. Melanie and Corinne spent hours with Kate on their first fashion shoots, coaxing just the right amount and sort of greasiness into her long and, by the time they'd finished styling it, suitably limp hair.

For Sarah Doukas, always keen to spot new talent and manage the girls she had, the rise and rise of the 'London Girl' proved a challenging time. She bewailed the fact that she and her colleagues had to spend fruitless hours drumming the concepts of basic grooming into their London girls. She used to send them to the Beauty Clinic on Kensington High Street in the hope that even if they didn't take the time to have their legs and bikini lines waxed regularly they would be won over by the aromatherapy facials and massages on offer. As for manicures and pedicures, that was a hope too far. In New York you could tell a girl to cut off her head and she would do it if she thought it would give her a better chance of getting a booking. In London you could tell a girl that Ralph Lauren was on the telephone and she'd still flinch about having a haircut and dither over the prospect of leaving her boyfriend for the weekend.

Such was the rebellious streak that shot through the girls who personified 'London Girl' spirit. It was refreshing and frustrating in equal measure, and it was, in its most pure state, at its peak in March 1993, with Kate at epicentre.

In that same March edition Kate is shown modelling the international collections in a football field in Croydon. Where else? The shoot was the work of Day, whose star was in the ascendance thanks to her endlessly exciting collaboration with Kate.

The previous year, 1992, Corinne had been awarded the prestigious Photographe de la Mode prize. More significant in terms of her financial status was a telephone call she received from Anna Wintour, editor of American *Vogue*, asking her to go to New York and shoot for her. It was an invitation that coincided with an approach to do the spring advertising campaign for Barney's, the upscale designer store that *Sex and the City* actress Sarah Jessica Parker once neatly explained, 'If you're a nice person and you work hard you get to go shopping at Barney's. It's the decadent reward.' It was also an unexpected one for Corinne, who prided herself on being a fashion photography visionary and not necessarily one for whom the Park Avenue princesses, their dear mamas and rich fathers and husbands were quite ready. In short, they were the sort of people for whom fashion and grooming are one and the same thing.

Corinne was not anti-fashion, but she was keen to photograph it on her own terms and had no interest in predictable or ostentatious dressing. Like Kate, who could now look at pictures of herself on billboards or in magazines and not quite recognize the face that looked back at her, Corinne felt a creeping disbelief at how big she had suddenly become. She openly wondered if *Vogue* was ready for her brand of photography, with its stark, documentary style, however overwhelming the enthusiasm with which it met the dawn of 'London Girl' style.

Her uncertainty was hardly surprising. After all, Corinne

had been instrumental in introducing Kate to the pages of *The Face* magazine, yet after more than a year working as a major contributor to the publication they had gone their separate ways. The magazine, she was informed, wasn't selling. They needed a more commercial look. Why should *Vogue* prove any less fickle? Why should any more store be set by the opinions of the fashion editors of *The Times*, who described Corinne as 'the perfect recessionary photographer', or an editorial in *Harper's Bazaar* that wondered, 'Could this girl photographer turn out to be the David Bailey of her generation?'

Fashion had a habit of cutting one off at the knees. Corinne was well aware, and even prepared, for that. What she could not have been prepared for was how swiftly that cut would follow – falling within months of her glorious recognition in *Vogue* – or that, when it came, it would be delivered by Kate.

Corinne and Kate had forged an intense friendship, having both embarked on a similar journey. They shared a passion for music and their minds were hungry for sensation and information. They shared a taste for clothes by Margiela and Galliano – designers who created items that looked like beautiful antique treasures . . . or rags. They shared clothes, period – a small thing perhaps but as any woman knows, it's a gesture that speaks volumes for the strength and intimacy of their friendship. Clothing and identity are so closely linked.

Of course they each found, even in the same item of dress, enough wriggle room to assert their own personality. When they both adored a completely see-through silver lamé slip dress by Liza Bruce – with thin straps, a scoop neckline and bias cut that skimmed their hips – Corinne wore it over a black T-shirt with big pants so she looked aggressively cool, while Kate wore it with nothing but a pair of black knickers and got her pictures in all the papers. In that detail the difference between life behind and before the lens was writ large, and it brought with it a pressure that would test even the strongest friendship.

In April, the month that Corinne flew to New York for her meetings with Anna Wintour and the advertising directors at Barney's, Kate appeared in a television advert alongside Naomi Campbell, Linda Evangelista and Christy Turlington. The advert was for the Vauxhall Corsa and featured the girls attempting to attack the car with circular saws and metal cutters in a vain attempt to distract men's attention from this new supermodel. It cost £4 million and was the most expensive television advert of the day, in part because of the large-scale special effects and filmic scope, but also because of the hefty fees Naomi and co. commanded.

Yet had it not been for Sarah Doukas's determined driving of Kate's career and dogged refusal to settle for anything less than market supremacy for her big discovery, Kate would never have been in it. When the advertising agency booked their supermodels Kate was not among them and Sarah wanted to know why. Her decision to create an inhouse PR machine was about to pay off big time for Kate and Storm. Paula Karaiskos, tasked with handling all press for Storm and its girls, contacted the advertising agency and enquired why they hadn't booked Kate for the shoot. They had never heard of her.

It seems incredible now, but what follows shows how orchestrated Kate's apparently organic emergence was. Paula Karaiskos had a courier take Kate's press book of advertisement and editorial work round to the advertisers, and in the final ad Kate ended up sitting on the bonnet of the car. The staff at Storm were thrilled, and perhaps slightly amazed, that their efforts had paid off. After so many set-backs and rejections, it must have come as a sweet vindication of Doukas's management style.

Before setting up Storm, Sarah had, after all, worked for a large agency where it was, in her words, 'all about making money'. As a result she didn't always feel comfortable with the direction in which she, and the girls, were pushed. In *her* agency she was determined to take a bigger-picture view and really invest in building a girl's image. It was more interesting for her and, as far as Kate was concerned, ultimately it was more profitable. It was this approach which led Sarah to question advertisers and ask, 'Why not Kate?' helping to promote her model as a brand in herself with an inherent, and product-enhancing, value.

For decades models had rarely been named in the credits of magazine or newspaper shoots. It was only the agency that got a name-check, along with the photographer, hair and make-up and, perhaps, a stylist. The focus was less on the model and more on the clothes on her back, the make-up on her face or the product in her hair. In the end, of course, the supermodels became so famous in their own right that the public were on first-name terms with many of them – Naomi, Linda, Christy, Helena – but none of them had an image; not really. They were just incredibly beautiful ciphers who commanded incredibly high fees.

By pushing the girls on her books, giving them names and identities and actually thinking about their image, Sarah was ahead of the game. But once an image is built, it must be protected. That was the tricky part and it called for some harsh decisions. In the same month as Kate appeared in the Vauxhall advert and Corinne shot the Barney's campaign, the pair collaborated on a job that would threaten it all.

Three months later the results of that shoot were published in the June edition of British *Vogue*. It was Corinne's second assignment for the magazine and, in her approach to the brief, she showed no sign of compromising her style for a more traditionally *Vogue* take on life. The fashion story in question was 'Under-exposure'. 'What to Wear Beneath Effort-Free Clothes?' found its answer in 'Barely-There Underwear. Naturally.'

Corinne chose as the location for the shoot Kate and Sorrenti's west London flat, and in the photos Kate was lit by the shrill, cold daylight of early spring rather than the warming glance of studio lighting. Her hair hung loose or was pulled back in a scrunched-up ponytail. The 'set' of each picture was bare and deliberately unluxurious. In one shot thin, lacy knickers, their label still in place, bunch and bag around her tiny bottom, and the look was finished with a stripy sleeveless tanktop. In the most famous image of the set, Kate stands against a wall, framed by an uncertain halo of fairylights stuck to the wall with masking tape. One hand rests on her hip while the other arm extends out of shot – the picture, like the model, seems badly framed, but deliberately so. Kate wears a pink vest and animal print knickers. She looks directly at the viewer with a bored, almost insolent, gaze. It is the gaze, not the knickers, which demand attention.

In another shot Kate is shown wearing what appears to be a tiny little skirt and lace bra. In fact it is a vest pulled down about her slight hips. In a more playful image Kate is shown kneeling on an unmade bed, the duvet rumpled around her, pillows and a star-shaped cushion apparently hastily shoved to one end. There is a television remote control in view and an old portable television behind her, set to one side on a small table. She wears transparent American-tan tights over faintly visible knickers and a plain white cotton T-shirt. Elsewhere

Kate tugs at the hem of a floral thermal vest, teamed with silver lurex briefs. She is standing by a radiator before a wide, uncurtained window. She looks cold. She looks like she needs that thermal vest.

This was Corinne poking fun at fashion. Truth be told the 'joke' ran far deeper than the simple look of the pictures suggests. While Corinne told her editor at *Vogue* that the underwear was the product of upmarket lingerie specialists like La Perla and Berlei, the knickers and bras Kate wore were in fact from Ann Summers, a store better known then for its sex toys and high-polyester content than fine silks and exquisite laces. The joke, according to Corinne, was that when she showed the pictures to Vogue they hated them, but when she lied and said the knickers were from Berlei, suddenly what had been unacceptable, or at least borderline in their judgement, became OK. It confirmed Corinne's later, perhaps rather bitter, feeling that fashion photography was 'crap', and 'dishonest'.

Few of fashion's big-hitters – nor society's self-appointed moral guardians who were, it transpired, both many and vocal – found any humour behind the grimy images when the magazine landed on shelves in May. (Glossy magazines seem to work to a publishing timescale based on the premise that by the time the month of the edition actually arrives anyone who is anyone should already be looking at the next month.) But even though she knew that Corinne's work was a world away from the traditionally sumptuous shoots published in her aspirational magazine, *Vogue* editor Alexandra Shulman says it simply didn't cross her mind that there was anything particularly controversial in the pictures.

Looking back it is indeed difficult to pinpoint just why the reaction against the pictures was so vehement and, for Corinne's career as a fashion photographer and for her friendship with Kate, so damaging. Yet the backlash was as swift as it was vociferous. Kate was nineteen years old, but the squalid appearance of the pictures, the apparent fragility of the model and the uncomfortable extent to which she met the viewer with those challenging, yet slightly deadened eyes, saw the shoot condemned as somehow paedophilic. Author Colin McDowell launched a stinging attack on Corinne and her 'fascination for the freakish and squalid'. Writing in the *Daily Mail* he confusingly both blamed Corinne for the movement towards a style of photography that, to his mind, bordered on perversion and damned her for unoriginality as this had 'all been done before with infinitely more artistry and intelligence . . . [by] Sixties American photographer Diane Arbus.'

The images were damned as exploitative, in spite of the fact that they featured a professional model, handsomely paid and well and truly 'of age'. The supposed glamorization of a squalid existence and a look that 'in reality, is achieved by fasting or starvation' was described as 'perverse in a magazine that has always been a byword for glamour'. This argument was flawed since in fact Kate's tiny dimensions were *not* the result of 'fasting or starvation', but the happy collision of genes and youth. What was really worrying for Kate's management, however, was that the criticism of the pictures and the photographer spilled over onto the model. Suddenly Kate was cast as a pin-up girl for all that was *wrong* with fashion's onward flow away from the glamazons of the Eighties.

Radio programmes discussed the 'issues' the photographs raised and pages were devoted to the debate that seemed to spring spontaneously from their publication. The debate was about paedophilia, anorexia and exploitation, not knickers and a joke poked at fashion. This was dangerous. Corinne actually received death threats and also suffered a more open form of attack – and threat of a professional death of sorts – from US *Vogue*. Anna Wintour, the editor with the nickname 'Nuclear Wintour', and the woman whose patronage had gone a long way to bringing Corinne into the mainstream fashion fold, neatly snatched back her invitation to fashion's powerful inner sanctum with an article in October 1993's American *Vogue*. Under the headline THE LOST YOUTH, photographs that Corinne had taken as fashion shots were run alongside documentary photography by Larry Clark. The photographers' pictures of squalor and young people with vacant eyes and scrawny frames were presented as indistinguishable. Only there was a key difference and Corinne knew it. She had never intended her work to be viewed as a documentary of drug addiction, or as embracing it as a fashionable look. Yet here were her pictures displayed next to Larry Clark's, only his were genuine images of American adolescents strung out on crack, reeling from their last hit or jonesing for the next. It was shocking, and in that moment Corinne's presentation of 'true beauty' was held up as something ugly. She was being placed in a category outside acceptability, or at least outside commercial viability. Grunge never sold a £1,000 dress.

There is a bitter irony in the fact that the June edition of *Vogue*, which featured the underwear shoot that provoked such outrage, ran in its inside pages a featurette naming the magazine's 'most covetable item'. It was 'the guarantor of recognition among the glossy posse . . . the fashion photographer'. A photographer, the editorial pronounced, was 'for life, not just for Christmas'. The point of the small section, printed on a page of what was 'in vogue', was to identify a new phenomenon – the power of a model becoming one half of a creative partnership with a photographer. Perhaps today that coupling has been replaced by a celebrity and his or her stylist, but in

1993 it was the photographer who had all the power and, in large part, the ability to make or break a model's careers. Cindy Crawford had Herb Ritts; Linda Evangelista had Steven Meisel and, first on the list, pictured right at the top of the page, was Kate Moss and Corinne Day. 'Kate Moss', the piece ran, 'might still be lost in SE20 were it not for Corinne Day.'

Whatever Sarah Doukas may have thought of that assessment she recognized a stark necessity in the controversy that followed Corinne's underwear shoot with Kate. In Storm she had created an agency that nurtured, built and protected girls' images. As summer gave way to autumn the fuss showed no signs of abating. Corinne was under attack and Kate was being presented as inextricably linked with a movement Corinne had instigated. Sarah felt that the link would have to be severed. Sarah had set her sights firmly on Kate's public image and it was time to get tough – it was her job to do so.

There was the small matter of Kate's career to considers never mind the friendship that had blossomed between the two women. It fell to Kate to tell Corinne that, on the advice of her agent, she would no longer be able to work with her. To this day neither woman will be drawn on what passed between them during that conversation. Both were profoundly shocked by what Corinne refers to as the 'stink' made by the press as a result of a shoot that she claimed not even to like. But though Kate understood the furore even less than Corinne, she understood the value of business. Did it pain Corinne to be carved out of Kate's professional and personal life? Of course it did. She recognized that her refusal to compromise meant that she was not always the easiest of people to work with, but still, she admits, 'I felt hurt by Kate, yes.'

In some ways Corinne was every bit as ambitious as Kate, but her ambitions lay not simply in making it commercially, but in doing so on her own terms. However, when those terms caused her to fall foul of the fashion industry's bible, while each public criticism saw her slip further and further down advertisers' most wanted list, she was wounded to find herself so swiftly deserted, whatever the circumstances, by the girl she'd been instrumental in bringing to the public's attention. She became the first victim of Kate's success and for a while it would seem that Kate almost tried to rub her out of her history.

Kate referred to the outcry as 'madness' – to imbue a model or set of pictures with such influence seemed 'just crazy' to her – but she stopped crediting Corinne for her early success. When asked about those early shoots for *The Face*, there was a time when Kate would refer simply to 'the photographer', with a casually dismissive tone that suggested 'the photographer' in question was nobody of importance in her life. Corinne too started to publicly distance herself from Kate and the *Vogue* shoot. She claimed not to particularly like the shots, finding Kate 'too beautiful' in them – too much like a model and a supermodel at that. Kate had become the very thing that Corinne had sought to subvert.

Recalling the shoot itself Day claims to have felt something end as she looked through the lens at her friend: 'Halfway through the shoot I realized that it wasn't fun for her any more and that she was no longer my best friend but had become a "model". She hadn't realized how beautiful she was, and when she did, I found I didn't think her beautiful any more.' Corinne has always insisted that she felt no bitterness when Kate told her she would no longer work with her. But it's impossible not to hear those words, spoken years after the shoot and viewed through the prism of perceived betrayal, without catching a whisper of the pain Kate's desertion, however necessary, caused.

At the time Corinne chose to be pragmatic. She claimed that she was 'bored' of fashion photography, and in the long run viewed the moment that her career stalled as 'destiny'. Of course, time and hindsight made such a view possible. Four years after the photos were taken, Corinne's picture of Kate, standing against a halo of fairylights, was hung in the Victoria & Albert Museum as part of their collection of fashion photographs, alongside prints by Irving Penn, Richard Avedon, Horst and Sir Cecil Beaton. By then Corinne's work was deemed beautiful once more, but by then the damage had been done and not enough time had passed for there to be a hint of rapprochement – personal or professional.

Alexandra Shulman has described that time when Corinne and Kate worked together as 'the most interesting time of the decade', and has called Corinne in particular 'one of the most influential photographers of her generation'. It's a statement some might find difficult to reconcile with what *Vogue* did next – or rather what they did *not* do – as they didn't commission Corinne for a decade. Kate and Corinne barely spoke for the next seven years.

Corinne's career in fashion stalled because she was effectively frozen out. Her career did not end there, but she most certainly embarked on a period of what might be most kindly described as re-evaluating and repositioning herself professionally. Ultimately she pursued the documentary style of photography that had always been her passion.

There may have been another cause for relief on Sarah Doukas's part that Kate and Corinne were less intimate than before, as Corinne has made no secret of her use of recreational drugs during that time and beyond. For Corinne it was not an occasional post-shoot spliff but serious chemical highs, and three years later it would prove something of a salvation when she suffered an epileptic fit as a result of 'all the drugs' she was taking.

'Everybody took drugs,' she later explained. 'So you think it's normal to be spaced out all the time, but it was great fun.' The fun stopped with that fit, though, and the subsequent routine brain scan that followed and identified a tumour. It was a shocking, but life-saving, wake-up call as the tumour was successfully removed and Corinne adjusted her lifestyle accordingly.

As an agent Sarah has always maintained that there is a 'line' across which she could not step into Kate's personal life. Some might argue that such delineation would prove rather convenient when, many years later, Kate found herself at the centre of a drug-scandal that looked, for a time, as if it might bring her down. However much Sarah stuck to her decision not to ask Kate about certain recreational aspects of her life, she must have experienced the odd, and entirely natural, pang of concern. Since spotting her five years earlier, Sarah had become something of a surrogate mother to Kate. This is not to suggest that she had in any way replaced Linda, but Kate's work and travel meant that she would speak to Sarah and her booker, Jess, pretty much every day. Few teenagers could boast of such consistent communication with their mothers. Sarah may not have pried into the details of Kate's friendships, but she can't have been wholly oblivious to the reality of Corinne's indulgences and Kate's proximity to them. For that alone a degree of separation must surely have seemed desirable.

Corinne was not the only relationship to fizzle out that year; travel, tensions and the natural process of growing up also brought Kate's romance with Sorrenti to an end. They gave up their London flat and Kate found another. The days of him cooking pasta and her cleaning were over. Truth be told they had been few and far between as their relationship was characterized by travel, adventure and the sort of youthful intensity that is almost impossible to sustain and endure.

The split was painful for them both and the passion they had shared could not be replaced by something platonic, however strongly they may have wanted it. Only time would make that possible. There would be little communication between them over the next couple of years, but ultimately, to the relief of both, friendship and abiding affection filled the space left by the romance. Years later Sorrenti would describe Kate as his first love. She had become 'family' to him and they would always be part of each other's lives.

With her rising profile, Kate's openness and natural tendency to be chatty and helpful to any enquiry, regardless of the inquisitor, was becoming a source of concern to her agent. Kate's giddy excitement back stage at runway shows was matched by her enthusiastic mingling and chatting at the numerous dinner and award ceremonies to which she was regularly invited. In September Kate went to the Face of '93 awards, held that year in London's Café Royal. It was a lunchtime affair sponsored by Highland Spring, and Virgin boss, Richard Branson, was there, holding court with Sarah and Kate. Kate looked far younger than her nineteen years that day. Her face was scrubbed of make-up, her hair tucked back behind her ears and she wore a plain white T-shirt, jeans and a John Galliano tailored jacket that looked as if it was cut from a Union Jack flag.

The event was a chance for the industry's young blood to mingle with the great the good and the sponsors. It was, as these events often are, a glamorous job fair of sorts, where contacts are made and connections worked. For Sarah the seating plan offered an opportunity for Kate to learn from one of the modelling profession's old hands, Marie Helvin. By then Helvin was also on Storm's books and had been seated next to Kate, where Sarah asked the older woman to give Kate some interview tips. Kate went on to work with photographer David Bailey, the man to whom Marie had once been muse and wife. The Hawaiian-born model was forty-one years old when she and Kate met and still an extraordinary beauty. She was internationally famous and had enjoyed a lifestyle of remarkable excess – she listed film stars and rock stars among her many lovers and didn't believed love needed to be expressed through sexual monogamy. Sarah could hardly have selected a more suitable person to offer advice to her young protégé. She certainly wasn't a stern authority figure who was going to lecture the young Kate – a wise move on Sarah's part as neither she nor Kate seem to have been enamoured or particularly influenced by authority figures.

Sarah explained to Marie that Kate had been chatting nineteen to the dozen to journalists, practically giving away her new address. Helvin did her best and counselled caution to Kate, who struck her that day as 'sweet and gawky, yakking away in pure Croydon'. She doubted she made much impact, though, recalling, 'There was clearly going to be no stopping her.'

By the close of 1993 the personal tumult and professional scandal of that year had been all but stamped out. But both Sorrenti and Corinne's lives were set to collide with Kate's again in the most extraordinary fashion when a personal tragedy drew comment from the President of the United States of America and saw Corinne's pictures return to haunt Kate once more.

6

The rooms on the third floor of South Kensington's Polish Club were a muddle of models, make-up artists and stylists. Half-drunk bottles of champagne and discarded tumblers of Pepsi Max vied for space on every surface, alongside ashtrays, make-up and hair products. Clothes lay in crumpled heaps while the straps of models' hastily discarded bras caught around the heels of those trying to navigate a path across the room. They were all gathered to take part in designer Bella Freud's fall season fashion show. There was less than an hour to go before the scheduled start, but the chaotic scene suggested that any hope of starting on time had been abandoned. There seemed to be an awful lot of chatter, fussing and preening, with very little evidence of any real headway being made.

Despite this, nobody was flustered or irritated. The eight models booked for the occasion were patient as their make-up was applied and reapplied and their wilting hair re-bouffed. They drank champagne, smoked an endless stream of cigarettes and nattered away. Music played and the atmosphere in the cramped communal changing room was positively sunny. The radiance was emanating irresistibly and irrepressibly from Kate.

Dressed simply in a white vest top and jeans, Kate crouched

in a corner of the room and pulled a folded scrap of newspaper from the handbag she had unceremoniously dumped on the floor a couple of hours earlier. Quietly, her back to the room, she unfolded it, looked at the picture and read and re-read the caption beneath it. 'I can't believe it,' she said. 'I can't believe it.' The story she found so compelling in the midst of what should have been a last-minute sprint to deadline, drawing her attention away from the business of the day and the hubbub of the room was simple enough and contained no shocking revelation.

It was the last week of February 1994 and the newspaper cutting that held Kate in thrall was a picture of her and Hollywood film star Johnny Depp. She clutched it as if she were clutching him, as if slackening her grip on the piece of paper would somehow loosen her grip on reality. That reality was that Kate was dating Johnny Depp, Hollywood heart-throb, bad boy, the works. She was now one half of a couple that *Vanity Fair* would later name the hottest – or is it coolest? – couple around. Kate was famous by now, but Depp was a bona-fide film star. Four years earlier he had starred in Tim Burton's *Edward Scissorhands* and it had proved a career-making performance. Other hits followed, including *Benny & Joon* with Aidan Quinn and Julianne Moore and *What's Eating Gilbert Grape* with Juliette Lewis and a young Leonardo DiCaprio. To Kate, Depp seemed, on paper at least, out of her league and beyond her reach, and yet here she was, in a romance with him.

It was, as she told anybody who cared to listen that February afternoon, 'unlike anything she had ever known'. This time it was 'different', this time she just *knew*, and with the utter certainty that accompanies such torrential love she was, of course, riddled with doubt. She was with Johnny Depp, yet somehow, however much she looked at the photograph in her hand, it seemed incredible. As her outfits were lined up in order on the clothes rail marked 'Kate' she drew a little heart on her wrist, no larger than a beauty spot, and toyed with getting a tattoo. The fact that Depp had 'Winona Forever' etched on his skin in honour of his previous grand passion, Winona Ryder, was a detail that evidently did not concern Kate. Whether or not she remained 'Truly, Madly, Depply' in love, as headline writers proclaimed that spring, a heart tattoo presented a safer option than a name, and before long Kate had a little heart shot in tiny bullets of ink into the pad of flesh between the thumb and forefinger of her left hand, while Depp amended his own body art to 'Wino Forever'.

It was a witty gesture, a canny solution to a problem that might have given some girls pause for thought. Depp was thirty-one years old and a devoted son to mother Betty Sue. Born in Kentucky and raised in Florida, he moved to Los Angeles with dreams of being a rock star and became a film star instead. More pertinently he had earned himself a reputation as a 'serial fiancé', proposing marriage to four women – Winona, Sherilyn Fenn, Jennifer Grey and Lori Allison – before meeting Kate. They had all said yes, but back in 1983 Lori had been the only one whose acceptance had led to a marriage – they divorced three years later.

None of this dimmed Kate's ardour, though. She had just embarked on what would be the most formative and, in its moments of intensity and the heartbreak it left in its wake, the most damaging relationship of her life. In later years she would seem to try to recapture a fraction of what she had with Depp many times over. Their relationship was so passionate that at times Depp wondered if it was love at all or 'just sex'. Kate was never in doubt, but then Kate was, it seemed, quite convinced that their meeting in New York in January 1994 was a moment akin to divine intervention.

The circumstances of Kate and Depp's meeting are pretty well documented, but what preceded them and underpinned Kate's request for an introduction is not. It was the day of the CFDA Awards (Council of Fashion Designers of America), a high-rolling bash in New York, and Kate and a group of friends had headed to the Café Tabac, a fashionable restaurant and bar in New York's East Village, for drinks after the black tie dinner. Depp happened to be in town and popped in for a coffee. He saw Kate's table – how could he not? – and recognized a friend of his, a photographer. He went over to say hello and asked Kate if she'd like to join him for coffee. For her, that was it – the thunderbolt. Depp's extraordinary looks must have helped, and Kate fancied him rotten, but so too did the presence of myriad – well a couple – of 'signs'.

Months earlier Kate had been working with the photographer who numbered among her party that evening. The shoot had been for Calvin Klein and the photographer had wanted to get a particular look or vibe that he had previously seen in photographs of Depp. As a result there were pictures of Depp all over his studio. Everywhere Kate looked on set, her eyes alighted on another shot of the actor. During the shoot, while the music played and Kate did what she does best – flirting, teasing and working each shot and move – a deal was struck. When the photographer asked Kate to 'find him a girl', she agreed on condition that he introduce her to Depp, on whom she had developed a perfectly understandable crush. In lieu of the real thing, she left that day with several of the pictures that had been scattered around the studio. Months passed and the photographs remained pinned on the wall of Kate's flat.

On her flight to New York in January 1994 Kate was reading

The Celestine Prophecy by James Redfield. It was not a choice that marked her out from the crowd, since hundreds of thousands of North Americans were doing the same back then. The book, published the previous year, was top of the *New York Times* bestseller list, and the mass of publicity that surrounded it had turned it into a cult book. It was the *Da Vinci Code* of its day: a work of fiction that fans treated as truth. At the heart of the book was the less than original suggestion that there was no such thing as coincidence and that by examining the apparent coincidences in your life you would start to see 'signs'. How you took that information and acted on it was down to you, but each 'sign' was a sort of divine intervention.

When Kate saw Depp that day at Café Tabac she took it as a sign, and from the moment they spoke she knew that they would be together. The following day brought with it another supposed sign. Kate accepted Depp's invitation for a drink and ended up going back to his hotel room. She was dressed as she had been for the award ceremony, in a tiny skirt and high heels, hardly appropriate garb for a blisteringly cold New York in January. That night there was a snowstorm, and by six in the morning they were snowed in and Kate was stranded. It took seven hours for clothes and boots to be couriered from Midtown Manhattan, and in those seven hours her relationship with Depp was cemented. Kate regarded the snowstorm as a sign. The fact that it left her straned had, to her, an uncanny parallel with the way her career began, stuck in a standby queue at JFK. Of course there are other ways of looking at it. She was, after all, already in Depp's hotel room before the snowstorm began, and if the clothes could come to her by courier then she, no doubt, could have gone to them by cab, but Depp was unlike anyone she had ever met and however predestined their meeting, Kate fell for him heavily.

Their relationship became public the following month when Kate accompanied Depp to the Los Angeles premiere of his film *Banter*. It was a rather worthy work – his directorial début – an eight-minute film in aid of Drug Abuse Resistance Education (DARE). He must surely have known from personal experience that such resistance was a hard lesson to learn, but the film had another reason for being meaningful to Depp at the time as its release came just four months after the death of his friend River Phoenix. Phoenix was twenty-three years old when he collapsed on Sunset Boulevard. He was rushed to the Cedars-Sinai Medical Center, but he was already dead. He had died in the street just outside the Viper Room, a Hollywood nightclub part owned by Depp, having overdosed inside on a combination of heroin and cocaine known as a speedball.

There was more than a ripple of 'there but for the grace of God go I' in the grief-stricken shock felt by his Hollywood friends and peers. To his fans, who had bought into the public image of Phoenix as a squeaky-clean golden boy, this glimpse of a darker reality was profoundly disturbing. Suddenly the youth of Hollywood were all about cleaning up their act, mourning such a waste, writing songs, painting banners and making worthy drug education films. For many weeks the Viper Room languished under threat of closure or of losing its liquor licence, which was tantamount to the same thing, but ultimately little changed. Less than twelve months after the release of *Banter* another of their actor friends would be rushed to Cedars-Sinai, having collapsed in the Viper Room at a party thrown by Depp for Kate, having earlier taken too much cocaine.

In February 1994 Kate was already extremely famous, but it was only when she went to Los Angeles to be with Depp that she truly understood the power and extent of her new boyfriend's fame. He was in another league and when she stepped out with him her own celebrity stepped up a notch. Critics noted that Kate and Depp looked 'very scruffy' at the *Banter* premiere and it is true that in her long bias-cut skirt, white T-shirt and battered leather biker jacket Kate was hardly dolled up like a Hollywood starlet. But her hair was notably more glossy and blonde and her make-up was perfect. With Depp, a more glamorous, grown-up Kate would begin to emerge.

It was not only her sense of glamour that increased. Kate may never have shown any enthusiasm for school, but in common with many who glean little from formal education, she had a voracious appetite for reading once school was over and she was left to her own devices. Now, with Depp, books like *The Celestine Prophecy* were set aside in favour of works by American writers like Jack Kerouac, Truman Capote, F. Scott Fitzgerald – first read at school but now re-read and adored afresh – and Hunter S. Thompson. It wasn't all one-way traffic when it came to inspiring and influencing each other, though. Depp may have introduced Kate to music like the Smashing Pumpkins but she played him Barry White and gave her rocker boyfriend what she described as 'disco fever' – so much so that when Depp and his little-known band P released an album the following November, it included an unlikely cover of Abba's 'Dancing Queen'.

Depp's mantra was that in life you should always surround yourself by people who are better than you because only then could you truly grow as a person. The terminology may sound rather west coast America, but the principle is sound enough, and in later years Kate would arguably suffer from being surrounded, however accidentally, by increasingly sycophantic acolytes.

When Kate met Depp she had already met some of the

most successful and talented designers and photographers, but her experiences and horizons had been largely limited to the fashionable world. Day, with her left-field outlook, had all but faded out of her life at this point, but now with Depp her horizons opened up and she began experimenting. In March she met country singer Johnny Cash when he played in the Viper Room. The meeting led to Kate's first appearance in a music video – something she would come to develop a taste for. The track was 'Delia's Gone', a classically bleak Cash number first recorded by him in 1962. In it Cash bewailed the fact that Delia was 'gone' as he had tied her to a chair and shot her twice with a semi-automatic gun . . . Delia was 'no good'. Kate's appearance didn't call for any particular acting skills. She wore a pretty, puff-sleeved dress in the sepia-tinted footage as Cash recalled her murder and burial. He carried her lifeless body to a hole in the ground into which she obligingly slumped. But in the end Delia got her revenge. She may be gone but she certainly isn't forgotten – Cash cannot sleep for the ghostly 'patter of her tiny feet' running around his bed, and in the closing scene we see Kate, standing above the camera, kicking dirt into the hole in which she was so recently buried.

Those early months of their relationship were, for both Kate and Depp, an intense and exhilarating time full of high emotion and grand gestures. Once when work forced the lovers apart – as it often did – Depp surprised Kate by having her hotel room filled with daisies, her favourite bloom. He also gave her a string of diamonds – a gift she had to retrieve from its hiding place down his trousers – which dazzled around her neck when they attended the London launch of Naomi Campbell's book, *Swan*, that autumn. In return she bought him a clutch of black pearls caged in a solid silver rattle. In April he saw her model for the first time at an AIDS benefit fashion show held at Manns Chinese Theatre in Hollywood – an event that neatly united their two worlds, fashion and the movies. After the show Depp, Kate, Naomi Campbell and Linda Evangelista headed to the Viper Room for a private party.

The passion that fizzed between Kate and Depp was clear, and in their four years together that physical passion didn't fade. It remained so intense and unshakeable – so 'pure' in Depp's words – that months after they split he kept a favourite picture of Kate in his wallet as a memento; proof perhaps, should he ever look back and doubt it, that what had passed between them had been all-consuming and real.

That summer Kate introduced her mother to Depp. She telephoned Linda and asked if she fancied joining them on holiday on Richard Branson's secluded Necker island in the Caribbean. Depp had booked the whole place for the week. Of course Linda accepted the invitation. The last leg of the journey had to be made by helicopter, and when she landed Kate ran across the landing field to meet her.

Some might find it strange that a young woman holidaying with her lover only months into a passionate relationship should even think of inviting her mother along, but for Kate and Depp there was nothing unusual in the gesture. Kate's relationship with her parents had always been a casual affair when it came to discipline and boundaries, and there was no sense that Kate would find her mother's presence inhibiting. Linda had always been keen to be Kate's friend, and who could criticize a mother's desire to be a confidante to her daughter? Certainly she would need one in the years to come, and while Kate's father may sometimes have seemed dependent on updates from Kate's booker or personal assistant, when it came to the pivotal moments and times of crisis in their daughter's life, it was Linda who would receive telephone calls late into the night.

As for Depp, he no doubt found Kate's relationship with her mother endearing, echoing as it did his own closeness and affection for his mother, Betty. To underscore his filial devotion to her he had her name tattooed on his arm. Kate may not have worn her affection for her mother quite so publicly, but however successful she was, she still needed her just as she had when, as a little girl, she would run to her for cuddles and kisses when her tummy hurt. However far life was taking Kate, Linda – and Croydon – was still 'home', though at times the gulf between them must have seemed surreal. Certainly her life with Depp was anything but run-of-the-mill. It was thrilling, passionate and wonderful. Linda witnessed that much when she first saw the couple together and she was glad for Kate's joy.

But it wasn't all hearts and flowers – no great romance ever is – and however tender, affectionate and adoring Depp could be, however much he *loved* Kate's tinkly little voice and the south London accent he strove to mimic, his Hollywood 'bad boy' image was not entirely unfounded. He could be rude and angry and jealous. Truth be told this 'dangerous' edge was part of his allure, though. What's the point in dating a bad boy if he's thoroughly, boringly tame?

Depp was never violent to Kate, but when yelling and screaming didn't release whatever pent-up frustration and rage he might be feeling, he wasn't averse to throwing things: books, lamps and items of furniture. Kate was with Depp on the night of 12 September 1994, and as the thirteenth dawned she witnessed his rage first hand. The couple were staying at The Mark Hotel in Manhattan's Upper East Side. It hadn't been Depp's first choice of hotel – he preferred to stay in The Carlyle when in town – and perhaps that had some bearing on his mood, though it can hardly explain what happened next. As night gave way to morning the front desk received complaints about noises emanating from Depp and Kate's suite. The complaint was not about shouts or screams or anything so mundane, it was that, for what seemed like hours, there had been relentless crashing and banging, as if somebody were hurling items of furniture around the room in a steady and systematic demolition job. Somebody was – Depp.

When the manager confronted Depp he offered to pay for the damage, later reported as amounting to £1,300, but it was an immediate checkout, not cash, that the manager required. Depp refused, and much to the horror of a tearful Kate, the police were called and Depp, looking dishevelled and faintly ridiculous in a green jelly-bean hat, sunglasses, tan jacket and jeans, was handcuffed and escorted from the building. He spent forty-eight hours in cells, having been charged with the confusingly playful-sounding crime of causing mischevious damage.

Later Depp would say that he had had a bad day and identify that date – or more accurately the forty-eight hours spent in a police cell in the nineteenth precinct afterwards – as a turning point in his life. Only Kate and Depp can ever truly know what sparked his actions that night and set light to his touch paper, but in a bizarre twist that might appeal to Kate's fascination with coincidences, the person who had complained to the hotel's front desk was Roger Daltrey, singer with The Who, a band famous for rampaging through life, and hotels, during the Sixties and Seventies. It seemed it wasn't only the noise to which Daltrey objected, but the amateurish fashion in which Depp wrecked the room. According to Daltrey: 'On a scale of one to ten I'd give him a one. It took him so bloody long. The Who would have done it in one minute flat.' Later, as hotel staff began to assess the damage they found the book that Depp had been reading; it was a biography of Marlon Brando, published the previous year. In all likelihood Depp was reading it not simply because he was fascinated by the man and admired him greatly but because he would soon work with him on the dismal flop of a film that was *Don Juan de Marco*. It was reported that there was writing scrawled in the margins, and across some of the pages were the words, 'Fuck you, Johnny Depp', and 'I hate you, Johnny.' Both Kate and Depp loved riding on roller-coasters: given the ups and downs of their romance, it was perhaps just as well.

Only a few days after Depp was bailed and emerged from the cells, his woolly-hatted head bowed in shame, he and Kate were in London together at the Lainsborough Hotel for the launch of Naomi Campbell's book *Swan*. Naomi's foray into the world of literature saw her savaged twice over by the critics, who damned the model for putting her name to such 'airport novel trash', before damning her once again for not actually having written the book which, far from being a swan, according to one critic, was more of a 'golden goose that failed to lay an egg'. Safe to say Naomi did not set the literary world alight as she had done the world of fashion.

Back in London, Kate decided to show Depp Croydon. If her mother Linda was at all overawed by the presence of a Hollywood star in her home, or put out by his recent hotel high jinks, she didn't let on. The visit followed a typically last-minute telephone call from Kate, but that was par for the course. What was the point of being young and loaded and in town if you couldn't do something impetuous, even if that impetuous something was nothing more outrageous than a trip home to see your mother? Linda welcomed Depp into her home as she had welcomed Sorrenti before him, chatting and watching while Kate and he prepared bangers and mash for everyone to share. Linda liked him. She always made a point of not interfering with her daughter's choice of boyfriend but, as with any self-imposed rule, it was easier to abide by when the boyfriend in question was somebody she approved of, and Depp most certainly was. Indeed, when he and Kate split almost four years later, it wasn't only Kate who longed for a rapprochement.

When Kate was with Depp there was always a new experience, always a new person for her – and sometimes her family – to meet, a new icon with whom to come face to face. She met Iggy Pop, a friend of Depp's since they had starred together five years earlier in John Waters' film *Cry-Baby*. She met Marlon Brando a man who, for all his advanced years, still 'had it'. Kate and her mother met Hunter S. Thompson, the American writer whom Depp would go on to play in the film of his book, *Fear and Loathing in Las Vegas*. Kate had read the book about Hunter S. Thompson's drug-fuelled drive across the desert as a teenager and thought, I want to do that, wondering if it could *really* be possible. She read it again after meeting the man, devouring the pages, and this time not questioning the truth of each tale of outrageous drug and drink ingestion.

Depp learned from Kate too. He may have been ten years her senior and a man more inclined to spend his fortune on rare books and art than flash cars and gadgets, but he could, by his own admission, be morose and overly serious. Depp called Kate his 'little girl'. Through her innate enthusiasm and childish capacity to enjoy life she lifted him out of the doldrums into which he could quite naturally fall. In later years that endearing trait would be Kate's downfall as it slipped, unchecked, into almost reckless abandon.

Back in March 1993, *Vogue* had identified the new spirit in fashion as London Girl style. The following month *Select* music magazine put a picture of Suede lead singer Brett Anderson on its front cover superimposed on the Union Jack flag. Beneath ran the words, 'Yanks Go Home'. Just as Kate had heralded a new movement in fashion, Anderson and that cover – an image he always hated – sounded the starting pistol for the music scene that would eventually become known as Britpop.

The independent music scene with its psychedelia and 'summer of love' sensibilities was growing old and Manchester, Hacienda, The Stone Roses, Happy Mondays and Inspiral Carpets were on the way out. That year a little-known Manchester band called Oasis, freshly signed to Creation Records, had been relentlessly gigging the length and breadth of the country, building a fanbase, spreading their name and preparing for the release of their first album. Noel and Liam Gallagher, in their Adidas hoodies and low-slung jeans, looked like just what they were, a couple of lads from a Manchester estate, but thanks to bands like The Stone Roses with their lead singer Ian Brown, they were also couple of lads who didn't doubt for a moment that 'their sort' could make it big.

Two hundred miles south, Damon Albarn, Alex James, Graham Coxon and Dave Rowntree had already released a top-ten single, 'There's No Other Way' but their band, Blur, hadn't come up with their signature sound. Albarn had yet to find his voice and 'There's No Other Way' was a cynical record-label choice designed to cash in on the dying days of Madchester. The fashion scene was all about London, and as 1993 came to a close, the music scene's centre of gravity was about to move south.

Noel Gallagher moved to London, leaving Manchester one Friday night with his guitar and some money in his pocket, and never looking back. Essex-born Albarn realized that he should write songs about what he knew, and in 1993 Blur released their album *Modern Life is Rubbish*, full of nostalgic tunes and caustic lyrics. The following year they brought out *Parklife*, and four months later Oasis released *Definitely Maybe*. The Madchester scene was over. London Girl style now had a soundtrack in the form of Britpop and a stomping ground in north London – Camden, Chalk Farm and, when the money really starting pouring in, Primrose Hill and Maida Vale.

On any given night of the week in any given pub in Camden or Chalk Farm there would be some hopeful group gigging. And on any given night of any given week in any given pub in Camden or Chalk Farm, even a sparse audience might include a clutch of pop stars – Albarn enjoying a pint with his girlfriend Justine Frischmann, the lead singer of Elastica; Jarvis Cocker, the scarecrow-like lead singer from Pulp, checking out the latest group with bandmate Steve Mackey. The Dublin Castle and the Monarch were favourite venues of the time. If there was a down-at-heel feel to the scene that only heightened the appeal to the lingering indie sensibilities of stars keen to 'keep it real' while their albums went platinum many times over. Oasis sang about the joys of life – cigarettes and alcohol and more – while Liam apparently spoke of once taking to the stage high on crystal meth.

By late 1994 the music scene – or at least the only one that mattered – was in London. It was vibrant and exciting and it had a long way to go before its inevitable implosion, when some of its stars succumbed to rehab and others stopped singing about houses in the country and moved to them instead.

For Kate, as 1994 drew to a close, her world was about to collide with that scene as it approached the peak of its powers and excess. The collision would unite Kate's great passions and lay before her new playmates who brought with them the prospect of unlimited temptation and indulgence. For performers with last-minute nerves, there was always a shot of vodka, or slug of champagne or line of coke on offer. It was hedonistic and fuelled by copious amounts of booze and drugs. Kate would fit right in. More than that, she would become lost in it all.

7

The Viper Room sits at the corner of West Sunset Boulevard and Larrabee Street. The building presents a dark, windowless façade to the Boulevard and eats back into the hill on the downward slope of the lesser-known road. Its brickwork is painted brown/black and the paintwork on the doors at the front and side is peeling and in need of some attention, while the brown/black awnings bear the club's name in scrawled white lettering over both entrances.

There is live music every night and every night, after say ten o'clock, a queue will have formed at the side door ready to part with the cover charge at the small box-office booth inside. Since the smoking ban a crowd of people can often be found at the front, too, having spilled out of the fire doors in the club's upstairs room for a quick cigarette on the sidewalk before sneaking back in. Inevitably one of the club's doormen will put an end to this nightly infringement, informing punters that if they want to smoke they will have to go back out the side door they came in and take their chances fighting their way across the crowded club and bar space on their return to reclaim whatever prime viewing spot they may have bagged as their own.

There are a handful of booths in a crescent around the

dance floor and a long, darkly lit bar. When Depp co-owned the club, as he did from its opening in 1993 until 2004, he kept one of the upstairs booths permanently reserved for himself, his agent and a friend, and along with the reserved tag nailed to the wall was the instruction, 'Don't fuck with it'. For the most part this is a small, dark, sweaty, noisy venue for live music and dancing, while downstairs is a more intimate lounge. The walls and floors, and what little furniture there is, are purple or black – it's hard to tell in the dim lighting. It has a bar, some seating and a screen on the wall transmitting action from the upstairs stage. The club only holds 250 people and is small, dark, awkward, seedy and consistently cool.

On 14 January 1995 it was filled with roses and balloons and given over to Kate's twenty-first birthday celebrations. It was two days before her actual birthday, of course, but that only added to the surprise in this surprise party, organized by Depp for the girl with whom he was utterly smitten.

Kate had been rather subdued for most of that day. Nobody had called her. Wherever she was in the world, be it Milan, London, Paris or New York, her telephone rarely stopped ringing, so this radio silence was unusual and unsettling. Depp told Kate that he was taking her out for dinner to a nice restaurant, so she should put on 'something cool'. She picked a slinky red satin floor-length dress. Depp took one look, lifted a pair of scissors and hacked the hem into jagged handkerchief dips. Depp told Kate that he just needed to pop into the club to sort out some business on the way to the restaurant. She would have waited in the limousine, but Depp said to come in, they might as well have a drink before dinner.

It took a moment for her eyes to adjust to the gloomy interior and another beat or so for her to absorb the scene before her. *Everyone* it seemed as she scanned the room was there – *everyone*. Naomi, Linda and Christy, Helena and her boyfriend Michael Hutchence from INXS. John Galliano had flown in from Paris with the white satin dress that would be his twenty-first gift to her: on the small stage in the far corner the curtain swept back to reveal her mother and father, Sarah Doukas and a large cake iced like the Union Jack. Moments later the icing erupted and out popped the auburn curls of friend and hairdresser James Brown. Kate was thrilled and blind-sided all at once. Her legs were shaking. She flung her arms around Depp's neck and kissed him so passionately that, had they been in other company, observers might have blushed. As it was the party simply began in earnest.

Kate has recalled that night many times over. She has spoken of how Gloria Gaynor sang 'I Will Survive' and 'Happy Birthday', how R&B singer Thelma Houston was there and some Elvis impersonator. She has recalled Depp joining Michael Hutchence on stage for an impromptu version of 'Gloria' and how it was like 'Christmas Day all over again'. Among the gifts that Depp showered upon her was a dress, 'same as the one Julie Christie wore in *Shampoo*'. They had watched the film together and Kate had admired the black sequined sheath, so Depp had had one made up her. He had also sought out a beautiful and rare edition of *Alice in Wonderland*, illustrated with twelve Salvador Dali lithographs. Only 200 such books were ever made.

It was an exquisite and appropriate choice. After all, Wonderland was both fantastical and frightening, nonsensical, compelling, unsettling and fun. Wonderland was an hallucinogenic realm that had, in common with all the very best children's stories, a ruthless heart, sinister characters with winning smiles and temptations and wrong-turnings there for the taking. Not so very different then from La La Land. And on the night of

Kate's party one guest in particular was experiencing the darker side of the evening's entertainments.

Few who were there that night could have been partying under the illusion that this was a drug-free affair. Some undoubtedly were, but should anybody have been indiscreet enough to really look, they would have found more than a modest dusting of various powders among the guests who drank and danced into the small hours.

Depp himself has admitted to – or boasted depending on your perspective – having taken 'every drug there is'. He is a man of experience and, a decade Kate's senior, he showed her a great many things during their intense relationship. On that night how much she was indulged and how much she may have been sheltered from the excesses of the night is a moot point. What is certain is that in the industries in which they both excel, drugs are available and so much the norm that it would shock those who have never come into contact with so much as the fringes of a drug scene.

Of course that availability is not confined to the film and fashion worlds. The music industry is the same, as is the world of print and broadcast media. The extent of the drug use, the finances to provide it, the size of the egos involved and the need to placate and cater for them, varies in all these walks of life. High-profile individuals in each realm may tut and disapprove and pretend that, of all the disciplines, theirs is above reproach, but it is not. This is not to suggest that the movers and shakers in all these industries pitch up for board meetings high on coke – that's far too excitable an interpretation – though the truth might be almost as shocking for those who view narcotics, in any form, as profoundly illicit. The fact is that cocaine, crystal meth and marijuana are only a telephone

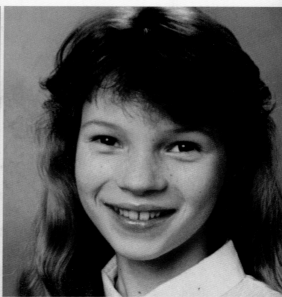

Above The eighties begin and the smile is sweet, but as Kate's personality blossoms her mother observes a defiant streak.

Above, right On the cusp of a difficult time: as Kate approaches teenage years, her parents' marriage begins to implode.

Right Kate's first ever shoot with a professional photographer, 26 October 1988. She is fourteen years old and wears a jumper she brought with her that day.

Fifteen years old
and freezing on
Camber Sands,
East Sussex, 1989.
Corinne Day's picture
on this gruelling shoot
would prove one of
the most important
of Kate's career.

Heavily under the influence of
a more worldly woman: Kate and
Corinne Day enjoy another night
on the tiles before their
friendship stalls.

Suntanned and happy:
the official 'London Girl' – now big
in the States – aged nineteen, drinking
beer on holiday with her brother,
Nick, and father, Peter.

Backstage in Paris, Kate flirts with photographer Mario Sorrenti,
the man who would become her first love, spring 1991.

Kate on the catwalk for designer Bella Freud's
October 1993 show – she is the most in-demand
model on the circuit.

Paris 1993: Kate's rapid success sees her living in hotel room after hotel room.
Speaking of that time she said, 'Whenever I get comfortable I have to leave.
That's the worst thing, having to leave all the time.'

Above Gianni Versace's Spring/Summer '94 show, October 1993. Kate takes centre stage among the supermodels, including (from left to right) Claudia Schiffer, Carla Bruni, Naomi Campbell, Yasmin Le Bon, Amber Valletta and Helena Christensen.

Left Getting into character on a magazine shoot in Paris, June 1994.

Right Kate in 1995: the poster girl for 'Cool Britannia', she personifies the optimism – and excess – of the Britpop years.

Below Fooling around in the south of France with Naomi Campbell, the Streatham girl who showed her the ropes, May 1995, Beaulieu-sur-Mer, Côte d'Azur.

Johnny and Kate leaving
The Big Breakfast television studios
in London. They are the couple of the
moment and used to dodging paparazzi
and questions of marriage.

Johnny and Kate with friends
Noel Gallagher and Meg Mathews
in Mustique, 1996 – a holiday
where the cracks in both couples'
relationships begin to show.

Kate and Johnny's
Los Angeles home and
Kate's first real taste
of A-list living.

call away from a glamorous party or a dull Tuesday evening at home.

Similarly, for those who see drug use, recreational or habitual, as a scourge, the etiquette at play must seem equally preposterous, but it's there nonetheless. The notion that a seasoned user, out of friendship, kindness, even love, would guide a novice through their first taste of some new substance, ensuring they don't overdo it, keeping them 'safe', perhaps offering a pill to ease the anxiety of 'coming down', is one that to many people seems tantamount to pushing and not an act of friendship at all. But to those who think nothing of such things, to those who were part of the world in which Kate now moved, it's no different from urging caution to some teenager who's made themselves sick on peach schnapps.

On the night of Kate's twenty-first birthday party, Jason Donovan would certainly have benefited from a more experienced person's guidance and cautionary advice. Donovan was at the height of his popularity and fame in Britain and Australia. He had long since left *Neighbours*, the Australian soap that made him famous, had a string of hit singles and albums to his name, thanks to signing with Stock Aitken Waterman, and had appeared to great acclaim as Joseph in Andrew Lloyd Webber's *Joseph and His Technicolor Dreamcoat*. He could never have been accused of being cool, thanks to the squeaky-clean boy-next-door image that, much to his frustration, hung on him however far from *Neighbours* he strayed. He didn't really know Kate or Depp in any more than a passing fashion. They had met at events, parties and so on, and he had seen Kate at clubs in London, like Billion Dollar Babes on the Tottenham Court Road, a place that had its moment during the early Nineties. Naturally Donovan had been thrilled, and a little amazed, to receive an invitation from Depp to her twenty-first birthday. He had just flown into Los Angeles from Sydney the day before, arriving exhausted but, as he recalls, in good spirits.

Donovan's hotel was situated just behind the Viper Room. Looking back he has admitted that the sensible thing would have been to check in, get some rest and get ready for the following night's party – it was, by his own estimation, 'going to be the party of all parties' – but after the long flight, jet-lagged and excited, Donovan didn't feel like sleep. Instead he made a telephone call and placed an order. 'It was', he remembers, 'as easy as ringing for room service, the only difference being that what they were delivering was drugs'. For a couple of hundred dollars he bought a large bag of grass and a half-ounce of uncut cocaine, and as soon as it had arrived he got stuck in.

By the next morning Donovan was, unsurprisingly, wired. Jittery from an absence of sleep and the effects of the coke he had consumed by himself throughout the night, he felt both energized and comfortably numb. He was still mindful of the scandal that had rumbled on after River Phoenix's death and of the increased scrutiny it had brought to bear on the club and any drug use within its walls. So Donovan vowed not to bring his stash of cocaine with him when, dressed in tailored hot-pink trousers and a tight Jean Paul Gaultier T-shirt, he left for the club. As his hotel was so conveniently close he planned to simply duck out of the party and back to his room whenever he felt in need of a little pick-me-up.

Realistically it was a ridiculous plan that would involve darting between hotel room and party all evening, during which his desperation for another line would be matched only by his desperation not to miss the party. But high as he was – and he was high – it seemed logical, even brilliant, in its simplicity. Inevitably, as the night went on Donovan's frequent trips to his hotel room and the accumulation of the past twenty-four hours' excesses took their toll. Midnight came and went, James Brown had burst out of the Union Jack icing on Kate's cake, 'Happy Birthday' had been sung and Depp and Michael Hutchence were on a small corner stage performing 'Gloria', but for Donovan the party was about to come to an ignominious end. His heart began to race, his vision became blurred, he could feel the room moving around beneath him and dizziness overtook him. Sweat beaded across his forehead and above his lips. He reached for a table to steady himself, reached for a chair but it was too late. His legs buckled and he collapsed in an undignified heap on the floor.

Donovan doesn't know where Kate was in the confusion that followed. All he can remember is that somewhere in the distance the music stopped and a circle of guests formed around him – or had the crowd simply parted where he fell? Somebody was rifling through his pockets, urging him to think and asking him repeatedly, 'Have you got anything on you?' It was Michael Hutchence, frisking him and explaining, 'It wouldn't be cool if anything was found on you by the medics.' That comment reveals just how obvious the cause of Donovan's collapse was. In another situation the confused aftermath of a guest's sudden collapse would surely have been heightened by a panicky uncertainty as to what was wrong. But when Donovan hit the floor of the Viper Room, the only uncertainty was what he had taken and whether or not he still had any of it on him.

An ambulance was called and Donovan was taken to the Cedars-Sinai hospital. The doctor who saw him had one simple piece of advice, 'Lay off the drugs from now on.' Seizures like the one Donovan had experienced could be fatal. After three hours Donovan discharged himself and headed into the cool Los Angeles morning and back to his hotel. He was understandably mortified. He felt, he remembers, 'racked with guilt' that he had ruined Kate's party and was in no doubt that, however groggy and ashamed he might be feeling, he had to go and apologize to his hostess and to Depp.

They were throwing an after-party back at his hotel – the celebrations would roll on not just through the night but for the best part of the following week, with barbecues, dinners, music and dancing. Donovan knocked on the door of their suite and Depp answered. Donovan started to make his apology: 'I'm really sorry for what happened, mate.' If Depp was in any way irritated, he didn't let it show. He probably was, as he said, just pleased that Donovan was all right. 'Now take some advice from me,' he said. 'Go to your room, get some sleep and for God's sake take it easy in future.' Depp had seen it all before, and then some.

To many of the guests at Kate's party that night and morning, there was nothing inherently shocking about Donovan's collapse. Drugs were just part of the world in which they moved.

More than a decade later, when asked in an interview to name the most glamorous night of her life, Kate answered without hesitation: 'My twenty-first birthday party in the Viper Room.' It was a revealing response. Ten years on, after a decade filled with nights both glamorous and sordid, there was not a single one that compared to that evening in Los Angeles. Kate's life is one that many look upon with thinly veiled envy, but the reality is that for much of the time Kate is bored, unchallenged and living a largely unchallenging life. Modelling is something she is very good at, but it's not something about which she is or ever has been passionate. At the age of nineteen she commented, 'It must make you feel secure if you know what you really want to do. I want to find something I really love, because I don't love modelling. I've got all these people around who're so passionate about what they do. I envy them . . . Fashion's not satisfying to me at all. You can't change the world through fashion because the average person doesn't look at fashion pictures. At the moment I'm always working, and when I'm not I just, like, relax and have a good time, but I'm gonna find something else to do.'

Of course she was only nineteen years old and views expressed at that age can be barely recognizable as your own within a few years, but it wouldn't be the last time that Kate admitted to finding modelling a less than satisfying career. She wasn't complaining as such, simply noting that, when it came to having her picture taken or working the runway, it came to her so easily that it ceased to be of any interest or enjoyment. It was boring, and that simple fact took the edge off everything that went with it turning 'fun' into compensation as well as reward. But on the night of her twenty-first it all fell seamlessly into place – save for that moment of drama with Donovan. It was genuinely exciting and thrilling. With Depp, anything seemed possible.

It is piquant that the girl who was, even then, living a life many girls dream of should be fostering more run-of-the-mill hopes. She wanted to live in the country and to have children – loads of them. She was toying with the notion of acting and certainly there was no shortages of offers. At this time dozens of scripts were sent to Storm each month, within two years it was forty a month, and so the figure would continue to escalate over the years. More recently, Lily Cole, an exquisite schoolgirl with red hair and porcelain skin who was discovered by Sarah many years after Kate, commented that, as a discipline, acting wasn't so very different from modelling. After all, she had, she said, 'been silently acting for years'. Yet how many stars of the silent film era imploded with the advent of the talkies? Kate has always been rather conscious of her voice. Those who like it describe it as tinkly, whispery, sweet, while those who don't use words like tinny, wispy and weak. If more people heard it, might she lose some of her appeal? Besides, as surprising as it may seem, maybe Kate was shy of pushing on with any acting ambitions: people might accuse her of piggy-backing on her boyfriend's success and perhaps she didn't honestly know if she was any good. Anyway, there was plenty time to explore such things in the future.

The point is that, at twenty-one, Kate was beginning to think of a world beyond the catwalk, and *that*, rather than the celebrity-filled Viper Room on her birthday party, or the free champagne – a daily fact of her modelling life – was what made the night so genuinely glamorous to her. There would be other birthday parties, but none would fizz with such excitement. Ten years on, when she recalled her twenty-first as the most glamorous night of her life, the excitement had gone and ambitions that had seemed within touching distance back then remained unfulfilled.

After all, so much of what Kate had done and went on to do followed a path, if not dictated, then certainly mapped out and pressed, by others. The previous year Kate acknowledged this with the extraordinary statement, 'I feel blessed to have come as far as I have come. I was discovered on an airplane by a woman named Sarah Doukas at the age of fourteen. I don't know why that happened. I don't know why any of this happened. The chain of events that followed has led me to where I am now, and I wouldn't attempt to question any of it, or ask why. It's none of my business.'

Kate wrote these words in December 1994 when she was in Aspen holidaying with Depp. They appeared as a foreword to a book published in April 1995. Called simply *Kate*, the book was a collection of pictures of Kate; some were already published images, some were not. There was a handful from her family album and a smattering of snapshots of her life and friends 'off camera'. There is no text other than the photographers' credits and the only narrative to speak of is the thin thread of the chronology of the pictures. Yet Kate in her many guises, her many faces, makes strangely fascinating viewing. This was not a book that Kate herself had wanted to do. Quite sensibly, she noted that putting together what was, in effect, a retrospective of her work at the age of twenty seemed 'just slightly premature'. When the project had been suggested to her by Storm, Kate had been, she admitted, 'adamantly against it'. 'But they – the infamous they – would not give up; the more I was pursued, the more I was forced to think of a different approach for the book.'

She talked it over with those closest to her – Depp, her mum and Jessica Hallett, Kate's booker and an assistant at Storm who had, in the years since they first met, become one of her closest friends. Jessica is credited at the front of the book with 'Production'. Given that, for many years, she and Kate travelled together, living in each other's pockets, and that Jess was instrumental in setting up, if not being physically present at, the majority of the shoots featured, it's a credit that could be taken literally. Were it not for Jess's work behind the scenes a lot of the material might never have been produced. Kate came to the conclusion that the only way she would be comfortable doing the book was to convince herself – if nobody else – that it was not about her at all. In fact, she wrote, 'To say this book is about me (which is the MAIN reason I was uncomfortable – me, me, me, me . . . Frightening!) is ridiculous. This book is not about me. It is more about all the people I have been lucky enough to work with . . . To me this book is a celebration of the photographers, of change, and of growth.'

No doubt Kate's words were sincere, but however she may have convinced herself to feel comfortable with the project, the simple reality was that the book was, of course, about Kate. It was called Kate and it featured page after page of pictures of her. It didn't take a genius to figure out what it was all about, though it took some months of mental acrobatics on Kate's part to deny it and agree to the project.

Kate's family turned out to celebrate the London launch of Kate – Linda, Peter and Nick sipped champagne and were united in their evident pride of their daughter and sister. There had been times since Kate's discovery when Peter and Linda had wished Kate would be more restrained in what she said, if not in her behaviour. The very month that the book was published, T-shirts went on sale in New York bearing the legend 'Kate Moss – Smack Head'. It was nonsense, of course, but Kate had never made any secret of her use of cannabis and her openness about this narcotic indulgence had evidently been taken on rather enthusiastically by some American wag. But on the evening of Kate's book launch, it was all smiles, as it should have been.

These days Linda recalls Kate as 'that funny little book', with a tone of affectionate bemusement at all the fuss generated about it at the time. Kate gave interviews reflecting on how she would 'be called a waif forever', and how much she hated that fact. She appeared on British television's The Big Breakfast, on This Morning and was interviewed on a double-decker bus for children's television. She spoke with wonder about how beautiful the other girls on the catwalk were. Christy Turlington, a particular friend with whom she often stayed in New York, was so beautiful that, Kate admitted, you couldn't help but stare. Yet could anybody really imagine a book coming out called *Christy*?

Somehow the exquisite beauty possessed by Christy, Helena, Linda, Naomi et al. was bland by comparison to Kate and however 'invisible' Kate claimed to make herself the opposite was true. Kate's success in front of the camera came, in large part, from the fact that however she was made up and styled, there was something irrepressibly and recognizably 'Kate' that burned out of the page. On the evening of the book's launch, Peter rightly commented that his daughter had worked very hard to achieve what she had. Of all of the Moss family he, perhaps even more than Kate herself, was aware of exactly how that success translated into cash.

The month before her literary début Kate bought a flat in London. Two years earlier she had called upon the services of a flat-finder, but found that she spent so little time in the city that she never had time to view the properties they found for her. Finally, in March 1995, on the advice of her father, who saw the purchase as a canny investment as much as a home-making exercise, she bought a property in Shepherd's Bush, west London. It was, she remarked at the time, within spitting distance of more fashionable Notting Hill but, unlike Ladbroke Grove, you could 'pop out for a pint of milk without bumping into loads of people you know'.

Kate must have known that she would spend very little time in the property, but still she poured considerable resources into having it renovated. Kate seemed to have no confidence in her own interior design skills. Living out of a suitcase must have meant that she considered herself rather inept when it came to buying anything too big to pack and, at twenty-one, her sense of style when it came to houses probably wasn't something she'd devoted much thought to. The west London flat she'd shared with Sorrenti had been painted various lurid colours, so this time she took advice.

There would be a stainless-steel staircase, French hardwood flooring and a vast circular bath, bang in the middle of the bedroom. She employed a builder and life, when in London, still meant living in hotels as work had begun on her home. However little time Kate spent in Shepherd's Bush, Linda must have been pleased that her daughter had finally put down some roots in the capital. During those hectic days of trans-atlantic flights, foreign shoots and runway seasons all over Europe, Linda used to telephone Kate to check if she was all right, and when Kate seemed determined to spend as much time as possible in New York she would implore, 'What are you *doing*? Why are you living in that *awful* place?'

Eighteen months later, work on the flat was still not fin-ished and builder Frank Neal was threatening to sue Kate, claiming she owed his firm £23,000. The stainless-steel stair-case that had been hoisted into the property by crane had had to be hoisted back out again when it transpired it didn't comply with local authority planning regulations, and a steel sink unit flown in from Sweden had to be flown back again because it turned out to be the wrong size. In the end the dispute was settled out of court and the work completed. When Kate sold the flat in 1999 she did so for £80,000 more than the purchase price and had barely lived there at all.

Five months after *Kate* was published in Britain it was released in America. Depp was at Kate's side at the September launch at the Danziger Gallery, a self-consciously hip venue on West 26th Street that specialized in photographic exhibitions.

Launching it there was a slightly obvious attempt to give the book artistic status elevating it from an exercise in branding, the brand in question being Kate.

Kate looked effortlessly chic that night in a navy dress so dark it looked almost black. It had a cut-away neckline and the high halter-style neck was linked to the body of the shift with straps of material. As the music pumped at the after party, Depp took it upon himself to make a political statement. In June that year the French President, Jacques Chirac, had announced the end of a three-year moratorium on nuclear testing and resumed the practice in French Polynesia. France went on to conduct eight underground tests in the South Pacific. That month the first of the tests had been carried out, and however vehemently the French government defended their reasoning, international outrage was intense. Depp decided to make his views known that evening at *Kate*'s launch.

Kate had bemoaned the fact that you couldn't 'change the world with fashion'. Well that much was true, but you could capitalize on the publicity. Holding a poster aloft, Depp shouted above the din, 'Ban nuclear testing!' Kate joined in enthusiastically, calling for a boycott: 'Don't buy French! Don't buy French!' Her eyes fell on the champagne flute in her hand and the golden bubbles it held. 'Oh dear,' she giggled. 'I'm drinking champagne and all champagne is French isn't it . . . ?' Momentarily troubled, she took comfort in the notion that whatever she was drinking probably wasn't the real deal or, as she put it, 'It's only a gallery opening, so it probably isn't.' Thank God she didn't enjoy French cigarettes – Marlboro Light was always her brand of choice.

The following month Kate met another man who made a lasting impact her and who she would list, years later, as one of the sexiest men she had ever encountered (a category with some stiff competition). Living the life of a supermodel was not without its perks and it guaranteed you an invite to some of the greatest parties.

On 19 November 1995 Kate was among several hundred 'friends' invited to help Frank Sinatra celebrate his eightieth birthday at the Shrine Auditorium in Los Angeles. The evening consisted of a vast tribute concert, with stars performing cover versions of Frank's greatest hits, followed by a lavish party. Bruce Springsteen sang 'Angel Eyes', Bob Dylan performed 'Restless Farewell' and among the guests were music legends Ray Charles and Little Richard and celebrities such as Jackie Collins and Tom Selleck. It was an eclectic guest list to say the least, but Kate took it upon herself to go and wish the birthday 'boy' a happy birthday. She had long been an admirer of Sinatra and was probably more than a little starstruck that evening. She put out her hand by way of introduction and he pulled her close and kissed her on the lips. Kate would later claim that Frank 'snogged' her, 'but not with tongues'. Then Sinatra lit up a filterless Camel cigarette and asked if she wanted a puff. He was, according to Kate, 'so fucking cool'. 'I don't think he did [recognize me],' she later said. 'I think he just fancied me.' Then she met Bob Dylan and it all got too much: she nearly fainted and had to go and sit on the steps outside, catching some of what passes for fresh air in the heart of Los Angeles.

That December she and Depp returned to Aspen, where they had spent the previous December in blissful isolation. This time Kate invited her brother and mother to join them for ten days in the snowy mountains of Colorado, and they rented a chalet with no staff, save the most basic housekeeping. There was no reason to have a catered holiday as they wanted it to be relaxed and informal. On evenings when nobody wanted to eat out they took turns to cook, and they enjoyed long boozy lunches after mornings on the slopes. Kate had skied for the first time the previous year and had been surprised to find she wasn't at all bad at it. Kate and Nick took to the slopes a few times and most days Depp spent time working out with a trainer in preparation for his next film role, but most of the time, for all of them, there was no pressure and no reason to do anything but enjoy everything that was on offer. It was blissful.

Back at the chalet they played board games like Monopoly and old-fashioned parlour games like charades. Unsurprisingly Depp excelled at the latter. He told stories, taking on each character's accent, demeanour and eccentricities until Kate, Linda and Nick were helpless with laughter. On a couple of occasions the party headed to the Caribou Club. This was no ramshackle mountain bar; however homespun much of the chalet entertainments are Aspen is a retreat favoured by some of the world's most wealthy and powerful inhabitants, and the Caribou is suitably elite. Established in 1989, it's a private members' club. To become a member, as Depp and Kate did, you must be sponsored by an existing member and part with an annual fee of $1,000, which only gets you in the door.

Inside there is a room given over to a small dance floor with a large bar adjacent, but this is not a club in the falling-out-the-door-at-three-in-the-morning sense of the word. This is an old-fashioned, sumptuous establishment that, could it boast a lineage predating its Eighties opening, would once have been known as a 'gentlemen's club'. A fire blazes in the wood-panelled Great Room in front of a plump sofa, easy chairs and a central ottoman covered with a heavy tapestry throw. Globe vases hold fresh flower arrangements and lend the room a feel that is part club, part hunting lodge, part country home. Downstairs the wine room stores more than 5,000 bottles of some of the world's most sought-after vintages.

The dining room is formal – white tableclothes, fine silver-ware, dark walls and a chandelier fashioned from the antlers of some unfortunate caribou. The menu is elegantly robust: five choices of caviar, carpaccio of sweet shrimp, baked oysters, 'camp fire' trout with corn-crusted potatoes and an egg 'sunny-side up', Maine lobster, prime Aberdeen Angus rib eye, battered onion rings and horseradish cream. Nobody who saw Kate tuck into a steak dinner at the Caribou Club would give even a moment's credence to the anorexia jibes that, every now and then, and much to her chagrin, are lobbed in her direction. Kate and her family loved it. Who wouldn't?

Little wonder if, at times, Kate almost had to pinch herself to believe that this romance, this life, was hers. Of course she and Depp argued . . . passionately and furiously – it was part and parcel of a relationship that could be as torrid as it was tender – but they genuinely loved and nurtured each other. Kate may have shaken her head in disbelief and wonder at the fact that she and Depp were together, but that Christmas in Aspen there was only one thing that seemed less likely than their being together, and that was their ever being apart.

8

There was no apology, no note of explanation, Kate simply was not there. It was New York fashion week, March 1996. She had 'done' London, Paris and Milan and now it was New York. Only she was not there. In the middle of the New York fashion industry's biggest week, and at the peak of her prolific runway career, Kate Moss went AWOL. That day's runway shows were simply bumped from her schedule without warning.

It was an act that was both troubling and gobsmacking in its audacity. Kate had never had any particular respect for authority – despite her boasts that a liberal upbringing left her with no need to rebel, she showed every indication of being a rebel at heart. Going absent without leave in the middle of New York fashion week showed both extreme nerve and profound insecurity. To be fair to Kate she would later say that she felt she was about to crack up and needed to get out of New York. Undoubtedly this is true but to many in the industry it must have seemed that with the insolence of a teenager she was effectively putting the fashion world back in its place, showing that it meant – really *meant* – nothing, while running away like a guilty child who knew she'd done wrong. She was taking an almighty 'sicky' and leaving her American representatives at Women Management to handle the fallout.

On the day in question, instead of turning up for the day's final fittings and run-throughs, Kate joined Depp on an aeroplane to Chicago to see John Malkovich star in Stephen Jeffery's Restoration-era play, *The Libertine*. Eight years later Depp would star in the film version of the play, produced by Malkovich and co-starring British actress Samantha Morton, by then a friend of Kate's. No doubt the subject matter appealed to Depp's sense of culture and theatricality since the play is about John Wilmot, second Earl of Rochester, a confidant to Charles II and a talented poet, satirist, wastrel and womanizer.

Rochester's poetry and lifestyle earned him the nickname 'the profane earl'. He conducted drunken brawls in court, ran naked through the streets and wrecked the king's treasured sun dial (roughing up a suite at The Mark Hotel paled into insignifance in comparison). He lived the sort of life Kate and Depp in part perhaps both longed for and feared. Samuel Johnson was blunt in his assessment of the earl: following Rochester's death from syphilis at the age thirty-three the never knowingly tactful Johnson declared that he had 'lived worthless and useless and blazed out his youth and health in brash voluptousness'. Rochester was rock and roll and debauchery topped off with a periwig. It must have seemed very much in the spirit of the late poet to have recklessly abandoned commitments for a night in his honour.

There was another parallel easily found in the restoration tale. Rochester's great passion was for the actress Elizabeth Barry, with whom he had an affair. The story goes that she was not much of an actress before they met and that acting numbered among the many things the older earl taught her. Depp and Kate's relationship was not simply one of teacher and pupil – Kate brought more to the table than that paradigm allows – but in the years that they were together Depp *was* a mentor to his 'little girl', as well as a lover. And the more she learned and experienced with Depp, and the more her stature in the fashion world grew, the less comfortable she became promoting herself as simply 'a model'.

She was twenty-two years old and under no illusions that what she got out of modelling was, first and foremost, money – and lots of it. Of course it was fun, but already Kate was starting to see what her mother had meant when, many moons ago, she had told her that you couldn't have fun all the time. It wasn't that you couldn't *have* it, so much as that having it ceased to be . . . well, fun. When Kate did her disappearing act with Depp she had apparently reached the point where the constant travelling, partying and working had simply got too much. She obviously thought she was going to crack up, but evidently she felt unable to say so until later.

She worked in a world where it was a sin to be tired and where the easy supply of products on offer to pep up the most jet-lagged catwalk-weary model made it unforgivable. When Kate returned from her trip to Chicago there were no real repercussions. She was back and ready to work and she was, she recalls, 'like "OK, now I'll do all my stuff and I won't be a nervous wreck."' Crisis over – at least for the time being.

Work, love and the taxman may have kept Kate out of Britain for large swathes of the year, but she wasn't unaware of what was going on there; far from it. It would be close to two years before Kate would really call London her home once more, but already she was forging relationships with people who would be at her side during some of the most hedonistic – and damaging – times of her life. Britannia was about to officially become cool and, as usual, Kate was several steps ahead of the game.

By the beginning of 1996 Kate was restless and loaded. She

had more money than she could have dreamed of – though she would go on to make much more – she had a boyfriend who she adored and who lavished attention on her – for her twenty-second birthday he booked out Julie's restaurant in Holland Park and once again surprised Kate by inviting friends and family to a celebration dinner, then picking up the tab at the end – but still Kate cast around for something to really satisfy her.

Inspired by Depp's activist streak, she involved herself in worthy campaigns, lending her name to the War Child fund and, during one visit to London, appearing on Channel 4's *The Big Breakfast* to speak up for the cause. Depp accompanied Kate to the show that morning. As it turned out, Depp was still in the shower when the car arrived to take them to the studio, and the pair barely made it there in time for the last five minutes of the show, where they sat side by side on the sofa. Depp had only intended to support Kate from the background, but what studio director could resist the opportunity to get both in shot?

Kate spoke about the charity with self-conscious serious-ness, yet however heartfelt her words, however genuinely keen Kate was to follow Depp's mantra and surround herself by people who were 'better' than her – cleverer, more talented and cultured – this was life, not the reading room of the National Library, and the truly luminous talents of music, film and fashion knew how to have a good time.

In London the party had begun in earnest with the revving up of Britpop the previous year and it was still going strong. The 'scene' had moved from Billion Dollar Babes in Tottenham Court Road to the pubs and clubs of Camden, Chalk Farm and Notting Hill, and the cast of characters who would become Kate's 'set' – at her side for some of the most indulgent times of her life – were drawing together and gravitating, with a certain inevitability, towards north London – St John's Wood, Maida Vale and Primrose Hill.

The previous summer Kate had set the seal on a fledgling friendship with design student Stella McCartney by modelling Stella's degree collection when she graduated from Central St Martins in 1995. Stella would always claim to hate the 'fame thing' that came with being a child of one of the Beatles, but her name as well as her undoubted talent would always be noted. In a strong year – Stella graduated alongside Matthew Williamson, Antonio Berardi and Robert Carey-Williamson – having her work modelled by Kate, Naomi Campbell and Yasmin Le Bon certainly drew attention to it.

It also didn't do any harm to have her parents, Paul and Linda, sitting in the front row, grinning broadly and showing their appreciation of their daughter's talents with a semiphoric display of thumbs-ups and peace signs. Stella had met Kate some months earlier, the way most of this set met, at a party. It was actually Naomi who made the biggest impact on the night in question. Some years later, fame-shy Stella recalled how she wasn't in the industry at the time of the meeting: 'I was just a nobody,' she explained. 'I got talking to Naomi Campbell and thought, Wow, It's Naomi Campbell. She took me home to her house and cooked me fried eggs or something at 4a.m. The next morning I woke up with Naomi next to me.'

It's hard to believe that Stella's rock-royalty lineage didn't hold some possible appeal for Kate. Kate was already friends with Marlon Richards, who lived in New York with her dear friend and fellow model Lucie de la Falaise. She would also forge close friendships and intimate relationships with Ronnie and Jo Woods' son Jesse and daughter Leah, as well as Mick Jagger's daughters, Jade and, later, Elizabeth (all four of these

Stones offspring had successful careers as models). It was timely that the new scene should include the offspring of both The Beatles and the Rolling Stones. It was an appropriate throwback to the last great battle of British bands at a time when the drama was being played out all over again in the British charts, this time between Blur and Oasis. The fuss was mainly down to record-company hype, but it certainly sold singles and filled the coffers of both the bands and their management.

In August 1995 both Blur and Oasis released singles – 'Country House' and 'Roll With It' respectively. The well-oiled publicity machine ensured that this simple fact and the battle for No. 1 made the BBC's six o'clock news. The key was that British bands were making the news and making the music people wanted to hear, and when they weren't, they were out enjoying the spoils of their massive success. In this, if not always in their music – Blur's 'Country House' reached the No. 1 spot – the Gallagher brothers of Oasis dominated the scene.

Noel Gallagher had struck up a relationship with Meg Mathews when he moved to London. Meg was an ambitious, party-loving girl who'd hitchhiked south to London from her family home in Norfolk at the age of seventeen. For the next four years she was virtually homeless, moving between squats in Brixton and Stockwell while doing a variety of jobs: selling wigs; an assistant in Joseph – where she would later repay her wages many times over from the other side of the counter – PA to pop star Betty Boo, and at a music management company, which is where she met Noel. By then she was twenty-eight years old and sharing a flat with Lisa Moorish, a model/ musician/DJ, depending on where you choose to place the pin on any given day and a girl who, in this incestuous world, would go on to have children by both Liam Gallagher and Pete Doherty (post-Patsy and pre-Kate respectively).

Meg was also close friends with Fran Cutler, a straight-speaking woman who set up Crack Management in 1993. Given the drug-conscious times in which the company operated, it is barely credible that the double entendre of that title passed over Fran's head. Five years later Fran formalized her business dealings with Meg when the pair established 2 Active Management, organizing parties and managing artists.

Together Meg and Fran were a formidable partnership – well connected, fun-loving and with a hunger and energy for partying that matched any, and bettered most, of their set. These women organized album launch parties and charity fundraisers while making it look as easy as blowing up balloons for a kiddies' party. It is testament to her ferocious energy and networking abilities that, within ten years of moving to the capital, Meg was at the heart of its fastest social set, living in a north London mansion with one of the most successful popstars of the decade. Fran, too, was romantically linked with the band and dated Liam briefly before he met and fell for Patsy Kensit. She also went on to date DJ Jeremy Healy, the man who provided the soundtrack for Galliano's shows.

In April 1996 Liam followed his brother's move south, leaving his home in Manchester and his mother, Peggy. One decade and two marriages later, Liam recalled that time and how unreal it all seemed. The band had just played their first gig at Maine Road football ground in Manchester, and didn't believe it could get any bigger – though it did. According to Liam, 'I remember doing the first Maine Road gig. I was still living at me mam's house that day. Done the first gig, come back home to me mam's and I'm sitting on me bed thinking, Fucking hell, that was insane. The next day I moved down to London. Moved in with Patsy [Kensit]. Out of me mam's into a fucking million-pound house in St John's Wood.'

The arrangement did not, however, get off to a promising start. Within days of Liam's move Patsy was, according to press reports, seen kicking his car in the street, apparently furious at time Liam had spent with a certain supermodel: Kate. He had gone back to Kate's hotel after a party, a decision that took some explaining as far as Patsy was concerned.

There was a seven-year age difference between Meg and Kate, but they'd known each other for some time and neither was interested in letting such unpleasantness pollute their relationship. From the summer of 1996 Kate and Meg's friendship, and their partying, moved up a gear. Liam and Noel married Patsy and Meg the following year, and by then the pattern of excess and indulgence that eventually destroyed both marriages was well and truly established.

A stage was being set – the characters assembled – on which Kate would play out some of her most glorious and turbulent days. The friendships at the very base of this scene would prove phenomenally significant to Kate in every way and they were woven with a dizzying intensity and intricacy. Their overlapping history and geographic proximity provided a sprawling genealogy of sorts.

While Oasis were tearing up the charts, a group of young actors was causing a similar stir in the film industry. Among them was a friend of Patsy's, Sadie Frost. The women's lives had already progressed along strangely parallel – at times even overlapping – lines. Both attended the Italia Conti stage school in London, though Patsy was three years Sadie's junior. In 1985 Patsy had her first tabloid experience when, at the age of fifteen, she dated Gary Kemp from Spandau Ballet. Three years later – at the same time as Kate was being discovered – twenty-three-year-old Sadie married Gary and twenty-year-old Patsy embarked on a brief marriage to Eighties popstar, Dan Donovan from Big Audio Dynamite.

More lasting than either of those marriages was a friendship Kate later struck up with Mick Jones, who numbered among Big Audio Dynamite's line-up and was a former guitarist and singer with The Clash, a group much admired by Kate whose musical sensibilities stretched from disco to punk. Twenty years on, Jones was present at two crucial moments in her life. By then he was the producer for The Libertines, and it was his partner, Miranda, who introduced Kate to Pete Doherty. Jones was also in the room when Kate was captured on camera in a recording studio, hanging out with Babyshambles and snorting line after line of cocaine.

In 1992 Patsy married for a second time, to Simple Minds singer Jim Kerr, and five years later she married Liam Gallagher, four years her junior. That same year Sadie also married again, this time to Jude Law, an actor seven years younger than her. Sadie had started dating Law in 1992 when they met on the set of the film *Shopping*. The film was released in 1994 and was such an abysmal flop that Law went scuttling back to the theatre. Of the two, Sadie was by far the more famous at the time, having starred in *Bram Stoker's Dracula* alongside Keanu Reeves.

Law was yet to get his big break, and it was in theatre that he'd started and shown great promise – the National Youth Theatre to be precise. It was there that he met Johnny Lee Miller, who later dated Natalie Appleton, of the girl band All Saints and sister of Nicole, who became Liam Gallagher's second wife. Actor Sean Pertwee also numbered among this group of acting friends. He had appeared alongside Sadie and Jude in *Shopping*. Pertwee was also a friend of actress and heiress Davinia Murphy whose father made his millions selling toilet paper, where there's muck and all that ... Her wealth gave her the freedom to indulge her innate fondness for fun, travel and partying. Add her discretion, and a touch of social ambition – who wouldn't want to hang out with the coolest of the cool? – and she was another ideal playmate for Kate, to whom she would prove a long and lasting friend. Ewan McGregor was another exciting young actor who missed out on a part in *Shopping*, which turned out to be something of a blessing in disguise given the Britflick's failure.

McGregor's film breakthrough turned out to be rather more assured. In 1996 he starred in the film adaptation of Irvine Welsh's book about drug addiction and life in Edinburgh's mean streets, *Trainspotting*. Coincidentally it was a film that put Iggy Pop back in the charts with 'Lust for Life'. Iggy had been a friend of Johnny Depp's since they worked together on John Water's Eighties film *Cry-Baby*. Kate had met Iggy through Depp and been blown away, so much so that when asked what her favourite song was the previous year, she said, 'Dumb Dumb Boys.'

It seemed that anyway you turned the film, fashion and music industry – or at least this high-octane section of it – overlapped in some way, and this cross-over carried on into the actual bricks and mortar of London's social scene. It wasn't until 1997 that Sean, Johnny, Sadie, Jude and Ewan officially cemented their working relationships by establishing production company Natural Nylon, though the company had existed in all but name for several years by then. When they did, they were accompanied by producers Damon Bryant and Bradley Adams. Adams's wife was an old schoolfriend of Sadie's and had him to her in 1991. While Bryant was a former cameraman who had rekindled his friendship with Adams when he and his wife opened 41 Beak Street, 'a mini Groucho with a dance floor' and, for a time, a place for the scions of 'cool Britannia' to congregate in the heart of Soho.

When they went home, these actors all lived within spitting distance of each other in Primrose Hill, near Patsy, Liam, Noel and Meg, who rented a property before finding their ideal home in the form of the now infamous Supernova Heights. They bought the neo-Georgian mansion at the beginning of 1997 and named it, tongue-in-cheek, after the massively successful single 'Champagne Supernova', which was released in 1995. Among the lyrics to that particular song is the repeated question 'Where were you when we were getting high?' In all likelihood, as Britpop, Britflicks, Britstyle and Britart reached its zenith, the answer to that question for some of the key players, men and women who were, for the most part, Kate's playmates, was Primrose Hill – and more particularly Supernova Heights.

There was always a party to go to and there was always temptation on offer. From the very outset the relationships between some members of this group of creative, talented and occasionally wayward characters were complicated and intertwined. If plotted with pins and threads on a wallchart the resultant tangle would be spun with more complexity than a spider's web. To an outsider the world of celebrity might seem a glamorous and impentetrable bastion, but the reality is far more prosaic.

Celebrities, like anybody else, settle into cliques. The same faces go to the same parties and hang out in the same VIP sections of the same clubs-of-the-moment. They attend the same launches, sit in the front row of the same fashion shows and see the same film premieres before going on to the same first-night parties. If, in between all this relentless glamour, they happen to rub up against like-minded people who think Let's blow this party and have a good time, then so much the better.

Kate had always been fun. At school she was a back-of-the-classroom kind of girl and on her early photoshoots she'd impressed photographers and endeared herself to everyone on-set with her ability to launch herself into any job, however uncomfortable. She was talkative and giggly, girly but street smart. She was twenty-two years old and she was worth millions. In 1996 her Calvin Klein contract was renewed, making it, reportedly, the biggest modelling contract ever signed, though that same year Kate admitted to feeling 'ambivalent' about the latest jeans adverts. Still, she was in demand for both catwalk and editorial work. Photographer Mario Testino called her his 'favourite girl', and he was not alone in that view. Galliano adored her; Versace pandered to and flattered her; Sarah championed her and her booker and assistant Jess shielded her.

Kate was the person everybody invited to their party, and when she showed up they couldn't quite believe their luck. There were still a few friends from the old days – hairdresser James Brown and Jess Hallett to name but two – even this loyal retinue had a vested interest in making sure Kate was, and remained, happy. Brown, though a talented hairdresser, couldn't really have believed that his meteoric rise from city salon to become the youngest session hairdresser for a *Vogue* cover, with regular bookings as hairstylist for some of the biggest magazine titles and photographers in the world was not helped by his friendship with Kate and her preference for having him style her hair rather than Brown's equally qualified peers. Meanwhile Jess, though a friend, was in the employ of Kate's agent, Sarah. She and Kate had formed a strong friendship, and when Pulp lead singer Jarvis Cocker took to the stage and 'mooned' at the audience as Michael Jackson performed his 'Earth Song' at the 1996 Brit Awards in June, thousands of miles away Jess and Kate had T-shirts made up proclaiming, 'Jarvis is Jesus'. But however much fun they had together, it would be difficult to view this, or many of Kate's friendships, as truly equal.

Kate, after all, was the 'talent' and brand on which many of her friends' fortunes depended. Under such circumstances it would take a strong person not to allow a certain spoilt petulance to creep into their character, however innately sweet it might be.

Pearl Lowe was another member of Kate's clique. In terms of musical success she was at the other end of the spectrum from Oasis. As the lead singer of indie band Powder, signed to Island Records in 1995, she enjoyed limited success before falling head over heels in love with Supergrass drummer Danny Goffey. Later Pearl would develop a similarly intense relationship with heroin. After many years and several attempts, she is now clean, but back then she, and for that matter Kate, was embarking on an exhilarating and torrid time. Pearl had known Kate for many years in the sort of chaotic passing fashion that spawned many of Kate's friendships, and Pearl knew Mario Sorrenti, Kate's first real love, with whom she once again shared a warm relationship.

By 1996 Pearl too was living in Primrose Hill in a rented flat. Pearl's friendship with Kate continued for another ten years and her recollections of her life back then are instructive of the mood and tolerance of the worlds that collided under the canopy of mid-Nineties 'Brit–' anything. She recalls how she and Danny had no 'social or moral issue' with drug taking: 'He believed, as I did, that so long as you kept it under control, then taking drugs with your friends was no different from enjoying a drink or two: it was just about having fun. Right from the beginning of our affair drugs had played a significant role in our relationship.'

The same was true for Liam and Patsy and Noel and Meg. Never mind the 'cigarettes and alcohol' that Oasis sang about, for some of the Primrose Hill set the party favours that circulated day and night were more likely Ecstasy, acid and cocaine. If you wanted it, somebody could procure it, and for some of the Primrose Hill playmates their relationship with drugs was every bit as intense as their relationships with each other.

There were of course other characters on the scene, and some would stay for the long haul, while others would drift away or deliberately distance themselves in the years to come. Like the Primrose Hill set, not all were involved in the drug taking and complicated relationships. There was Anna Friel, the pretty Lancashire actress who earned a certain notoriety for performing the first lesbian kiss on Channel 4's primetime soap *Brookside*. She was very much a girl about town at the time and was enthusiastically taken up by Kate. Another integral to the clique was actor Rhys Ifans, a gangly, cool, erudite chap. He was a prime example of how closely the worlds of music, fashion and acting were linked. Rhys was lead vocalist with the band Super Furry Animals before they made it big, but his real talent lay in acting, though he remained good friends with his former bandmates and was the first to congratulate them when they made it big, having been signed to Creation Records (the same label as Oasis) by Alan McGee. In May 1996 Meg Mathews organized their album launch party at the Aquarium Bar in London. Of course Kate was invited, as was Sadie etc., etc. It wouldn't have been a party without them.

Drugs were the hazard, or the perk, of success in the music, fashion and film industries. For many in these industries which category they fell into depended on your point of view and whether or not you got caught. As Pearl puts it, 'Taking drugs was nothing more than a laugh . . . so long as you kept it under control.' But keeping it under control was the tough bit.

Fortunately for Kate, for the time being at least she was still very much in love with Depp – there is a certain irony in the fact that this notorious bad boy provided a much-needed anchor in Kate's life. When it came to partying he had, after all, seen and done it all before. He may not have been a choir boy, but Depp was the calm voice of reason and experience, and he was a man intent on furthering his career from acting into directing and writing.

While the London scene hotted up, Kate still spent much of her time in New York, where she rented an apartment and struggled to decorate it with thrift-store and antique-shop finds.

After her abrupt exit from New York fashion week, Kate had returned to fulfil what remained of her work commitments and life had calmed down ever so slightly. At the end of the New York fashion shows Kate and Naomi hosted a Vegas-themed party to raise money for Cancer Research. Kate has never had much of a reputation for philanthropy or charity work, but throughout her career she has quietly and steadily donated to this particular cause. That spring, when the fashion week mob decamped from New York, London's most desirable party guest was content to play at home in America with Depp. He was due to spend three months filming in Manhattan, three months during which he and Kate could live together. They had already bought a mansion in Los Angeles and placed the initials 'M' and 'D' on the large electronic gates, while Kate's rented apartment in the Pigalle district of Paris had been replaced by a millon-dollar duplex. And though there was no ring on her engagement finger, Kate made no secret of her dearest ambition: to have babies, a dog and a house in the country. Depp added a couple of goldfish when reciting his inventory of an ideal life.

For all their dreamy talk, though, by the early summer of 1996 there was less than twelve months left of the relationship that Kate and Depp hoped would last a lifetime. Tensions were beginning to show and, in later years, each would blame themselves for allowing those strains to overwhelm what they had together. Depp was thirty-three years old and had reached a stage in his life where he wanted to get serious about work and, to some extent, about life. He was young enough to believe that anything was possible, but old enough to know that while possibilities may be endless, time is not. He didn't want to end up, according to his own definition of a pretentious failure, as somebody who referred to himself as a 'serious actor'. He was, he said, 'just an actor'. But he wanted to do more than act, and he wanted to have children.

Kate was at a stage where, having worked for eight years, she too sensed that there must be more to life. In early 1996 she tried her hand at being a stylist on a shoot for *Mirabella* with friend and photographer Glen Luchford. For Kate it was a revelation, and she loved the voice the role gave her, though the money, she admitted, was far less appealing. Speaking a few weeks after the shoot she explained, 'I'd be there and I'd say, "I'm not sure about that, let's shoot it over here," or whatever. And he'd listen to me. Then a few weeks later I was working with him as a model. I'd be like, "Oh Glen, I'm not sure about this," and he'd just look at me. Models don't have opinions basically, you just can't say anything.' But though she was old enough to appreciate this and feel a hunger and ambition for more, she was still young enough to feel immortal. She was twenty-two; there was no rush. The tension between the two outlooks on life and between Depp and Kate was inevitable.

In June, Depp, Kate, Noel and Meg holidayed in Mustique. Depp and Kate, who was by then a close friend of Jade Jagger and had met and impressed her father, were staying in Jagger's house. It was, Noel later remembered, 'really fucking surreal', and the problems between the two couples were writ large in the rhythm of that Caribbean holiday. While Depp took himself off to a small room at the back of the villa to work on a script he was co-writing for *The Brave*, Noel sat in the front room surrounded by original Andy Warhol paintings, playing his acoustic guitar and working through songs for the band's next album. Both Depp and Noel were, and remain, serious about their considerable talents. Meanwhile Meg and Kate were, in Noel's words, 'out the back getting fucking pissed as arseholes'. But while Kate was having fun, part of her must, surely, have felt frustrated by the extent to which it was work, and not her, that commanded Depp's attention.

That August, one event more than any other served to crystallize the pull of the life of full-throttle indulgence that sprawled before Kate with her new London playmates, as opposed to the life flecked with something more profound – some sort of future and earnest endeavour – on offer with Depp. And that summer those worlds competed, consciously or otherwise, for Kate's attention.

On 10 August 1996 Oasis performed in the grounds of

Knebworth House, Knebworth Park in Hertfordshire. It was the biggest rock event of the decade. The band who, less than a handful of years earlier, had been rehearsing in the basement of the Boardwalk club in Manchester and who had released their first album only two years earlier, were now so phenomenally successful that they needed an estate to accommodate their audience. Close to 3 million people applied for tickets and only one in ten was successful.

Noel has recalled being driven through the early hours of the morning to see the venue for the first time. He was in his chocolate-brown Rolls Royce – a gift from Creation Records boss Alan McGee. Dawn was breaking as the gates opened on to the vast gothic country house used as Bruce Wayne's mansion in the Batman films. Coming down from the night before, still 'out of it', drunk and wanting to remain high rather than embrace the onset of the anxiety attacks that followed hot on the heels of a night spent inhaling a blizzard of cocaine, Noel remembers getting out of the car, sitting on the bonnet and making a telephone call to his management to say, 'Let's fucking do it.'

Weeks later, while the ground seethed with fans and the Primrose Hill set were barely a drop in the celebrity ocean that flooded the VIP area backstage, Noel decided to take a bath in the house itself. A liveried servant brought him a bottle of champagne, which he duly popped and sank. It was only later that he was told the 'servant' was Lord Cobbold, owner of the house and bath in which Noel bobbed. Kate was there for the two days that the concert – more miniature festival than massive gig – ran. Sitting in the palatial Creation Records hospitality tent, she turned to Alan McGee, Glaswegian founder of the indie label, and declared, 'This is just the best thing ever . . .' Kate had enjoyed five-star hotels, private jets, luxurious yachts, penthouses and mansions, but nothing could compete with the sheer thrill of being backstage at an excessive rock concert. She must have been utterly seduced.

9

The scent of sweet thyme filled the air, carried over the Provençal hillside by the warm spring breeze. High above the Cote d'Azur coastline, in the medieval village of St Paul de Vence, the Colombe d'Or hotel was an exquisite refuge, away from the buzz of Cannes and the clatter of the town's main beachfront drag, La Croisette, which was always oppressively busy during the film festival. Kate and Depp drank champagne with the rest of the guests invited to the small celebratory dinner that May evening. They took in how pretty the gardens were with their fig and orange trees lit by the soft evening sun, they toasted actor Gabriel Byrne's birthday – the reason for the gathering – and they posed dutifully for pictures together before the evening's celebrations got underway. It all looked idyllic and effortlessly glamorous, but Depp for one was not as relaxed as he appeared.

His film, *The Brave*, had premiered the previous day on 10 May 1997 and the reaction from the all-important Cannes audience and critics had not been positive. Depp had poured all his energies into the project and the subject matter was significant to him personally. The hero, Raphael, is a Native American Indian, struggling and failing to support his wife and children. In desperation he makes a Luciferian deal: he will 'star' in a snuff film, allow himself to be tortured to death by a bunch of rednecks for a fee that, he believes, will ensure his family's welfare. The film follows him during the week before he must make good the deal. Depp is part Cherokee and the story of the Native American's plight resonated with him. He wrote the script along with his brother D.P. Depp, as well as starring as Raphael and directing the film – it was the first time he had done so. He put his own money into the film and called in a few favours too. Marlon Brando took a small part for no pay. Brando famously got a Native American Indian to collect his Oscar in 1973, and his involvement with *The Brave* was part an act of friendship to Depp and part a political stand. Long-time friend Iggy Pop also made a cameo appearance and wrote the music score. Depp spent three months filming in the Californian desert during which time everything else came second, including Kate. Then the American critics savaged it. Depp was devastated.

He raged against the critical drubbing the film received, and though his own performance was nominated for a Palme d'Or it was little consolation to him. Making the film had been a painful process, and looking back he berated himself for even attempting it. 'It was way too much work for one person,' he said. 'You get up earlier than everybody, go to bed later than everybody and when you're asleep you're dreaming about it.' It had hurt him and his relationship with Kate, and it hadn't even been worth it. Following its Cannes screening, Depp refused to release the film in America.

Twenty-four hours after the premiere, Depp was not in a party mood. He had been, by his own admission, 'a horrific pain in the butt to live with' for many months. Little wonder then that in the months before Cannes he and Kate had spent barely any time together at all. More than that, their once daily telephone calls, during which Kate would stop whatever she was doing and melt into their conversation, had dwindled away. Depp seemed not to have any time for Kate, paying her little or no attention when before he'd showered her with gifts and parties.

After spending three months in New York, living together in Kate's little apartment, Depp had spent three months filming *The Brave,* and no sooner had he finished filming that than he threw himself into his next film project – starring as writer Raoul Duke in Hunter S. Thompson's *Fear and Loathing in Las Vegas.* The character was one that inhabited him to an alarming extent. He lived with Thompson while preparing to play the character, holed up in the basement of his fortified compound, reading and absorbing the man, with nothing but Thompson's books and his roll-ups for company. During this research Thompson and Depp built a bomb in his garage and detonated it by firing a 12-bore shotgun at the device. The explosion caused an 80ft-high fireball. They had, Depp recalls, 'quite a time together'. Kate had met Thomspon – as had her mother Linda, who was frankly terrified of the man – and not even Depp liked the side of him that 'being' Thompson brought out. 'The greatest danger of playing someone like him, he said later, 'is that he doesn't leave you. That also made me hell to be with for a spell. It took me two months just to shake him off. He would just "appear" without warning.'

Depp was overloaded with work and it was affecting him profoundly. When he wasn't working he was 'getting loaded' because he was 'sick of looking at the guy in the mirror'. Sometimes, he admitted, it was 'almost a letdown to look in the mirror and realize, I'm not Edward [Scissorhands] . . . there's nothing cynical, jaded or impure about him.'

All in all this hard-working, hard-living, sometimes morbidly gloomy phase of Depp's life was not conducive to romancing Kate.

Kate, too, was taken up by work, though she would never claim to be as emotionally involved in it as Depp. She did the season shows and posed for an advert for Absolut vodka, though the brand she carried from shoot to shoot and job to job in her trusty little hipflask was Stolichnaya. She knocked it back neat, eschewing 'fucking mixers', and demonstrating an iron constitution and capacity for alcohol that, by this time, had earned her the nickname 'the Tank'.

Bit by bit Kate and Depp's lives, which had seemed to be pulling together only months earlier, were drifting apart. The previous year reports of them rowing had appeared in a smattering of gossip columns. In December they spent time together once more in New York, but had found that, after so many months apart, being under each other's feet was not as blissfully harmonious as they had hoped. Still, they tried to make the best of things.

In the New Year they travelled to England. Kate had always had a fondness for rural England and the previous year had toyed with buying a place in the Cotswolds. January 1997 found Kate and Depp in Buckinghamshire, spending afternoons meandering through antique fairs, poring over examples of period stained-glass windows, rummaging through trinkets and wondering what would look best in her west London home or the Los Angeles villa they shared.

But however comforting such interludes were, the reality was that, bundled up in his work, obsessing over the final cut of *The Brave*, holed up being Raoul Duke or giving interviews to push *Donnie Brasco*, Depp was increasingly absent from

Kate's life. More and more when it really mattered, he was emotionally not there for her, and in the early months of 1997 she needed him perhaps more than ever.

On 4 February Mario Sorrenti's younger brother, Davide, died. He was twenty years old and he was addicted to heroin. His death made the front page of *The New York Times*, where it was wrongly reported that he had died from a heroin overdose. Heroin had indeed been the cause, but less directly. Davide died from complications caused by a combination of his drug use and the painful blood disorder, thalassaemia, which he had been born with. Such detail seemed of little importance at the time, though. The bottom line was that heroin lay behind the demise of a talented young man, and in that irrefutable fact a dark side to the fashion world was laid bare.

Davide, like his brother Mario and mother Francesca, was a fashion photographer. The side of fashion that his death exposed was one that nobody wanted to acknowledge; the dirty little secret induldged behind closed doors at 'glamorous' parties; the stain to which a blind eye was repeatedly turned to the cost of Davide and others like him. He lived in a loft apartment in the East Village with his eighteen-year-old girl-friend, Jaime King. Tall, blonde and beautiful, Jaime had been spotted by a talent scout at the age of fourteen and was a hugely successful model. She made a lot of people very rich and earned a great deal herself in the process and she learned quickly that great wealth brings with it great temptation. She, like Davide, was a heroin addict. For her, drug use that had started as recreational had become a necessity, though after his death she quit modelling, got clean and moved into acting.

There was simply no denying that the industry was shot through with serious hard-core drugs. That's not to say that the designers, photographers or agents were pushers, but it was remarkable what passed unremarked and unreported. In common with the film, music and media industry, fashion was a competitive, high-pressure world where the vulnerable and insecure rubbed up against some monstrous egos and demands. Given the money, the temptation and the certainty that there would be no reprimand as long as the job was done, it's little wonder that, for some, narcotic escape turned into drug-induced oblivion. Somebody had to take a stand and be the adult at this children's party, and Davide's mother, Francesca, made it her business to point that out.

In the weeks after Davide's death she gave numerous interviews in which she railed against the 'glamorization' of drugs, and by that she meant the images of elegantly wasted models – pale, thin and apparently 'out of it' – that graced the pages of glossy magazines and sold the clothes of fabulously expensive designers. Francesca knew better than most that often the appearance of being 'out of it' was a reality, but that there were those in the business whose only concern was getting the shot and getting paid. 'I've been thinking about what people in my world and Davide's – the fashion world – can do ... No boy or girl goes into this industry saying, "I am going into modelling because I want to be a drug addict." No. He or she wants to be a model make money, have fun. But sometimes they fall into something else. If someone comes to a photoshoot so far off their rocker that they can't stand up, I think the most horrible thing you can do is wait until they come down or feel better so you can get on with your pictures. What you do is sit them down and call the agency or the parents. You take that person home.'

Her words provoked outrage because they revealed a callous disregard for models' welfare that nobody outside the business could imagine and few inside would admit, and the fact that this cold surface was held up as some sort of glamorous ideal made it even worse. Davide's death was a bereavement that affected Kate both personally and professionally. She had lived with Mario's family when she first went to New York and they were like a second family to her, so Mario and Francesca's grief mingled with her own. Given the genuine loss she felt, it seems deeply unfair then that Kate would soon find herself somehow blamed for giving drugs a glamorous gloss.

In March Kate was at Depp's side in Paris at the French premiere of *Donnie Brasco* and afterwards at The Queen nightclub on the Champs Elysée. They laughed off recently published reports of a split, saying that it didn't really matter what the press said, they themselves knew the truth: their relationship was still fun and still fresh. Kate could make Depp laugh and surprise him with her sheer enthusiasm for life and capacity to embrace it. He could still impress and wow her with his taste, his knowledge and his artistic and intellectual ambitions. All this may have been true, but it was not the whole truth.

For Kate and Depp turned their faces away from that until it was inescapable and unstoppable. The truth was that their grand romance was running out of steam. Kate thought she had found 'the one', and so did Depp. Perhaps they were right for a while, but not for keeps. They loved each other, but increasingly it was not enough.

When they were together in America it was wonderful. In Los Angeles, when Depp wasn't working, their friends would come over and they would go out 'all the time' and have fun. But Depp was away a lot, and increasingly Kate found herself communicating through a variety of assistants. She went shopping, she did the whole 'ladies-who-lunch crap', she 'faffed around', and she got bored in a place that was, without Depp, lonely, shallow and remote from the people she loved. Kate got sad, brooded and they grew apart. The harsh reception of *The Brave* and Depp's gruelling work schedule combined with Kate's grief at Davide's death conspired to make those first few months of 1997 peculiarly battering for them both. And for Kate it was about to get a whole lot worse.

That May President Clinton stood in the White House and addressed thirty-five mayors, invited there to draft a plan to control trafficking and the use of illegal drugs. A few days earlier he had happened to read an article in *The New York Times* that referred to the death of young fashion photographer, Davide Sorrenti, and characterized his work as using models that looked drugged and haggard. The article went on to quote some magazine editors admitting that glamorizing the strung-out look reflected a use of heroin among young people in the fashion world and that appearances were not, in this case, always deceptive. Evidently it struck a chord with the President and he pulled no punches as he criticized the fashion industry for making heroin seem 'glamorous, sexy and cool', delivering a speech where he coined the phrase 'heroin chic'. 'You do not need to glamorize addiction to sell clothes,' he said. As for this 'glorification of heroin', it was tantamount to 'glorifying death'. He pointed to campaigns – giving as an example Calvin Klein's Obsession adverts featuring Kate – to illustrate what was to him, and the logic ran to any reasonable individual, an 'ugly' practice.

In the furore that followed Kate found herself and her image held up for particular criticism. She had always been 'the waif', and now the look that had launched her – or that she had launched, depending on your perspective – was given an altogether darker interpretation. The pictures that had brought her working relationship, and very nearly her friendship, with

Corinne Day to an end when they appeared in the June 1993 edition of *Vogue* were once more wheeled out for criticism. At the time they had been lambasted as paedophilic and now Kate's tiny frame, blank eyes and the squalid flat in which she posed were interpreted as the epitome of 'heroin chic'. The previous year a picture of Kate, topless and smoking a cigarette had appeared in US *Playboy* to the disgust of the anti-smoking lobby. She had been blamed for anorexia, paedophilia, lung cancer and now heroin addiction.

Kate didn't comment at the time, though years later she would roll her eyes at what she regarded as the madness of it all. Besides, she was mourning the sudden loss of a dear friend. Little wonder that Kate was feeling ever so slightly bruised. But however much she may have needed a little coddling, it was not to be. Kate and Depp's relationship was giving way under the strain of the past year and the brutal beginning of 1997.

That June the couple apparently spoke for the first time about separating. What had once been such a close and powerful romance was unravelling and they had to address that. Only two people will ever truly know what passed between them in those conversations. No doubt there were tears – certainly many were shed by both sides in the weeks and months that followed. Depp retreated to his room, sick to his stomach, and wept and smoked for a week. Chivalrous in heartbreak, Depp later claimed it was he who shouldered the blame for the break-up that began that summer. He had blown it with Kate and he was racked with the guilt that brought and the fear that he would never come close to happiness with another person again. He had been impossible to live with. He had allowed the critical failure of *The Brave* to eat away at him and, coming hot on the heels of all those months of brooding and sulking, he'd allowing himself to be consumed by work. It was more than Kate could bear.

Despite everything, Kate did not really believe that the distance that had opened up between them that year was the end of the road for her and Depp – neither of them could really believe that – and so the relationship limped on. Kate and Depp saw each other several times and tried to breathe new life into their dying affair, but the twice-daily telephone calls had dwindled to once a fortnight or less; the momentum that had been so irresistible had gone and there was no getting it back. The reason why was hard to fathom. Depp had been so convinced he'd met his Miss Right. He had felt ready: ready to settle down, marry and have children. Kate, however, had not. She was, after all, ten years younger than Depp. She had viewed it as a natural enough progression of their relationship.

Then, quite unexpectedly, something happened that would put any thoughts of her ailing relationship with Depp abruptly to one side. The fashion world was hit by news so devastating that it seemed to make no sense at all: Gianni Versace had been murdered.

It was 8.45 in the morning of 15 July and Versace was walking back towards his villa on Miami's Ocean Drive. He had been to the nearby News Café to buy a newspaper and some magazines. It wasn't his usual routine, but it was such a beautiful Florida morning that he decided to walk there himself rather than ask a member of staff to make the short trip. He bought *Vogue*, of course, and *People* – well, we all like a bit of gossip – and he was nearly home. He had walked up the steps to his front gate, put his key in the lock and was on the point of turning it when Andrew Cunanan approached him. Cunanan shot Versace twice at close range: once in the face, once in the neck.

There was no motive for the crime – Versace was just unlucky. His murderer, Cunanan, had killed four times that year in a violent spree that took him across America and ended eight days after Versace's death when he committed suicide to avoid capture. Kate was working in Jamaica when news of Versace's death broke. It must have been so shocking as to seem almost absurd. Only a few months earlier she had modelled his Fall '97 collection in Milan. Gianni – kind, funny and phenomenally talented – had been part of the fabric of her modelling career. She had modelled for him as a freshly found girl and her brother had been booked by him for his catalogue work.

Now the Miami mansion, the location of many flamboyant parties, was a crime scene and the Milan headquarters of the family's billion-pound empire were shuttered up and silent. Kate sent a personal message of condolence to Versace's sister, Donatella. Publicly she issued a statement saying only, 'I am stunned and lost for words.' Work commitments meant that she could not attend Versace's memorial service, which was held in Milan the following week. The vast Roman Catholic cathedral was packed with celebrities as one might expect. There were 2,000 mourners, among them Naomi Campbell – one of the designer's favourite models – who was so grief-stricken she appeared to struggle to stand. Designers Karl Lagerfeld, Carla Fendi, Georgio Armani and Tai Missoni paid their respects to their esteemed colleague. Sir Elton John, always a fan of Versace's flamboyant designs, wept openly as he sat in the congregation next to Diana, Princess of Wales, who placed an arm tenderly around her bereft friend.

One month on, Elton would be singing at Diana's funeral and the world would mourn and try to make sense of another shockingly sudden death, when Diana was killed alongside with her lover Dodi Al Fayed in a car crash in the Alma Tunnel, Paris. Amidst the tributes sung in Diana's honour, one is now largely forgotten – dedicated to her by Elton but overshadowed by his reworking of 'Candle in the Wind'. 'Something About the Way You Look Tonight' was the second track on the CD. Kate appeared in the video – tanned, carefree and incredibly beautiful – filmed in a roomful of models and dancers, drenched in warm colours and lighting.

Back in Croydon, or more specifically nearby Haywards Heath, Kate's world was undergoing an upheaval of a more modest – yet for her more affecting – nature.

It was nearly ten years since her parents' divorce and Peter, like Linda, had found a new relationship. There is nothing to suggest that Kate was anything other than happy for him, but it must still have taken some adjusting when he broke the news that summer that his partner, an elegant Norwegian woman called Inger who he'd met through work, was pregnant and their baby was due in January. Moss family mark two was about to take shape.

Of course Kate had her own life and was no longer a child – she was barely even in England half of the time – but coming in the midst of a tumultuous year, the news must have been as unsettling as it was happy. It would be impossible not to hear it and feel, rightly or wrongly, that her father's attention, if not his love for her, would turn away from her in the coming months. For a second time that summer, however minimal or temporary it might prove, Kate had lost a man in her life.

Perhaps that creeping feeling played its part as Kate *sans* Depp began to reposition herself socially. After all the upset, fun was now high on the agenda, and the significant others in her life were female. That is not to say there weren't men in Kate's life; far from it. For the next two years, or even longer, there were men to whom she would be linked, but there were none to whom she gave her heart.

Instead, Meg Mathews, Sadie Frost, Davinia Murphy, Jade Jagger and, to a lesser extent, Pearl Lowe and Anna Friel became the constant playmates in what proved to be an increasingly inconstant life. There was the old guard too – Anita Pallenberg, Annie Nightingale and Marianne Faithfull – but they would not truly come into their own until Kate wilted, just for a little while, in the face of the dervish-like spin of her post-Depp frenzy. In the summer of 1997, as she and Depp contemplated the prospect of separate lives and drifted inevitably apart, Kate began living at an unsustainable pace, physically, spiritually and emotionally.

It had now been five years since Kate had been signed by Calvin Klein and she was on the books of three modelling agencies: Storm in London, Women Management in New York and Marilyn in Milan. Her Klein contract – by then worth £2 million a year – was the biggest modelling contract of the day. She had worked the world's catwalks, some many times over regularly appearing for designers such as Galliano, Alexander McQueen, Vivienne Westwood and so on. Her name was so dominant, her image so strong, that she had been asked to appear in One2One mobile telephone adverts for a British television campaign. 'Who would I most like to have a One2One with?' she asked wispily, before answering the question: 'Elvis.' Kate was nervous of speaking in public. She was well aware that, as a model, nobody expected her to speak, and to a degree it suited her to be 'just a face or a body' to the world at large because she has never been fond or confident of her voice.

Her uncertainty was unnecessary, but in the extent to which it came across as she spoke, it remained an endearing, and bankable, trait. For all her fame and fortune Kate could still morph from supermodel to excitable Croydon girl. The moment she said 'Elvis' with a self-conscious bite of her lip and barely controlled giggle, she turned into a slightly gushing fan whose dream of meeting her idol was no more attainable than it was for any of the million others who shared it. Had Kate named a living musical icon it would have been a rather different story: Mick Jagger, Ronnie Wood, Paul McCartney, David Bowie, Johnny Cash, Iggy Pop – she could have called any of them up for a natter if she'd fancied, and she could have thrown in a few film stars, some world leaders and captains of industry while she was at it. In the light of such possibilities, it seems almost modest to have picked an imposs- ible dream, and reassuringly human that she still had such a thing. Barely a month went by when she wasn't either featured on the inside pages or pushed onto the cover of the glossiest and most hip magazines in the world.

In September it was announced that Gianni Versace's younger sister, Donatella, would take over as head of the fashion empire. There had never been any doubt that the Versace show would carry on without Gianni, nor that Kate and her friend Naomi would continue to have a lead role in it, but there had been a discomfiting air of uncertainty since Gianni's murder, so the announcement, when it finally came, was met with relief at Storm. It was good news for the fashion house and good news for Kate. It's a truism that people like working with people they like. Donatella liked Kate and liked working with her, so there was no question of bookings dwindling with her at the helm. It made good business sense, but it certainly did no harm that when Kate was booked for a job, there was one less catwalk diva to manage.

While Naomi worked her hips like twin pistons and spiralled into a full-blown tantrum if she perceived another girl to look better in an outfit than she did, Kate would wonder aloud whether she mightn't wear something different, but button her lip and whatever dress had been hung on her rail if it was obvious that a rethink was not in order. Similarly, when Storm flew Kate out to South Africa that September for a triple launch – the advent of their South African branch, Virgin's new flight route to Cape Town and CKJeans – and the barman failed to turn up for the after-show VIP knees-up, Kate simply slipped behind the bar with Richard Branson and began serving up the champagne, joking, 'The tips are terrible in this job.'

In the years since her discovery, Kate had become a strange blend indeed: a down-to-earth 'sarf London' girl whose feet hadn't touched the ground for a long, long time. While Donatella's fashion style might have been out of kilter with the underplayed, almost haphazard glamour Kate was personally fond of, and which she was increasingly becoming associated with, her lifestyle certainly chimed with Kate's enthusiastic fondness for excess all areas.

The month before flying to Cape Town, Kate could be found on the deck of the *Sevrilor*, lapping up the sun, and limitless booze, off the coast of St Tropez. Liam Gallagher had chartered the 54ft superyacht and turned it into something of a floating gin, or perhaps more accuarately, lager palace. Patsy was there. It was more than a year since she reportedly confronted Liam – and his car tyres – over his visit to Kate. Now she had calmed down and got over her earlier insecurities. Besides, Patsy was no stranger to partying herself. Noel, Meg, Fran Cutler and Kate's assistant Jess made up the rest of this decidedly merry party.

Later Noel recalled that period of his life as one of sheer madness. It seemed that everything after Oasis's massive performance at Knebworth came as an anti-climax. There was no natural high to be had, so they drank and took drugs 'every day all day', and marvelled at the simple fact that, no matter how badly they behaved, they could do no wrong: 'Being famous is a good laugh when you're on drugs. You meet people and go, "Nah, nah, fucking, nah," and everyone goes, "Wow, hasn't he got loads of charisma." And really you're just hammered.'

Back in Britain life was not short of opportunities for Kate to show just how much charisma she had. In September she was invited to Rolling Stone Ronnie Wood's fiftieth birthday party, which had a Wild West theme. Kate was deeply tanned from her summer spent working and playing in the sun and she wore tiny Daisy Duke hotpants, cream ankle boots and a cream hide top that was little more than two ragged strips of material stitched together at the front and tied at the back.

It might be natural to assume that Kate was there more as a friend of Wood's son, Jesse, with whom she would go on to have a brief relationship, than on the ageing rocker's request, but it would be wrong. Kate had met Wood and his wife, Jo, at Noel Gallagher's house and the friendship that bloomed between the three would bring out a part of Kate that her more febrile relationships sometimes threatened to swamp: a thoughtful, inquisitive side that has always been part of her make-up and the genuine sense of fun and childlike delight that drugs and sensual indulgence sometimes dulled.

Perhaps it is simply because, having 'been there and done

that', it takes more than an outrageous capacity for drink or drugs to hold the attention of a Rolling Stone. Perhaps it is, as Depp always tried to counsel Kate, proof positive that you should always surround yourself by people who are better, more talented and cleverer than you are. Certainly the time that Ronnie, Jo and Kate have spent together over the years has been about more than just knocking back vodka and that, in part, is why the friendship has endured while others that sprang up around the same time have fizzled out. Many years have passed, but it seems that Kate still wants to impress Wood. It is a healthy instinct and presents Kate with a challenge – something that, over the years, her life has come to lack.

According to Wood, 'Kate is my favourite DJ. When you're at her place she blows you with her musical taste. It goes from Sinatra to Mozart and The Stones, but it's always incredible. I'm always surprised and I tell her, "I didn't know you knew that!" She has such exquisite taste.' The pair can talk and listen to music all night and, probably refreshingly for Kate, there is no sense of Jo feeling threatened. She is far beyond the petty dramas that accompany many of Kate's other friendships. Jo can afford to indulge Kate because she is fond of her and Kate cannot touch Jo's life or relationship with Wood. They do not compete together, they just have fun, rummaging through the attic of the Wood's London house for Jo's old Seventies clothes and mementoes from wilder days.

As far as Jo is concerned Kate is like her – 'One of the guys', albeit one who enjoys trying on her old catsuits. Still, it would be a more grown-up Kate who took much of an interest in Jo's knowledge of alternative therapies and her promotion of a health-boosting lifestyle. After all, it would be naive to believe that, at the age of twenty-three, Kate's initial respect for

Ronnie went much deeper than admiration for his legendary wild-man past and impressive wild-man present. There is no getting away from the fact that Kate is drawn to bad boys – even those who have reached their half century – but their recklessness has to be cut with talent . . . or at least it did back then.

Towards the end of the year Kate was back in New York. There was still much to draw her there and, regardless of Depp's increasing absence from her life, there remained an emotional appeal about the city. Her friend the model Lucie de la Falaise, was now married to Anita Pallenberg and Keith Richard's son, Marlon, and had given birth to the couple's first child, a little girl called Emma, and Kate was her godmother. On a less emotional level New York is also Kate's favourite city for shopping – Paris and London come second and third in that order.

On 8 December, five months after he was gunned down on the steps of his Miami mansion, New York's Metropolitan Museum of Art staged a gala dinner to mark the opening of an exhibition in honour of Gianni Versace and his work. It was a predictably star-studded affair and it was testament to the shift in Kate's social positioning of herself that she attended not with a man but Marianne Faithfull, a friend of some three years standing who happened to be in the city at the time.

Over the next year and beyond, Kate would not be short of male attention, but while she held an obvious appeal to many men, none proved to have much hold over her. Again and again over the coming months it would be Kate's female friends to whom she would turn – old and new, young and old. Her relationship with Marianne in particular would prove close, complex and compelling. On the evening that Kate invited Marianne to join her at the Versace gala dinner the friendship was relatively young, though the acquaintance stretched back three years or so to an introduction by Anita Pallenberg at an aftershow party in Paris. Marianne had never known Gianni, though she would become reasonably familiar with his sister, thanks in part to her friendship with Kate and a resurgence in her own career as she branched out into serious, and on occasions acclaimed, acting.

As they arrived at the Metropolitan Museum on that December night, Kate and Marianne adopted a pose that would become familiar over the next couple of years as Kate, *sans* Depp or any man, showed herself to be utterly comfortable with being as tactile with her female companions as she was with male ones. Kate and Marianne arrived in black Versace – Kate's knee-length off-the-shoulder dress was one she had owned for several seasons, while Marianne's floor-length number was given to her for the evening. They walked hand in hand and it was hard to discern who was drawing strength and chic from whom.

The evening was wonderful, but it was after everybody had left the museum, when a small, camp collection of guests headed to Versace's New York residence, that the party began in earnest. Kate was there, of course, along with Marianne, Donatella, Antonio D'Amico – a former model turned cutter and designer and Gianni's partner for eleven years, to whom he reportedly left a monthly income of $26,000 for the rest of his life – Rupert Everett and Cher. The house was exactly as one might imagine it – impossibly grand and Romanesque; in Marianne's words, 'Nero's Palace'. It was freezing cold outside, but they wandered across the mosaic-tiled floors barefoot. They drank champagne and spoke about death and there, as night gave way to morning, what had begun as a celebration of Gianni's work turned into a wake in honour of his death.

It was Kate who started the singing – or rather it was Kate who demanded, as only she could, that they all had to sing. Marianne sang an old Irish folk song and Donatella began to cry, then Kate turned to Cher and informed her it was her turn to sing. It says a lot for Kate's self-possession – and perhaps for the amount of champagne that had been consumed over the course of the evening – that she not only took it upon herself to galvanize this odd, starry gathering into action, but that she wasn't in the least bit starstruck. Cher, according to Marianne, 'is a wonderful and genuine person, but not exactly spontaneous'.

Yet as Marianne, Donatella, Antonio and Kate – the only guests left by then – reclined on chaise longues draped with leopard-skin throws in a Nero's Palace of a New York apartment, replete with frescoed walls, fluted columns and fountains, Cher rose to her feet, stunning in a tight green Versace sheath. Marianne has since recalled the moment: 'My God she was amazing, plastic surgery or not . . . She looked like a supernatural being, unearthly and breathtaking. With her hair down to her waist, a siren from Greek mythology standing before us in this fabulous temple. She stood there and sang "Danny Boy"; her voice, echoing through the colonnades and resonating somewhere high above us on the gilded ceiling, was spine-tingling. Of course by the time she finished we were all sobbing . . . We couldn't take our eyes off her.'

10

Marianne Faithfull called it the 'tyranny of hip' when she described herself as the 'victim of cool' – a force so powerful that she credited it with nearly killing her. She had been a rather sheltered convent girl when, at the age of seventeen, she was spotted at a music industry party and propelled to fame with the haunting song 'As Tears Go By', written by Mick Jagger and Keith Richards. She had fallen for Jagger and fallen hard, and with him came a lifestyle that took first her reputation – in the most old-fashioned sense of the word – and then very nearly her life.

In February 1967 Marianne was the only female guest present when a party held at Keith Richards' Sussex home, Redlands, involving the Stones, a couple of the Beatles and assorted luminaries of the day was raided by police in a drugs bust. Marianne was naked save for a fur rug and the whole bust became mythologized as having interrupted some sort of orgy – something she and the rest of the partygoers have always denied. Jagger actually took the rap for Marianne that day, claiming that the pills were his, but there was no escaping the drug addiction into which the youthful Marianne was about to descend. The scene consumed her.

By the age of twenty-three she was living on the street,

anorexically thin and a heroin addict so desperate and weak that she needed to ask others to help her inject the needle in her arm. Back then she had bought into the romantic notion of the artist as a figure who must plunge himself into the abyss of drugs and wretched excess. These days she regards that as 'utter crap', saying, 'It doesn't create anything. It's a supreme form of narcissism.' Yet it took Marianne years to come to that conclusion, and still there is a part of her that fears being sucked back into her self-destructive old ways. If she had to do it all again, would she resist from the start? Would she be able to?

Marianne understood the temptations with which Kate was presented and she knew the consequences and cost of succumbing to them as wholeheartedly as she had. At the end of 1998, when Kate stood at the edge of the abyss, wobbled and struggled not to fall, Marianne showed her a level of friendship others did not dare. She was a voice of caution distinctly absent among many of Kate's then crowd and with an authority of friendship that trumped parental interference.

In November 1998 Kate checked into the Priory clinic in Roehampton, and Marianne drew from her own considerable experience of life and helped as best she could. For that, and for Marianne's many kindnesses to her daughter, Linda would long be grateful. Perhaps Marianne recognized in Kate something of herself before the fall. Back then she had had nobody to tell her, 'Enough! Stop!' Certainly for the best part of a year, before she buckled and checked into rehab, Kate was careering towards a similarly perilous state.

On the surface the year began well. Kate's half-sister, Charlotte, was born on 9 January at The Princess Royal Hospital. Later that month Kate celebrated her twenty-fourth birthday in New York with Depp. It was the last birthday she would enjoy with him. For the sake of symmetry it would sometimes be pointed to as the end of their romance proper – four years on the nose – but life is rarely so neat and cuts rarely so clean, and the end had in fact been dragging on since the previous summer. Still, that birthday evening proved an amazing, and long, night.

It began with watching the Rolling Stones perform at Madison Square Garden in New York and rolled on to Ron Wood's Palace Hotel suite, where the music, drinking and general revelry sprawled on until morning. When dawn broke, Kate left alone. She had commitments to keep. She had promised Island Record founder, Chris Blackwell – a man whom Naomi Campbell regards as her stepfather – that she would be at the opening of the Aveda Spa at his Jamaican resort, Strawberry Hill. She flew out on a commercial jet and spent four hours there before work compelled her to return to New York. Blackwell was touched by her loyalty, though noted, with a distinct lack of chivalry, 'She looked like she had been through hell, but I was impressed that she kept her word and decided to show.'

At the beginning of February Kate travelled to Cape Town, South Africa, once more with Naomi Campbell and Christy Turlington. The girls were due to model in a charitable Versace fashion show in aid of Nelson Mandela's Children's Fund. The South African had founded the charity, which raises funds for the country's impoverished children, shortly after he was elected president in 1994 and donated one third of his annual salary to the cause. On 13 February Kate, Naomi and Christy stood alongside Mia Farrow and presented Mandela with the last shirt Gianni Versace had designed. It was a lurid creation, as one might expect, and so too were the tales that would later emerge about how Kate and Naomi spent their downtime in Naomi's Table Bay Hotel.

According to claims made by Gavin Maselle in a Sunday newspaper, the blizzard of cocaine that blew around some of the coffee tables in Primrose Hill was replicated in Naomi's luxurious suite in South Africa. Maselle, who worked as a booker for Storm in South Africa for eight years, during which time he knew Kate well, claimed that a 30-gram bag of the powder was delivered to the girls' hotel and spoke of the use in terms of addiction rather than recreation. Naomi has spoken of her drug use and claims that these days, wherever she is in the world, she tries to attend a Narcotics Anonymous meeting. But her rehabiliation, according to her own time frame, didn't begin until 1999, and until then her drug of choice – the drug she first took aged twenty-four when she was offered it backstage at a rock concert – was cocaine. Naomi, who refers to Mandela as her 'grandfather', would look back on her meeting with him as 'the happiest day of her life', and certainly it seems fair on Maselle's account to describe it as a high point.

From South Africa, Naomi and Kate travelled on to Cuba for a photoshoot with *Harper's Bazaar*, where they were about to meet two revolutionaries in a month. Kate and Naomi together were a fearsome, and fearless, combination. They wanted to meet Fidel Castro, so they wrote him a letter, telling him they had just been in South Africa and had met Nelson Mandela and that now they were in Cuba they wanted to meet him. They handed the letter over for delivery and awaited a response, never really believing they would get one.

Two days later they were told that one of the president's representative would be joining them for lunch. Kate recalls, 'He was very official looking; he had hooded eyes, sunken cheeks, he was drinking Cuban coffee and smoking cigarettes. He said, "What kind of modelling do you do?" and things like that and eventually he said, "Mr Castro is a very busy man, but I will see what I can do."' Every night, dressing after the shoot that took place predominantly on the beach, Kate and Naomi wondered if that would be the day that the telephone call came and they would be summoned to Castro's offices. It never was. Then, on the last day of their stay, the aide who had lunched with them two days after their arrival showed up at the beach and told them, 'Mr Castro will see you at six o'clock.'

There was still three hours to go before the photographer was satisfied the job was done, and the moment he called it a day, as the assistants packed away lights and equipment, Kate and Naomi ran for the hotel. News of the meeting had, unsurprisingly given the nature of Castro's regime, travelled back to their hotel and the staff were there, waiting, holding the doors of the elevators for the models as they rushed to their rooms to shower off the sand and put on what Kate refers to as their 'First Lady dresses'. Within half an hour they were at Castro's offices, sitting across from the man who once joked that if avoiding assassination were an Olympic sport he would be a gold medallist.

It was a remarkable meeting between two young women and a communist revolutionary. They were the faces, in a very literal sense, of a world from which Castro and his nation was economically exiled and to which he was vehemently politically opposed. Castro could not have made his views any clearer than when he simply stated, 'I do not like capitalism.' But he seemed to find it in himself to like the capitalists who sat winningly in his office that evening. Naomi and Kate were given an audience lasting one hour – thirty minutes longer than the Pope got.

Of course Castro, or one of his aides, had done his research on Kate and Naomi. He admired both for being what he referred to as 'revolutionaries' in their own field – Kate supposed he was referring to her height and Naomi assumed the comment was a reference to her colour. Castro pulled a book about his own revolution from the shelves and talked the girls through every photograph. There were things they wanted to ask, but it had been made clear to them that Castro would do the talking and lead the conversation.

As the audience came to a close Castro gave Kate a copy of the book in which she had taken a great an interest. In it he wrote, 'For Kate Moss, frantelamante, brotherhood, Fidel Castro.' He walked them to the elevator and, as the doors closed, he saluted. 'That and the thrill of meeting him made me feel as if I was on a roller-coaster,' Kate explained when she recalled the meeting a year later. 'I was screaming all the way down in the elevator, all the way to the car and all the way back to the hotel, where we had to do a press conference which we were late for. Naomi, who is brilliant at things like that, sat down and said, "Sorry we're late, we've been with your president." It was the most amazing thing.'

But such thrilling moments could not disguise the fact that Kate's life was riddled with contradictions and temptations, and that she was increasingly finding the former hard to reconcile and the latter hard to resist. She was an extremely wealthy young woman, with contracts including Calvin Klein, Cerutti 1881, Versace, Christian Dior and L'Oréal, and a fortune rapidly approaching the £15million mark, but on a personal front her life had never been so vapid. Work drove

Kate hard while surrounding her with playmates and recreational drugs.

Pearl Lowe recalls one particular fashion party that year. Had there been a theme it would, she says, 'have been sheer opulence'. 'Everywhere you turned there was a famous face: Hollywood stars, supermodels, famous photographers, film directors. Everyone in the room was beautiful . . . The food was to die for, the wine was exquisite, the atmosphere electric. After pudding was served the coke came out. Silver trays covered in neatly drawn lines of white powder were brought to the tables . . . no one batted an eyelid. It was as if it was the most normal thing in the world to be served cocaine at the end of dinner, but then again, in the world that we were in, it was.'

Pearl's recollections give more than a flavour of the hedonism of the scene in which Kate was a star. It offered sparkling fun that would take Kate, and many of her friends, to dark places and seemingly endless opportunities for indulgence that could not last forever. It allowed her to meet some of the most inspirational world figures and travel to some of the most remote places on earth, but when she came home it was always to the same square mile of London, the same claustrophobically tight circle of friends and the same seductive enticements.

Kate didn't really know what she was worth until the previous year (1997), when her accountant sat her down and told her. She did several things straight away. She went shopping with Sarah [Doukas] and spent £800 on a Vivienne Westwood sheepskin rug. She gave her mother a chunk of money and bought her the grand Surrey property in which Linda continues to live, placing her name on the title deeds alongside her mother's. She acquired a portfolio of stocks and shares. She helped her father, Peter, set up his own travel company. She developed a taste for real jewellery, treating herself to a huge natural pearl. And, in spite of a lingering guilt at her wealth – 'I s'pose I didn't think I deserved it,' she admitted – she traded in her flat in Shepherd's Bush for a grown-up house.

That October Kate had ceased to be one of north London's most famous party guests and became one of its most party-loving residents when she bought a cottage in St John's Wood. The term cottage is perhaps rather misleading, conjuring up as it does images of a thatched roof and a doorway surrounded by roses.

The cottage that Kate bought was a semi-detached house, carved off the end of its neighbouring Georgian townhouse and tucked at the end of Melina Place, a dead-end lane off Abbey Road. When she sold the house almost exactly ten years later it had an asking price of £3.25 million. During her years there Kate would make many changes to the property, both decorative and structural. She added an extension to the side, eating into the pretty walled garden to the front and side of the building, and adding a light dining kitchen to the otherwise relatively small living space.

To all intents and purposes Melina Place was a bachelorette pad. It was bought and designed for adult living and socializing, which, after Kate became a mother with the birth of her daughter, Lila Grace, would be viewed by some as childish and selfish.

At the top of the house are two garret-like rooms, one with a bathroom, the other a small box, with just enough room for a single bed and a few small items of furniture. Ultimately those rooms would be occupied by a live-in nanny and Lila respectively. It must have proved a slightly impractical arrangement given the tight curve of the spiral staircase and the amount of lifting and carrying that a young child, her toys and clothes require.

Meanwhile, Kate converted the entire first floor into a master suite, kitting out what might have been a spacious bedroom with cedar-lined rosewood wardrobes and drawers to create a fabulous dressing room in which there was also a walk-in shower/steam room. Downstairs she sectioned off a windowless study at the back of the house, and at the very rear of that study she carved out a little store room, a cubby hole running off from the large L-shaped living room.

Should the new occupants of Melina Place care to look behind the mirrored panels that run across the lower section of the back wall of that cubby hole, they will find, on the exposed surface beneath, evidence of the lifestyle for which the house was originally bought and to which it was always best suited. There beneath the panels lie drunken scrawlings by Tracey Emin, the artistic detritus of past parties and of the days and nights of excess at Melina Place, of which there were many during Kate's decade in residence.

Of course the party wasn't always at Kate's place, but it was never far away. If the three most important things in buying a house are 'location, location, location', then St John's Wood certainly ticked all the boxes as far as Kate was concerned during this stage of her life. Sadie Frost and Jude Law, Noel Gallagher and Meg, and Liam and Patsy were only a square or so away on the A–Z in their Primrose Hill abodes and even Pearl Lowe and Danny Goffey's white stucco house in Stratford Villas, Camden was within spitting distance. As long as they were in London, on any given day or night the party need never end. There was no reason for this core of playmates to ever be out of each other's company and head home; they already *were* home, or as near as damn it.

It was the very relentless intensity that made that spring and summer of 1998 such an incredible time for those involved and such an impossible one to sustain. By the beginning of July, Noel Gallagher for one had had enough of the all-night parties and of finding half-naked friends and drug-addled strangers wandering around his Primrose Hill home. Within those walls, taking drugs was as normal as having a cup of tea, for some, but the effects were unavoidable. It was just a matter of how quickly they caught up with you.

Noel describes what he went through: 'I would wake up at four or five in the morning having these wild, wild panic attacks,' he recalls. 'Anxiety attacks, sweating. On the verge of tears. Constant racing heartbeat. Cold sweats then hot sweats. Getting the shakes. The demons come to visit you in the middle of the night. I was trying to get off the drugs [but] the house where we lived in London was constantly full of people. I just thought, I'm not going to end up in the Priory clinic, a sad, miserable cunt who is either getting high or coming down and always moaning about something. So it came to the point where I thought, This is it.'

That moment of truth came in September 1998, but it became inevitable a couple of months earlier, during the World Cup, when he called a doctor to Supernova Heights in the middle of the night. 'He looked at me and said, "I'm not even going to ask you if you take drugs." He said, "There's nothing we can give you. The longer you go on, the more intense the [panic attacks] are going to get. Stop doing it."'

Part of the problem, Noel has since reflected, was that he was rich beyond his wildest expectations, and for large swathes of time he had nothing to do but enjoy it. There was no reason to set boundaries and nobody close to him – just as there were very few close to Kate – would dare do so. Self-medication, not regulation, was the order of the day. Pearl Lowe recalls how during that time she struggled and failed to balance out heroin and cocaine-induced highs with a variety of illegal and prescription drugs. For every anxiety-riddled narcotic comedown there was a Mogadon, Rohypnol, Valium or the anti-anxiety drug Xanax. 'I had repeat prescriptions for them all,' she now admits. 'Courtesy of a doctor acquaintance who was happy to oblige.' He must have been a useful person to know.

Kate zigzagged across timelines when she worked and lost track of the hours when she played. The core members of her group of friends were fixed, but there were a few new faces that year and they spoke volumes for the direction in which her life was heading. There was hard-core jungle DJ Goldie, a Midlander with a metallic grin in keeping with his name, who returned to London that year having plied his trade in Miami and boasted of having such 'an abyss of energy' that meant he needed only three hours' sleep in every twenty-four. There was Nellee Hooper, a phenomenally successful music producer who started life as a club DJ in Goa and Ibiza, and made a name for himself with dance-orientated mixes. Then there were the artists who were tearing through the Britart scene.

It was a movement that had only really broken through to the wider public consciousness the previous year and still had some way to go before becoming truly established. At the forefront was Damien Hirst, the angry young man who would go on to become a rather more mellowed multi-millionaire; art dealer Jay Jopling who, along with his wife photographer Sam Taylor-Wood, ran London's uber-cool White Cube gallery; Tracey Emin, the angry young woman who would go on to become another more mellowed multi-millionaire and brothers Jake and Dinos Chapman.

Kate's interest in art was genuine and over the years she has invested tens of thousands of pounds in it. She has many original works, including paintings and sculptures by Damien Hirst, a nude of herself sketched by Tracey Emin, and a work by illusive graffiti artist Banksy, who took Andy Warhol's famous 'Marilyn' print and reworked it as 'Kate'. It is revealing that the art in which Kate has always shown most interest came complete with a frenetic 'scene'. That is not to suggest that the pleasure Kate took in her friends' considerable talents was insincere, but it was heightened by something else.

Kate loved the whole 'sex, drugs and rock'n'roll' ethos. She saw Edie Sedgwick as an inspiration – certainly Edie was its embodiment. In parts of the Britart scene, in the clubs some went to and the excesses in which some indulged, Kate relished the degree to which it was a throwback to an earlier era: to Andy Warhol and his Factory. She saw Edie Sedgwick as an inspiration, and when Kate had her long hair cropped two years later it was after looking at pictures of Edie. This is a troubling and revealing fact, since Edie was a feckless, mixed-up heiress – a groupie by any other name. Kate has admitted, however tongue in cheek, that were she not a model she would be a groupie.

There were parallels between the two if one cared to look, or perhaps, more accurately, sought to find them. Kate had first appeared in *Vogue* as 'Fashion's New Spirit', while Edie appeared in its pages in August 1965 as a 'youthquaker'. Though she had many relationships, Edie admitted there was 'only one true, passionate and lasting love scene [Bob Neu-wirth], and I practically ended up in the psychopathic ward. I had really learned about sex from him, making love, loving, giving. It just completely blew my mind – it drove me insane. I was like a sex slave to this man . . . But the minute he left me alone, I felt so empty and lost that I would start popping pills.' In spite of what would prove an irreconcilable split, Kate may have viewed Depp as her 'lasting love scene'. While Edie Sedgwick may have been many things, a healthy role model was not among them. She burned out, as Kate very nearly would after a year of living a distinctly empty life to the full.

It was not that there was any shortage of talent amid the bright (relatively) young things with whom Kate surrounded herself during this period. Indeed there was still, in her choice of friends, an earnest attempt to better herself by being in the company of people she considered better than her. But some-how, somewhere along the line, the aspiration to self-improve-ment was going awry and morphing into an undiluted fascination with a certain dark glamour, and that was always going to be problematic when taken – as she took her vodka – straight.

In May, Sarah Doukas threw a party at the Kensington Roof Gardens (owned by Branson) to celebrate ten years of Storm model agency. It might as well have been ten years of Kate, the two were so intrinsically linked. After Branson's original invest-ment of £250,000 the agency had bloomed and now turned over close to £7 million. In keeping with her desire to pick girls who didn't conform to the classic notion of a model, Sarah continued to sign against the prevailing wind, though there was every evidence from her agency's success that this policy was causing the wind to turn.

By now Sarah had signed Sophie Dahl as a mainstream model when, as a size 14, she would more usually have been advised to slim to a 12 before being considered for 'outsize' work. She had also signed Sudanese model Alek Wek and part

Japanese, part American Devon Aoki. Revealingly, Sarah had signed the then fourteen-year-old Devon the previous year on Kate's suggestion. It was Kate who had seen Devon in an American magazine and been struck by her exquisite, doll-like beauty. Unlike some models, Kate was not protective of her own status to the detriment of others. She saw something remarkable in Devon and championed her, regardless of the fact that, with her distinctive look and delicate frame, she could be seen as a potential rival to Kate. Even so, Kate brought her into her world and introduced her to her friends, in particular Bobby Gillespie of Primal Scream.

The year that Devon was signed by Storm she appeared with Kate in a bizarre video for Primal Scream's track 'Kowalski'. In it the girls are depicted as vigilantes of sorts, tearing up the road in a red sports car with Kate at the wheel, before taking on a series of male thugs and kung-fu kicking their way through them all. It's an odd, and not entirely convincing, scenario, and it's also one that includes an aspect to Kate's life about which speculation and rumour would become increasingly persisitent: sapphism. As Kate drives at high speed, Devon is shown applying lipstick to the older girl's pouting lips, she then leans in to kiss Kate's neck and mouth, which curls in a certain lazy satisfaction.

The year that Storm celebrated its tenth birthday Devon replaced Naomi Campbell as the face of Versace. She was another of Sarah's success stories, but she was well aware of just how much she owed to Kate. 'I have a lot of love for her,' she says. 'Because she is a wonderful person – she is a true icon.'

There is no doubt that Sarah shares that fondness for Kate, and the belief that she is both 'a wonderful person' and an 'icon'. But managing an icon was never going to be easy. After

ten years Kate still spoke to Sarah every day, but their relationship was not entirely full and frank. How could it be? According to Sarah, 'There are some things I know I can never discuss
with her. We're close, but when you're an agent, there's a line.'
And when there are vested interests and a complex balance of
friendship and business, that line must be difficult to draw.

As the woman who spotted Kate at such a young age, and
who regards her as her fourth daughter, Sarah must have felt
some responsibility for her welfare but whether she could have
acted is another matter. The balance of power between the two
is far from straightforward, after all, Kate isn't only Storm's
golden girl, she's their golden goose. That year, as she spiralled
out of control, Storm made sure to protect their business
interests and, in 1998, registered Kate Moss as a trademark. If
only protecting Kate from herself were such a simple matter of
administration. Looking back on that time years later, Kate
admitted, 'It was like a circus. We'd be up all night and then I
would have to do nine shows the next day. We were pretty
naughty. To be honest, seeing what we could get away with
was half the appeal.'

Barely two weeks after the celebration of Storm's decade in
the business Kate made headlines in a most unfortunate fashion. She had been asked to leave one of the most exclusive
hotels in the French Riviera – the Hotel du Cap in Antibes –
after guests complained about the noise coming from her room
at all hours of the night and into morning. At 5a.m. the hotel
concierge went to Kate's room and asked her to stop making
such a racket. She refused, so he rang the general manager,
Jean-Claude Irondelle, who went to the room and asked Kate
to pack her belongings before arranging for her and her bags
to be driven to the nearby Hotel Majestic. Kate insisted that
her room had been next to the bar and that *their* music was

blaring so loudly that she didn't think anybody would notice if hers did likewise. 'But they just got cross, and then they asked me not to wear a bikini around the hotel and it was like, *excusez-moi.*' She seemed oblivious to how spoilt she sounded.

Kate was in Cannes as a guest of L'Oréal and had been flown there with Claudia Schiffer the previous week. She had been at the festival's opening-night gala, a screening of *Primary Colors*, based on the book of the same name – a fictionalized account of Bill Clinton's first presidential campaign in 1992. At the gala she met the film's leading man, John Travolta, and was frankly starstruck in his presence. Far more significant was her reunion of sorts with Depp, who was at the festival for the premier of *Fear and Loathing in Las Vegas*.

Of course Kate went to the film with him, but the rumours of a rapprochment were wide of the mark, as she had promised to be by Depp's side many months earlier. After all, she had been by his side throughout the making of the film, or at least as close as their respective work would allow. Kate and Depp made a brief appearance at the official after-party, but soon moved on to Planet Hollywood, where they danced until early in the morning before moving on to another nightclub and heading back to the Hotel du Cap. The following day – Saturday – Depp cancelled all his interviews. When normal service resumed on Sunday he blamed jet lag and was quite categoric in his assertions that he and Kate were no longer together and that both knew, deep down, that there was 'no going back'.

How difficult it must have been for Kate to hear the heartfelt expressions of regret for the end of their romance, which filled Depp's Cannes interviews that year. Though he had been married before, and engaged to Winona Ryder, he claimed never to have really loved before the age of thirty – the age when he met Kate – and gave every impression of a man who was far from over her. Little wonder then that Kate didn't want to think about the loss and heartache, and instead chose to abandon herself to partying.

11

Back in London there was always another job or another party to go to: the launch of Damien Hirst's restaurant, Pharmacy; the *Vogue* magazine party at the Lisson Gallery, the Lenny Kravitz party, the Aveda party, the Spirit of the Himalayas party (seriously), Rock for Dockers (or for any other reason you fancied) at the Sound Republic, and when there wasn't a party there was dinner at the Ivy, Momo or San Lorenzo or, less glamorously perhaps, Bill Wyman's restaurant Sticky Fingers. Wherever she was, it seemed that Kate fizzed with energy, often displaying a seductively naughty sense of humour that bordered on the cruel.

Not many people can make the loud-mouthed Jeremy Clarkson cringe, but Kate managed it when she met him at the aftershow party on the opening night of Steve Coogan's show, *The Man Who Thought He Was It*. Coogan's wild-man credentials were pretty modest by comparison to the company Kate kept. He had first taken cocaine in 1992 and had been admitted to hospital as a result. In 1996 he 'enjoyed' his first red-top scandal when he was reportedly discovered with a couple of lap-dancers in a bed covered in ten-pound notes. Coogan reportedly said that he had no idea his lovely young companions were sex-workers, but thought they were Latvian refugees in need of shelter for the night.

By 1998 Coogan was very much the man of the moment; he was cool on stage and wild off it, and his stage show's premiere was a predictably starry affair. Kate was there with Noel Gallagher, Goldie and a few girlfriends when Jeremy Clarkson approached the group, thrust his hand out to Kate in greeting and announced, 'Kate, hello. I'm Jeremy Clarkson. I'd like you on *Top Gear.*'

'I don't do drugs,' she replied.

Slighty panicked by this perceived misunderstanding Clarkson tried again: 'No, no, you don't understand. I'd like you on *Top Gear.*'

Kate, by now in the swing of things, raised her voice in punchy indignation and explained, 'S'cuse me, mate, I don't care what type of gear you've got – I don't do drugs.'

In desperation an almost hyperventiliating Clarkson turned to Goldie and implored, 'Please, mate, tell her I'm not a drug dealer!'

Whether at home or abroad, Kate was rarely alone and rarely asleep, and that's how she wanted it to be. She was the life and soul of the party as far as her world was concerned, and there was always somebody to call on to ensure the party need never end. Kate's tight Primrose Hill circle was surrounded by a daisy-chain of generous friends and associates.

One Saturday morning that summer, still up from the night before and mortally hung over, Kate was filled with a desire to get out of the city. So she telephoned her friend Lord Cholmondeley and suggested they go to his country pile – or one of them – Houghton Hall in Norfolk. Kate's friendship with David Cholmondeley, a man fourteen years her senior, dated back to the early days of her romance with Depp, who was on good terms with the aristocrat having met him as David Rocksavage, film director and screenwriter. His professional name came from the courtesy title, Earl Rocksavage, which Lord Cholmondeley had gone by until his father's death in 1990, when he became seventh Marquess of Cholmondeley, Viscount Malpas and Baron Cholmondeley of Namptwich. He is also the hereditary Lord Great Chamberlain, a title that requires him to walk backwards down the aisle of the House of Lords as the Queen makes her way to her throne at the annual opening of Parliament.

However steeped in tradition his titles and however grand his inheritance – he has an estimated wealth of £60 million and the seats of Houghton Hall, Norfolk and Cholmondeley Castle, Cheshire – the earl is a thoroughly modern man. He studies art, listens to jazz, is well read and a great film enthusiast, as well as practitioner. He began by making documentaries drawing, unsurprisingly, on his own elderly and rather outré relatives, such as his grandmother Sybil Cholmondeley, an Edwardian beauty and great patron of the arts who died in 1990 at the age of ninety-five. As a girl she was heiress to the Sassoon and Rothschild fortunes, but was cut off by her family for marrying an English gentile. Under the name David Rocksavage, the earl has adapted Truman Capote's *Other Voices, Other Rooms* and directed *Shadows in the Sun* starring Jean Simmons and James Wilby.

Keeping the company of film stars, models and musicians is far more his speed than having a seat in the House of Lords, which he declines to take on the basis that he is, frankly, not qualified to do so. 'Many of the lords are', in his view, 'and would probably win their seats in an election, but birth shouldn't give anyone the right to have a role in running the country.'

Still, it has given him the right to call 10,000 acres of that country 'home'. The tract of Norfolk in which Houghton Hall sits is particularly beautiful and, on the Saturday summer morning in question, it was there that Kate decided, with enthusiasm bordering on petulance, that she wanted to go. Lord Cholmondeley did not disappoint. He told Kate to meet him at Battersea heliport. She put on a Galliano dress, threw a tiara in her bag and set out, sleepless and shoeless.

During the flight to Norfolk they drank champagne and smoked Malboro Lights. At Houghton Hall they walked through the vast stone hall, beneath gilt chandeliers, through the grandly rococo saloon and out into the gardens which swept down to the grand park beyond. They drank Sea Breezes, listened to the peacocks cry and watched the white deer peculiar to this estate graze in the distance. As the sun set and the moon rose, Kate was filled with a sense of how fantastical the scene was and how extraordinary her life had become. Suddenly she was filled with the thought: 'Oh my God. I am in *The Great Gatsby.*'

It was a seductive fantasy, and even now Kate will return to the books of F. Scott Fitzgerald and read and re-read them. She makes no secret of the extent to which she relates to the American author's tales of desperate, destructive, decadence, and just as she has been drawn to the books again and again, so she has returned to the lifestyle many times over. It was an existence that Kate enjoyed, perhaps for the first time, that summer, and its ending was one she did her best to postpone. Like the characters in her beloved novels she was almost afraid to stop: she didn't want the party to end because, when it did, she would have to start actually *feeling* something.

*

It was after midnight by the time Jason Lake and his small, rag-tag group of friends finally made their way down to the beach at Atlantis. By the time they arrived they were already tanked up on tequila, cocaine and MDMA powder, and one of their party owed Jason his life.

Back then Jason's sand-coloured hair reached almost to his waist. He was twenty-eight years old, suntanned and lithe with a hard body honed by days swimming in the sea off the Ibizan coast and nights partying in the island's clubs and on its beaches. He had been living on Ibiza for three years renting out a finca – once a Buddhist monastery – high in the hills above Benirras beach on the north of the island and a world away from the bright lights and fairground, package holiday-style attractions of San Antonio.

The party on Atlantis beach that mid-August night in 1998 was a rave. There were neither tickets nor flyers; this was strictly word of mouth. If you knew about it at all then you were cool enough to be there. If you could find it – Atlantis is a place imbued with mystical powers by the island's more bohemian dwellers and isn't signposted or marked on any tourist maps – then you were welcome.

Most partygoers that night arrived on the secluded beach by boat. Certainly if they'd been sensible, Jason admits, that's how he and his friends would have made their way there. Instead they opted for the alternative – a perilous scramble across a rocky mountainside and along an exposed cliff edge that would prove the first unsteady steps on what he now reflects on as a 'very strange evening indeed'.

'We'd all been snorting coke, taking pure MDMA powder, snorting lines of it, dabbing it, drinking tequila. This was kind of the norm because we knew there was a party in Atlantis that night and we thought, OK we'll get warmed up – a couple of bottles of tequila, a few spliffs, a few lines, all that ... get ourselves all revved up for the evening. We thought we'd drive up as far as we could, park up, then walk over the mountain. Pretty soon we were thinking, Jesus where is this party? It's a bit dodgy up here.

'It was really high, with a sheer drop on one side. My friend was walking at the front, laughing and larking about a bit and suddenly he trips and just disappears. Straight over the edge of the cliff. We all did a double take. It was like, "Did that just happen?" We all run over and there he is about 12ft down and he's landed, lucky bastard, on the only bush growing out of the cliff and behind him there's a 400ft drop.

'Suddenly we all sobered up. I said, "All right, mate. Don't move and whatever you do don't look down. I'm coming to get you." Eventually we managed to pull him up over the edge of the cliff and he was shaking and tanked up and he just said, "You saved my life." And gave me a massive bag of MDMA powder – pure Ecstasy.'

It was a generous reward for his heroism and one that Jason would put to good use over the next forty-eight hours.

The first person he recognized on the beach that night was Jade Jagger. She owned a finca not far from Jason's, but while his home was inland, hers was perched on the cliffs overlooking the hippy haven of Benirras. They had met the previous summer on that beach. Jason had been swimming in the sea when he saw Jade and looked over and smiled. 'She stuck her nose up and looked away,' he recalls. 'So I went right up to her and said in a laughing way, "Listen, love, you're not the only one round here who's got famous parents all right?" She goes, "Why, who are you then?" And I told her that my mum was Diana Dors. She laughed and we instantly clicked.'

Celebrity and hedonism were not new to Jason. When it

came to those two topics he, perhaps more than Jade and certainly Kate, was a veteran. As the son of Diana Dors and her actor husband Alan Lake, the notions were stitched into the fabric of Jason's childhood.

It is easy to forget these days, but in her youth Diana Dors was one of Britain's greatest screen icons, and her social life was peopled with the biggest, and wildest, stars of the day – Oliver Reed and Keith Moon were regular guests at her house parties.

But where Kate's world opened up for her with that chance encounter at JFK airport when she was fourteen, Jason's had shut down in the most appalling fashion. When he was fourteen his mother had died of ovarian cancer, and four months later his father took a shotgun and killed himself.

Fourteen years on, in Ibiza, he was, he reflects, 'a cathedral full of ghosts'. He opted for the oblivion of drugs, partying and sexual excess – his way of postponing the inevitable moment when the merry-go-round, the party, had to stop. Fourteen years on, on that August night in Atlantis, he met Kate.

'The whole beach was properly set up – there were bars and fires and lighting, big sound systems and backdrops and projectors. It was like a proper Goan tribal rave. I saw Jade and made a beeline for her, and she was there with this girl. I said, "Who's your mate? Who's the pretty girl?" She said, "Kate."'

The name didn't mean anything to Jason. He had submerged himself in life on Ibiza and before that he had been travelling in Goa. When it came to popular culture he was remarkably out of touch. At first the lack of recognition put Kate off her stride. He asked her what she did. 'I'm a model,' came the bemused reply. Then, perhaps hoping to prompt some realization of the scale of her celebrity, 'I've just split up with Johnny Depp.' That name also meant nothing to Jason. 'Never mind, love,' he consoled. 'I've just found out my girlfriend's been unfaithful to me, so I'm a bit on the rebound myself.'

At that Kate burst out laughing. She had thought he was winding her up, but it was clear that this wild-looking guy was the real deal, utterly removed from the reality she was doing her damnedest to escape, oblivious to her fame, unmoved by her celebrity and out to have fun.

That night on Atlantis beach Jason and Kate danced and flirted amid the throng. Jason recalls how they all 'got tanked up on MDMA powder', and as the night wore on and the drugs took hold the dancing became more sensual, the atmosphere more fetid.

'I suggested we all go for a walk along the beach,' Jason explains. Jade and Kate were good friends and not about to abandon each other simply because some man had pitched up and shown interest in one of them. So they all went for that stroll.

'We kind of settled on the beach for a while and had a bit of fun and eventually the sun was starting to come up, so we all decided to go back to Jade's.

'We carried on partying, drinking, dancing, getting high, having a good time. We spent the day listening to music and moving between the inside and outside of the house. It must have gone on another twenty-four hours and then it started getting dark again. It was a real mash-up. I said to Kate, "I've got this lovely house, do you fancy coming back?"'

A taxi was called and Jason and Kate drove inland to his whitewashed finca. Kate seemed enchanted by what she saw. It was a beautiful old house, basic and rural with a vast fireplace for the winter months and walls three feet deep. Mosaic tiles covered the floor and walls of its bathrooms, the furniture was old and solid and big and the garden was as lush as Eden: there were fig trees, orange trees, persimmon, almond, plums and pomegranate trees, and all around was cool and green. There was a pool and a roof terrace. Kate declared it 'lovely' and the party continued *à deux*.

The next morning, Jason recalls waking up feeling 'less than average' and having a fleeting moment of doubt. 'Kate was like, "Awright, Jason? Shall I make us some tea and toast?" She was really down to earth, but I'm hearing this voice, this Croydon accent, and I thought, Is it just me or is she a bit of rough? She's really pretty, but is she a bit of rough? I couldn't work it out because I'd been on such a bender. Then I looked at her and thought, Yeah. She's really pretty and she's fucking sexy. She's got a bit of a gob on her but she's lovely. We basically chilled out that day because we were both absolutely fucked. That day was officially cancelled.'

Over the next two weeks a rhythm developed – partying with Kate and spending time with her either at his own or at friend Jade's finca. In the mornings Jason would make smoothies for Kate. They'd relax round the pool, soaking up the sun as it intensified towards noon, then plunging into the water and drying off in the sun. After doing that a few times they might have the first vodka of the day, then, if they were at his place, Kate would hop on the back of his scooter and they would head to somewhere like Camrayet, a favourite little seafood restaurant near the coast, where they would eat swordfish and salad and drink cold beers. Then they might telephone Jade or simply meet her down at Benirras beach where she and Kate loved to sunbathe topless or nude.

'Skin,' Jason recalls, 'was definitely in that summer. Kate wore very little. People used to call her and Jade the Dynamic

Duo, cos they looked so amazing that year.' An affection developed between Kate and Jason. Make no mistake, this was never going to be any great or lasting love affair for either of them. It was fun and frolics, but it wasn't soulless – not as Jason remembers it anyway. There were days when they talked about life and love, albeit with the sort of profound inanity that comes with booze, drugs and sunshine.

'She spoke about Johnny a bit. She was upset about it, really upset. We'd talk about relationships and she'd say, "Isn't it hard? Aren't they shit?" And I'd say how life was a mixture of joy and pain. I was trying to console her, I suppose. I remember telling her I had a child from a previous relationship – a daughter, Ruby. She turned to me and said, "We'd probably have nice kids together wouldn't we?" It was really sweet the way she said it.'

Kate, according to Jason, was a perplexing combination of wholesome dreams – she spoke of wanting to have children, a house in the country and to make jam – and raucous fun. 'I found her very lovely really, very down to earth, very straightforward, very pretty, very sexy.'

In the evenings they would go to the Rock Bar and knock back vodka, champagne and tequila. Kate's volume, Jason remembers with a faint cringe, would increase as the night wore on. 'We'd both get really pissed, but she could get really loud. That voice carried, it fucking carried.'

Looking back, Jason describes that time as a strange, exhilarating, fun, sexy two weeks – weeks during which Jason became caught up in Kate's world. 'She was quite out of control when I met her,' he reflects. 'I was out of control. We were all out of control in 1998.'

For Jason those two weeks were a last hurrah of sorts – the high point before his own personal crash. Kate's would not be far behind his. His ticket out of Ibiza and back to reality had already been booked before that night in Atlantis when he had met Kate. She and Jade drove him to the airport on the day of his departure. After so many days and night of fun the atmosphere in the car was subdued. Jason and Kate exchanged numbers and wished each other luck. It had been an intense and enjoyable chapter in their lives but now it was over.

Looking back Jason reflects that some of that intensity was borne, in part at least, of desperation – the desperate need to escape. 'We were all escaping something, I suppose,' Jason said. 'Basically we had a major overload of experiences. It was escapism, getting really pissed, getting really out of it . . . then we both crashed and burned. I hit the [crack] pipe big time. I hit the drugs. I had loads of fun there, a really great time, and the next thing . . . rock bottom.'

Kate's fall would not be as catastrophic as the one Jason describes, but it would come nevertheless, hot on the heels of that hedonistic blur of summer.

Looking back on that 1998 summer Kate recalls, 'I was living fast. It was, "Sleep? Why? Why not go on? There's too much to do. There are too many places to go." I was working, I was travelling a lot. I was playing and I didn't stop. It got to the point where it wasn't much fun any more. It all became unbalanced. I was not very happy. I was doing things that weren't good for me. I had tried to stop certain things before; I had tried to get focused on other things. But I always ended up back in the same place and it wasn't making me happy. It is quite amazing what I didn't feel after a while. I didn't really want to feel things probably.'

Perhaps the most remarkable thing about this time is how long it took for Kate to bow out, exhausted. Even if she were a passive spectator, the parties that went on day and night, combined with a still punishing work schedule, would be enough to floor the sturdiest of creatures. It was all starting to get just a bit messy. A clinch with Anna Friel at the Groucho Club and a very public snog that summer might have shocked those who read of it with their morning toast, but such things were more likely to raise a laugh than an eyebrow between Kate and her friends. For her part, Anna explained away the moment with the words, 'Yeah, but Kate's just too beautiful.'

The problem was that with such an overload of sensation, and such limitless options to indulge them, it was becoming increasingly hard for Kate to get a kick out of anything. At first Kate turned to Anita Pallenberg for guidance and the two went on holiday, trekking for a week in India, in an attempt to find spiritual rejuvenation on Kate's part. But a holiday was never likely to really do the trick – it was escapism when what Kate really needed to do was face up to and address some old demons. In November, life conspired to bring those demons rushing to the surface when she learned that Vanessa Paradis was pregnant with Depp's child.

Something surely ended for Kate that day. After all, that could have been *her* future, her future with Depp, and it had all dissolved so rapidly with the appearance of Paradis on Depp's horizon barely five months earlier, in June. He was in Paris filming Roman Polanski's film *The Ninth Gate*, and if Kate was still looking for the 'signs', as she had been when she herself met Depp, then she would find an uncomfortable persistence at play in the uniting of Depp and Paradis. They had met once before, in 1994, at a mutual friend's house, and Paradis would later admit, 'He made a big impression on me . . . during my years of solitude he never left my thoughts.' Four years on, the French actress auditioned for Polanski's film. She didn't get the part, but it brought Depp to Paris and, one fateful night in June, it placed him in the bar of the city's Hôtel Costes where she was dining with friends. Depp approached Paradis with the words, 'Do you remember me?' and she was 'caught'.

Kate was once asked what she thought made life worth living. Her answer was 'hope'. On the November day that Vanessa Paradis announced she was pregnant with Depp's child and Depp committed to her and their unborn child, any hopes Kate harboured of a reconciliation with Depp ended.

Later that month Kate made a difficult admission. Something was terribly wrong. She needed help. She no longer felt in control of her life and it was a dizzying, fearsome realization. Over dinner at the Ivy with Meg and Noel Gallagher and Alan McGee, during which Kate ate nothing, she tearfully shared her anxieties. By the time she left the restaurant Kate's mind was made up. She was going to the Priory.

12

It was after midnight when the telephone call came through to the home that Linda shared with her husband Geoff. It was four days since Kate had checked into the Priory in Roehampton. Kate told her mother that she planned to stay in the facility for two weeks. Kate's wealth had allowed her to look after her mother, but now the balance had shifted once more and Linda sought to support her daughter.

Once news of Kate's attendance at the Priory reached the newspapers, as it inevitably did, Linda found her divorce and relationship with Geoff hauled up for criticism and cited as the reason for Kate's 'troubled' state. In truth, there were a great many issues that, by her own admission, Kate had to work through in her weeks of therapy. But it was a cruel twist of the knife that Linda was pilloried as a mother at the very time when she was doing everything in her power to help her daughter. It is notable too that, with sorry predictability, it was Kate's mother not her father who bore the most personal criticism, yet it was her mother to whom Kate turned in her hour of need.

Peter, naturally concerned, was kept informed of his daughter's progress by her assistant, Jess. Meanwhile Linda did what any loving mother would and in the weeks that followed Kate's admittance she sought out guidance from others who had found themselves in similar straits and attended several Al Anon meetings – the organization set up to provide support and advice for the relatives of people whose life is affected by drink.

For her part Kate must have been beginning to learn how much she had pushed to one side, refused to feel and refused to deal with, in favour of escaping by being 'out of it'. The Priory group may have become synonymous with celebrity rehabiliation, but there is nothing glamorous about the white, gothic hospital in Roehampton where Kate checked herself in on the morning after her dinner with Meg and Noel Gallagher and Alan McGee.

Towards the end of Kate's stay, her usual habit of bringing candles, incense and throws wherever she travelled, in an attempt to personalize hotel rooms, caused a flurry of excitement when a candle caught the edge of a scarf she had draped over a lamp to soften the light. The fire alarm was set off and fire engines promptly arrived as Kate and Jess, who was with her at the time, looked on with embarrassed giggles. For the most part, however, her days were regimented and reassuringly predictable.

The girl who once boasted that her parents allowed her to 'do anything' found herself in an institution where rules were made to be kept and the hours between sunrise and sunset were accounted for. It was, Kate later reflected, 'like boarding school', and she loved it. Tellingly, part of what she 'loved' was meeting 'normal' people. 'I did that whole walking in with dark glasses thing,' she said, 'but after five minutes it felt ludicrous.'

Kate intended to stay for two weeks but ended up staying for five (the Priory recommends a stay of twenty-eight days for the treatment of addictions). 'You're supposed to go back to when you first started,' she explained. 'You regress. Because you stop growing when you start doing . . . because you don't deal with pain and stuff, you just go and turn to drink, so you don't grow.'

Not once, she claimed, did she crave a drink, though she couldn't remember a time in the past decade when she had walked down a catwalk sober or woken without a hangover. She could not in all honesty 'blame' the state into which she had fallen on modelling. She would probably have 'got there in the end whatever', she reflected. 'Modelling just speeded things along.' Within days of her arrival, a package of books arrived from Marianne Faithfull. It contained C.S. Lewis's *The Chronicles of Narnia*. Marianne had read the children's allegories when she was going through a similar experience in her own youth. Kate had read the stories as a child, but she read them again, gratefully escaping into their fantasy world. 'I just loved them . . . it would completely be the whole heavy day and then go back and get into bed and read these books. It was such a treat.'

Kate changed her mobile number and stepped off the merry-go-round. She had lost interest in her life and she needed to regain the enthusiasm that had made her such a success in the first place. Where once she had fizzed with energy, she felt down and tired. She had thought that having fun all the time would be, well, fun, but instead excess had made her miserable. It took her five weeks in the Priory to figure out why she had been unhappy, five weeks to be able to sit calmly in a room and not be – in her own words – a nervous wreck.

'I was a bit all over the place,' she later admitted. There was no truth in the reports that a BMW was delivered to Kate from

Depp in an extravagant gesture of support. He was supportive, but such a gift was not his style, and nor was it Kate's for that matter. A car *was* delivered, but it was a Mini Cooper sent by the manufacturers in a generous, though hardly out of the ordinary, example of the perks that came with the 'unreal' life Kate lived.

As for Depp, while his affection for Kate was still strong, the finality of their split had been underlined by the news that Vanessa Paradis was pregnant. In interviews given earlier in the year, Depp had not only berated himself for letting Kate slip through his fingers, he had admitted, 'There's a big part of me that really misses her and I keep wondering why we aren't together, thinking about starting a family.' Little wonder that Kate felt emotionally exhausted, torn and confused.

Before going into the Priory, Kate had felt certain that her unhappiness had begun to affect her work, though she felt quite confident that it did not show – in the end product at least. 'I'd get away with it,' she said, 'but I wasn't completely there.' Reflecting on the months, even years, which led her to the Priory Kate said, 'I was in denial for a long time, I think. I was beginning to be not very happy. It stops working after a while. A bit messy. I did it for a long time. It was a long period of going for it. And I think I drank more [than was normal for a twenty-four-year-old]. Yeah, I don't think I was being over-dramatic when I went into treatment, that's for sure. It just got out of control really. Alcohol can't make you happy. I wasn't clear-headed; I couldn't really think properly because I was always hungover. So I didn't really know what was going on – it wasn't real any more.' Her own life didn't seem 'real' to her any more. 'In the Priory,' she explained, 'they believe that you're either an addict or you're not an addict, or you have an addictive personality and there are patterns, and all addicts have the same patterns. So being in there with other alcoholics and drug addicts and people, then you realized – you see your patterns.'

While Kate struggled to understand just how and why her life had veered off track, she was not without support. There was and remains a certain quality about Kate that inspires women to mother her and men to protect her. It's a powerful vulnerability. When she emerged from the Priory in December 1998 she returned to find her north London home had been purged. There was no trace of alcohol left. Not even her trusty hip flask – an accessory on many a photoshoot or night out where a little bit of extra vodka might be required – remained. The clear-out did not stop with the purely physical either. Kate had Melina Place exorcised too – twice. The first ceremony was a traditional Christian one performed by a priest who said prayers in every room, while a Thai lady conducted the second. Both the priest and the Thai lady sensed the presence of an angry man in the kitchen and a sad little girl in the house. According to some accounts of the house's history it was once used as a home for the mistresses of royalty. It occurred to Kate that the sad little girl in question might have been the illegitimate product of a secret royal romance. Less poetically, it crossed her mind that the little girl in question might be her.

During the ceremony, the Thai lady pinpointed one particular artefact in the house as an 'anchor for evil'. It was a tribal mask, bought by Kate from an antique dealer friend for a few hundred pounds. She removed it immediately and left it in the small garden in front of her home. Unfortunately, the dealer in question spotted it there on a visit and, understandably put out by the fact that the precious object was festering in the damp and cold, he asked to buy it back. Kate refused. It was hers and she would burn it and bury the ashes in the garden as she'd been advised to do, though as a concession to her friend's feelings she housed the offending object in the shed until that time came.

Kate's sojourn at the Priory gave her vital time and space to take stock of an extraordinary decade of excitement, success, excess and heartbreak. As she had become 'Kate Moss' she had started to lose sight and control of who she really was and she must have been grateful to the specialists at the Priory for helping her regain some focus and perspective, however temporary that proved. In later years, when others close to Kate struggled with their own addictions and demons, Kate was always on hand to help.

Pretty much the first thing Kate did on leaving the Priory was work, flying to New York on a day trip for a Versace jeans shoot with Steven Meisel. For the first time in a long time she didn't drink between set-ups. This time, when she called for a shot it was of nothing stronger than coffee, and when that didn't hit the spot she took another puff of the cigarette permanently on hand between takes. She was, she joked, a 'cliché of recovery', propped up by the dual crutches of cigarettes and caffeine.

If she felt uncertain and exposed in her newly 'clean' persona then she didn't show it. Perhaps, after so many years in the business, she came to the blissful realization that she could walk into a room full of some of the most established names in the business, as well as a clutter of strangers, and feel a confidence in her own abilities that had eluded her in the years she spent in a fug of dope and alcohol. ('In France and London,' Kate once observed, 'we're allowed to smoke pot all day. After the first picture, "Skin up!"') In fact, to some extent, the presence of nerves provided a frisson that had been sorely lacking in latter months. What little challenge she might have found in her work had been flattened away to nothing, courtesy of a nip of vodka or suck on a joint.

None of which is to say that, after five weeks of therapy, Kate had morphed into a twelve-stepping, born-again teetotaller, but she seemed determined to be more than the image she had become and not allow her personality to be subsumed beneath the legend writ large on billboards and advertising hoardings around the world. On the set of a shoot she knew that part of her talent was her ability to become another woman, with other drives, passions, needs and ambitions. She genuinely felt that she set herself to one side and became whatever version of 'Kate Moss' the photographer needed. That was the challenge, and it was one she was extremely good at meeting.

As Christmas approached Kate's mother wanted her home. She got her wish but, however enjoyable, it was hardly a conventional, quiet Christmas. Tracey Emin once commented that she had never done cocaine and that, when she was in Kate's presence, there was no need to. Now, refreshed and having shed some of the darkness that had crowded about her over the previous months, Kate was buoyant, enthusiastic, playful and childlike. Christmas at Linda's was a high-spirited affair in the company of Kate's 'new friend' Twiggy. Not, as Linda might briefly have imagined, the Sixties model, but Twiggy Ramirez, bassist with the Los Angeles rock band Marilyn Manson.

In fact, Twiggy's stage name was a combination of the famous model's name and that of serial killer Richard Ramirez, and the choice pretty much summed up the band's outrageous approach to music and their darkly flamboyant stage shows and personas. Twiggy's real name is Jeordie Osborne White, and he met music journalist Brian Warner when they worked together at a second-hand record shop in Fort Lauderdale. Warner became Manson, the self-styled Antichrist Superstar. Ramirez apparently claimed various influences for his bizarre stage look, among them a desire to ridicule Courtney Love. As members of the band Marilyn Manson, Twiggy and Marilyn dressed with disturbing androgyny. They wore colossal heels; heavy, nightmarish make-up – part Queen, part Kiss – they fondled each other on stage and Manson acted out grinding bones and drinking blood. When high school students Eric Harris and Dylan Klebold went on a shooting rampage in their school in Columbine, killing twelve fellow pupils and wounding twenty-three before committing suicide, Manson's music was cited by some sections of the press as an example of the sort of 'violent rock' that had inspired the youths. It seemed a hysterical response and was one that Manson for one met with an eloquence that dumbfounded his critics. Manson and Ramirez may have presented themselves as grotesque horrors on stage, but it was, to a large extent, a persona that they wiped off with their panstick and black kohl.

Twiggy Ramirez was, no doubt to Linda's relief, a charming, articulate man, which is not to say that he was a choirboy. Over the two days before Christmas, Twiggy and Kate stayed in London before joining her mum in Surrey for Christmas Day. They watched the *Star Wars* trilogy and played the trailer for the prequel, *Star Wars: The Phantom Menace*, over and over on Twiggy's computer. They punctuated such wholesome entertainment with Twiggy trying to persuade Linda to go to a strip club with him. 'He calls her "Mum,"' Kate said. 'He's, "Mum, let's go to a strip club." She's, "Let's have more champagne."' On Christmas Day they had dinner together, watched *Starship Troopers* and played Cluedo, then on Boxing Day they drove out towards Marlow in Buckinghamshire, where Kate had bought an eight-bedroom house that was in need of some renovation.

It was a sound investment. She bought it for £1 million and sold it barely six months later for a reported £1.7 million. The work that Kate had done on the property was executed according to the guidance of a Mr Chang, her feng shui oracle (Kate had also developed an interest in yoga and meditation). He told her that the house was 'shaped like a pistol' and that she must add a conservatory or it was curtains for her career. She added a conservatory. The notion of living in the country and escaping the buzz and noise of the city had never left Kate.

That December they were joined on their country walk by the little puppy Linda gave Kate for Christmas. Rather inauspiciously, Kate named him Sid, after Sid Vicious, 'because he looked a bit naughty and he's got really sharp teeth'. He was, she surmised, supposed to represent 'a bit of responsibility' in her otherwise feckless, single life, but within a week Linda was left holding the puppy as Kate headed off to Dublin to see in the New Year with Marianne Faithfull. There was no ill feeling on Linda's part. What mother wouldn't be glad to know that her daughter was in the company of a woman who had recently shown herself to be such a good friend? As far as Kate was concerned, Marianne was her 'mentor'. For her part, Marianne called Kate her 'naughty little girl'. After Dublin, Kate went on to Marrakesh for a brief holiday.

As post-rehabilitation plans go, Kate's would have struck even the most dispassionate observer as unusual – hanging out with a member of Marilyn Manson, kicking back with Marianne Faithfull, then travelling to Marrakesh – but as far as Kate was concerned, 'it all seemed to work'.

Before checking into the Priory Kate had spoken of giving

up modelling, a theme that would recur in the coming years. But after five weeks shut away from the world, or more accurately from *her* world, she appeared more eager than ever to embrace it once more: she was straight back to work and straight back into the company of the people with whom she'd spun out of control. Did that really suggest a person who had changed the destructive patterns she'd identified?

An oft-repeated and key part of the advice given by Alcoholics Anonymous is 'change your playground, change your playmates'. It's an excrutiatingly difficult thing to do, but for many it is vital for recovery. Kate did neither. The reality was that, however much she hadn't been made happy by her life of indulgence and the sex, drugs and rock'n'roll ethos, she was still attracted to it. When she first read Hunter S. Thompson's *Fear and Loathing in Las Vegas* she thought, I want to do that. Among the books that she kept by her bedside were *The Picture of Dorian Gray* by Oscar Wilde, works by Henry Miller and erotica by Anaïs Nin, the author after whom Meg and Noel Gallagher would name their daughter. 'I don't think you have to not like sex, drugs and rock'n'roll just because you stop,' she said. 'I'm changing, but I don't feel like I'm turning into a person who doesn't like that kind of lifestyle.'

But Kate's continued fascination with 'that kind of lifestyle' was only part of the story. Alongside these works was a copy of Benjamin Hoff's *The Tao of Pooh*, a book that 'calls for living without preconceived ideas about how life should be lived'. According to Hoff: 'The one chance we have to avoid certain disaster is to change our approach, and to learn to value wisdom and contentment. These are things that are being searched for anyway, through Knowledge and Cleverness, but they do not come from Knowledge and Cleverness. They never have, and they never will. We can no longer afford to look so desperately hard for something in the wrong way and the wrong place ... Within each of us there is an Owl, a Rabbit, an Eeyore, and a Pooh. For too long, we have chosen the way of Owl and Rabbit. Now, like Eeyore, we complain about the results. But that accomplishes nothing. If we are smart, we will choose the way of Pooh. As if from far away, it calls to us with the voice of a child's mind. It may be hard to hear at times, but it is important just the same, because without it, we will never find our way through the Forest.'

There was an unmistakably comforting tone about this wisdom, depicted as it was through the familiar characters of A.A. Milne that Kate, like so many others, had loved as a child. It may not have been exactly what Hoff had in mind when he wrote of Pooh, Piglet and co., but there is no doubt that part of Kate's irresistible appeal was the childlike quality she brought to even the most adult side of life. It was only when she lost that that she felt herself to be lost.

Now, once again, she approached life with a sort of wide-eyed wonder that presented as a surprising naivety given all that she had seen and experienced. Kate was younger than many of her closest friends – Sadie, Meg and Pearl are all a decade her senior – and she inspired a confusion of protect-iveness and submission in them all. When John Galliano called her his Lolita all those years ago in Paris, it had been a consummate piece of casting.

At the age of twenty-five Kate was not a child. She was an extremely wealthy young woman who had lived fast and already come close to burning out. She had been through rehabilitation and 'regressed' back to find the root of her problems, yet when she returned to what passed for the 'real' world, all those facts seemed to lose their punch. They seemed to carry no weight when set against the girlish enthusiasm with which she once more embraced her friends. Kate's life was riddled with temptations, and with people who were unwilling to resist them, herself included.

Still, she did her best. For several months after checking out of the Priory Kate attended Alcoholics Anonymous and Narcotics Anonymous meetings as often as work would allow and saw a psychiatrist once a week. She realized that, while she had never consciously wanted to be famous, she had 'craved the attention'. It had all got too much. There had been no normality. 'I felt like everyone was sucking me away,' she said. Kate was trying, however shakily, to change the rhythm of her life; to allow 'normality' to seep back in. But it was a struggle. In January 1999 Kate made her catwalk comeback at Donatella Versace's couture show in Paris. The audience kept bursting into spontaneous applause, for which Kate was eternally grateful; it was, after all, the first time she had been stone cold sober on a catwalk in years.

In an extravagant gesture of support and birthday celebration, Donatella gave Kate a clutch of sapphire, diamond and ruby bracelets and threw her a party in Paris at Les Bains, one of the city's coolest nightclubs and a converted Turkish bath. Friends flew over from London to fête Kate and her return to 'life', and to cheer as she blew out the candles on her cake, which was shaped and decorated like a blazing diamond. Linda was there too, watching Kate like a hawk – it wasn't long since she had received those distressing nocturnal telephone calls. Daft Punk and Mushroom from Massive Attack DJed and Kate had a ball, until about three o'clock in the morning when, sober and clean, she looked around the room at her friends and wondered to herself, What are you doing? Everyone's tweaked and out of it. She went home with her mother, 'like a good girl'. 'I wasn't going to get anything past her,' she later reflected.

Shortly after her twenty-fifth birthday, Kate took the first positive step towards fulfilling her acting ambitions. She had always felt self-conscious admitting that she wanted to act when she had been with Depp. Only once, when she had expressed a genuine interest in one of the numerous film scripts she was sent, did he show the enthusiasm she longed for. They had never really discussed any projects before that. Kate just 'got the feeling that he wouldn't be very happy'. In fact, Depp was warmly encouraging, but ultimately it was Kate who backed out, saying that she didn't feel ready. Now things had changed and she wanted to be in a 'hard-core earthy British film', something like *Breaking the Waves*, she said. That film, released three years earlier, may have been English actress Emily Watson's film début, set in the Scottish Highlands, but it was not a British film. It was a mongrel of Danish, Dutch, Swedish and French talent, directed and co-written by Lars von Trier.

Nevertheless, it was an interesting choice on Kate's part. Von Trier described his film as a 'simple love story', but that doesn't quite cover the story, set in the Seventies at the peak of the North Sea oil boom. Emily Watson plays Bess McNeill, raised in an oppressive and isolated Presbyterian village in Scotland, who meets and falls in love with a Norwegian rigger named Jan. They marry and Bess's sexual awakening begins. The film shocked many audiences for its unflinching portrayal of Bess, her sexual pleasure and the descent of this love story into dark, manipulative territory when Jan is badly injured on the rigs. He returns paralysed and tells Bess that the only way he can feel like a man again is for her to sleep with other men, then come to his bed at night and recount her affairs. Her love for Jan is so desperate that Bess does this in spite of the village elders' brutal condemnation, driven on by a twisted sense that she is helping her husband.

It's a profoundly disturbing and frankly harrowing film, and it was the sort of film to which Kate, with her love of all things dangerous, was drawn. She knew plenty of actors to ask for advice – Jude Law, Rhys Ifans, Sadie Frost, Anna Friel, Samantha Morton, Sean Pertwee, even Marianne Faithfull, and for once Kate did not feel inhibited in the face of their superior talent and experience. Instead, she asked for their help and took it, though it would be a while before she felt ready to show her acting skills to a wider audience. She performed a workshop version of a David Mamet play to test herself and was encouraged by the results.

Kate was engaged in the world of art, film, photography and literature in a way that she hadn't been for some time. It was as if she had paused to look back at something that, in the whirl of her life, she had rushed past, lost sight of or realized she might have missed: a cognitive double-take of sorts. It was this double-take that gave Jefferson Hack more than a fleeting role in her life, allowing a decent, if less than charismatic, man to make a lasting impact where he might have made barely a ripple.

Jefferson had the sort of pseudo-literary credentials to which Kate has always been a tad susceptible. He is not without talent, nor was he without ambition and achievement. Kate met Jefferson when he interviewed her in his capacity as editor of *Dazed & Confused*, and the interview appeared in the magazine's February issue (number 54) along with a phenomenally raunchy series of photographs, styled by Kate's friend and long-time collaborator Katie Grand – a woman who, like Kate, has been referred to as 'the most influential' practitioner of her art many times over – and shot by Jefferson's better-known business partner, Rankin. The magazine cover featured Kate wearing little more than long dark hair extensions and a sultry expression. Her 'outfit' consisted of a ribbon of suspender belt tied in a bow and black stockings, resting snug beneath her pert rear.

More than ever, and arguably more than any other super-model, pictures of Kate had become about *Kate*, not the clothes that she was or wasn't wearing. Our fascination with her was official and her stay at the Priory had only added an intriguing dimension to the girl of the moment – a past. That spring, writer Julie Burchill recalled a time before the arrival of the supermodel, when models 'had not been especially spectacular: they had perfect size 10 sample bodies, but their faces were often plain, so as not to detract from the clothes'. How times had changed. Kate was the unlikely supermodel who had 'out-supered' them all. She was, as Burchill eloquently put it, 'one of the most singular and shimmering icons this damp little island has ever produced'. If you wanted to shift copies of a magazine, it was enough to have an image of Kate, practically nude with 'all the matter-of-factness and endless grace' she possessed.

Jefferson, Rankin and Katie Grand had all known each other as students at the London College of Printing. It was there that Jefferson and Rankin first launched *Dazed & Confused* in 1991 – Katie came on board after a drunken night of conversation with Rankin in 1993. By the time of their degree show in London's Smith's Gallery everybody was talking about the publication. Well, everybody within the elite little clique of art and design students at LCP and its rival Central St Martins.

There was a great deal of overlap between the contents of

the magazine and the friends of Jefferson and Rankin who appeared in the pages of its early editions, as well as Kate's aesthetic inclinations and the friends who shaped them. The publication provided a platform for Alexander McQueen, viewed by some as a pretender to Galliano's crown, who was a friend of Kate's and the magazine's fashion editor-at-large. It featured interviews with and picture stories by artists such as Jake and Dinos Chapman, Damien Hirst, photographer Nick Knight and Sam Taylor-Wood. All friends of Jefferson and also friends of Kate. Equal billing was given to experimental art and music and established celebrities. There's a fine line between being a geek and being cool, and Jefferson, Kate decided, was cool.

He was also a thoroughly sweet man, with a background that sounded far more exotic than the man who sat before Kate and interviewed her one cold January afternoon. Jefferson is the son of a Swiss-German mother, Teresa, and English father, Douglas, who worked as a salesman for tobacco companies. Douglas's work meant that he and his wife were based in Montevido, Uruguay, in 1971 when Jefferson was born. With a hippy sensibility, they named their son after the band Jefferson Airplane, a decision that made being cool in later life not so much a matter of choice, but of survival.

By the time Jefferson was nine and his family moved to Ramsgate, Kent, he had lived in South America, Singapore and Belgium. When he was eleven, Jefferson was sent to Pangbourne College, a naval school in Berkshire that boasts of encouraging its students to be 'proud to be different'. From the name on his birth certificate to his interest in art-house films and desire to chart and shape youth culture, Jefferson was certainly that, though as far as his first words to Kate were concerned, he may have taken the attempt to be 'different' just a bit too far: 'You smell of pee,' he said with a smile as they settled down for a chat. Kate feigned outrage before dissolving in a fit of giggles. It had piqued her interest and taken her by surprise. This was going to be fun.

The interview itself was hardly penetrating stuff. Perhaps, for all his apparent insouciance, Jefferson was a little bit too smitten with his subject. Kate admitted that it was 'hard to say no' when, as Jefferson succinctly put it, your job means that you are 'offered free alcohol, all the best-quality drugs and the first class excuses to party anywhere in the world'. It was also a novel experience. According to Kate, 'I've never said, "No," to having a good time, to anything.'

In a teenage turn of phrase Kate bemoaned the fact that she didn't have a crush on anyone, 'not in the whole world. Not even on somebody who you'd know there was no way in a million years . . . it's quite annoying, because even a crush is quite exciting.' The response must have come as something of a blow to Jefferson who, along with many, had harboured a bit of a crush on Kate for some time. Still, he soldiered on with his next question, 'Are you into the idea of being in love?' Her reply must have left him thoroughly winded. Certainly, as personal moments go, it may not have been Jefferson's finest, but in the context of the interview, what Kate said next was the most touching, and most revealing, comment of all. 'I don't think I've completely got over my relationship with Johnny,' she said. 'So it's hard for me to think about being in love with anyone else. It was so intense for four years and it's still quite strange.'

Still, when the time came to publish that month's edition, Jefferson couldn't help but allow his feelings to seep through in the note 'From the Editor' which began the magazine. He was careful not to overdo it, of course; careful to retain something of the 'cool' that had piqued Kate's interest when they'd met. His words were stylized, but the sentiment was there for all to see. The previous month he had used his editor's note to publish a resignation letter. Since then, he explained, he had executed something of a volte-face: 'It's a compulsive disorder, this editing business, I had to face up to it, I was an addict and I needed my fix. "One issue is too many and a thousand is not enough," I would mutter . . . So I'm a c**t. After jacking it all in for the high life I'm back. And as soon as I settled into my editor's chair, I was pulled back out by the gregarious and gorgeous Kate Moss. You see, she too had had a break at the end of last year, she too was making a comeback, she too would understand what it was like to be addicted to things and she too would have had enough of self-indulgence and hedonism. We had to meet, we had to talk, and we did, but that's about where the comparsions end.

'It's great to be back, it's great to meet Kate, it's great to be a professional question mark.'

Kate and Jefferson kept in touch following that meeting. There may not have been an irresistible animalistic attraction – not on Kate's part at least – but something about Jefferson's calm, kind manner, his pale, searching eyes and delicately handsome face appealed to Kate in her newly sober mindset. Jefferson is a nice man and Kate recognized that. But nice wasn't going to be enough to hold sway just yet, and it would be more than a year before their friendship became anything more passionate. By the time the magazine hit the shelves, Kate was dating Anthony Langdon, the Leeds-born guitarist from rock band Spacehog.

As with so many of the friendships and relationships in Kate's life, Langdon was not some random addition to her circle, but was practically woven into the DNA of the group.

As a member of Spacehog he had known Supergrass drummer Danny Goffey, Pearl Lowe's partner, for many years. The bands had played and partied together on tour and at festivals. While the band members were all originally from Britain, they had formed, haphazardly, in New York, which is where Langdon's brother, the group's bassist Royston, met Kate's good friend, model and actress Liv Tyler. Liv went on to marry Royston in March 2003 and the couple had their first child, Milo, the following December.

Kate's relationship with Anthony lasted through to the early autumn. It was passionate and fun but ultimately nothing more profound. A rash of excitable rumours flurried up that summer, suggesting an engagement and October wedding in Ibiza, but they all blew away like confetti in the cooling autumn breeze. Some rumours, however, were more persistent.

In March 1999, Kate was in New York for Anna Friel's opening night in the Broadway production of Patrick Marber's play *Closer*. At the aftershow party Anna looked stunning, dressed in a diaphanous silver gown with a see-through bodice, which gave way to a billowing organza skirt. Of course Anna was thrilled that her friend was there to support her. They held hands, they embraced, and they were so tactile that one photographer tasked with covering the party claimed that his film was confiscated because the pictures were so 'hot'.

It was not the first time that Kate's physically affectionate relationship with her female friends had been commented on. She and Anna had already famously shared a playful kiss in the Groucho Club in London – the pair clearly enjoyed winding up the press – while the celebrity pages of newspapers and magazines featured images of Kate holding hands with, draped around or perched on the knee of Meg, Sadie, Pearl, Davinia,

Jade, Samantha (Morton) or Marianne with far more regularity then they did images of Kate and any man. Her New York agent, Paul Rowland, commented, 'Kate is just very affectionate.' But there were other factors at play too. Female friends are often more tactile than their male counterparts, but Kate's demeanour was palpably more flirtatious than many. Years of stripping off for photoshoots had altered Kate's sense of her own body; the adolescent modesty had gone, leaving a disconcerting matter-of-factness about nakedness and an almost defiant sense of her own beauty. But there was more to it than that. Kate is, by nature, flirtatious and tactile, and drink and drugs are great inhibition liberators.

By her own admission, Kate was struggling to come to terms with life after Depp. In May that year, Depp and Vanessa Paradis celebrated the birth of their daughter, Lily-Rose. Kate must have been upset at the news. It would not have been made any more bearable by the fact that, in his elation at his daughter's birth, Depp said, 'I feel like there was a fog in front of my eyes for 36 years. The second she was born, that fog just lifted.' He added, 'Anything I've done up till May 27 1999 was kind of an illusion. Existing, without living. My daughter, the birth of my daughter, gave me life.' Of course he did not intend to hurt Kate with his words, but they must have been crushing nevertheless. Depp's life had moved on and Kate tried to do likewise.

She pushed herself to make something of her acting ambitions, and in August she nervously took her first television role as Maid Marian alongside Rowan Atkinson, Tony Robinson and Rik Mayall in the one-off film, *Blackadder Back and Forth*. Safe to say that Kate's performance was not quite the revelation of acting prowess for which she might have hoped.

She twinkled seductively in the fleeting appearance – her Marian was of the minxy variety – but the whole enterprise seemed more a bit of fun than a significant screen début.

However earnest her post-Priory ambitions to make more of herself and her opportunities, Kate was already in real danger of tumbling back into the same old relentless routine. The same old routine that had failed to make her happy before. 'Nothing really changes does it?' Noel Gallagher once observed. 'Same shit, different day.' Nights out at the Cobden Working Men's Club – a rather more chi-chi Notting Hill venue than the name suggests – downstairs it might be darts boards and pool tables, but upstairs it's a private members club, decked out in velvet and gilt and listing Jade Jagger, Will Self and Leonardo di Caprio among its members – or the Groucho ended back at Primrose Hill at Davinia's, Sadie's or Kate's.

But it wasn't quite 'the same old shit', as Noel so succinctly put it. The cast had been slightly modified. Supernova Heights was no longer the property of Noel and Meg. On Noel's insistence the couple now lived in a house, a very big house, in the country – Chalfont St Giles, Buckinghamshire, to be precise. Now Davinia Murphy was chatelaine of the house, having bought it on the strength of a drunken early-morning conversation with Noel. The parties continued unabated, but Noel was no longer one of the revellers.

Years later he reflected that Kate was 'a really nice girl', who just 'got lost in it all'. It was something he did not want for himself. Nor did he want it for his wife. In March 1999 Meg became pregnant (Samantha Morton fell pregnant the following month). For about a year leading up to Meg's pregnancy, Noel had been filled with a certain dread that their marriage wasn't going to last. With news of her pregnancy that changed, and for a while things looked more promising. But this was one battle he was destined to lose. Noel was not the only one whose priorities were subtly changing, and nothing lasts for ever. People marry, they move on and they move up. The Primrose Hill set was no more immune to the vagaries of its members' individual fortunes than any other group of friends. And the tectonic plates were shifting.

13

There was no pause for deliberation, just a sort of exhausted exhalation. She was quite clear: 'Tell them I can't.' Kate was sprawled on a sofa in the Bristol Hotel, Paris, an exquisite establishment on the Rue du Faubourg Saint-Honoré, north of the Seine and a Gallic shrug from the Champs Elysée. Her instruction was directed at her American agent Paul Rowland, who seemed unconcerned as he delivered the warning, 'If you don't commit, they say they're going to use a new Kate.' Kate's eyes widened in mock horror, much to the amusement of Marianne Faithfull, who sat by her side, quietly observing the show. Laughing, Kate concluded, 'I've had a good run. Tell them to use the new Kate, then, if they can find her.'

It took a while. But in 1999 'they' thought they'd done just that. It had been Calvin Klein's people at the end of the telephone that afternoon, calling to book some of Kate's time to shoot a major new advertising campaign. The conversation had been conducted before Kate had checked herself into rehab, but the deed, and the damage, was done. When Klein had signed Kate back in 1992 he had never, he later admitted, 'meant to create a monster'.

In December 1998, as Kate emerged from her Priory cocoon, the girl who would be her replacement took a day off work as a dental nurse and went to the Clothes Show at the National Exhibition Centre in Birmingham. Lisa Ratliffe was seventeen years old. She had planned a day of shopping and watching the catwalk shows with her friends, then she bumped into Chrissie Castagnetti, co-owner of Select Model Management, a woman who prided herself on noticing the slenderness of a girl's wrists, the delicacy of her bone structure and the tone of her eyes – details that distinguished a workaday model from a modelling sensation. In Lisa she saw the latter. She gave her her business card, and within a week Lisa was handing in her notice at the dental practice. The following February the seventeen-year-old was standing in Calvin Klein's apartment, trying on clothes and trying desperately not to show how nervous she was.

As images of Kate were rolling out in Calvin Klein's spring advertising campaign across America, in the February issue of *Vanity Fair*, in an eight-page insert in *The New York Times*, in *Elle, Harper's Bazaar, Vogue, W, Details, GQ, Sports Illustrated, Entertainment Weekly, Interview, Spin, In Style* and *Cosmopolitan*; as billboards bearing her image went up in Chicago, Los Angles, New York, Miami, San Francisco; as the campaign took hold in Belgium, France, Germany, Italy, the Netherlands, Portugal, Russia, Switzerland, Spain, Turkey and Britain; as it seeped into the United Arab Emirates and the Middle East; as it launched in Asia and the Pacific, Australia, Hong Kong, Indonesia, Japan, Malaysia, Philippines, Singapore, Taiwan and Thailand; as this mighty advertising colossus straddled the globe, Kate was being replaced. 'I really didn't realize how big the campaign was at that time,' Lisa recalls. 'And I certainly didn't know I'd taken it away from Kate Moss. That was huge.'

Yet by the time the deal was done, Kate seemed surprisingly laissez-faire about the whole thing. Certainly it must have come as something of a surprise that her challenge should have been met head on. But she was right. She *had* 'had a good run' with Klein. She had launched his perfumes, jeans and season after season of clothes. Now, however much of a boon the contract had been back in 1992, Klein's safe, simple cuts and pure sheath shapes seemed an increasingly awkward fit for Kate, in terms of style at least. She had become too edgy, too interesting, to wear such fastidiously hemmed, neatly pressed garments with any real conviction.

Truth be told, Kate's working relationship with Calvin Klein did not come clattering to an absolute halt with the end of her contract in 1999; it merely stalled, albeit for seven years. In 2006 it roared into life once more when Kate returned to the Klein fold in a campaign for CKJeans, thanks again to the vision of Fabien Baron.

On paper the loss of the Klein contract might have seemed a blow, but in reality the hiatus of this high-profile contract didn't trouble Kate. She had contracts with Luis Vuitton, Dior, L'Oréal, Cerutti, Gucci, Versace . . . the list went on. The year that she lost the Klein contract she gained a campaign with Burberry, posing alongside Lord Freddie Windsor – a perfect example of the sort of rackety young aristocrat with whom Kate might be expected to hang out off camera. She was fêted by the editors of glossy magazines the world over and was a regular cover girl for them. Any designer worth his or her cotton socks (should anything so anodyne make the collection) wanted them paraded down the catwalk by Kate. She may have expressed a desire to be something other than 'just' a model, and she may have felt frustrated and unfulfilled by being one, but it was hard to say no to the riches the job brought her. She must have been understandably torn.

Perhaps what the loss of the Klein contract did more than

anything was serve as a pointed reminder that nobody in this business was indispensable. Sarah Doukas had to employ two members of staff to manage Kate's bookings, such was the volume of business she generated, but still Kate could be dropped, showing that even the most dazzling career could be snuffed out in an instant given the right – or wrong – circumstances. 'A girl can go out of business overnight,' Mario Testino once observed in conversation with Kate. She agreed, saying, 'I've seen it happen . . .' It could happen more quickly than that. In the world of modelling, success really was here today, gone today.

Of course Kate didn't want that, but there was a certain ambivalence about her awareness of, and surprise at, the comparative longevity of her career. She had never thought that the attention, lifestyle and money would go on for as long as it had and kept thinking, They'll get over it. And if they did, then would it really be so frightful? What, she wondered, was there to end anyway? 'Being in the newspapers all the time?' Was that really worth so very much? What did Kate want? The answer was simple: both personally and professionally she wanted more and less than she had.

As 1999 came to a close Kate had embarked on what would be a brief and affectionate romance with Jesse Woods, the model and son of Ronnie and Jo. Right from the outset Ronnie doubted that Jesse and Kate had a future as a couple. Knowing Kate as he did, he didn't fancy any man's chances when it came to forming a lasting relationship with her. Add to that the fact that Jesse was fresh out of a four-year relationship with Jasmine Guinness, and pretty broken-hearted, and the odds seemed heavily stacked against the pair being love's young dream, however pretty a couple they made (sure enough, the relationship fizzled out within a matter of months – four to be precise). But like Kate's mother, Ronnie and Jo knew better than to judge or interfere in their offspring's relationships. Besides, they were both fond of Kate and happy to welcome her into their home in Kingston-upon-Thames that Christmas. Afterwards, Jesse, Kate and a group including many of the usual Primrose Hill suspects headed to Phuket, Thailand, to see in the Millennium.

But not everybody was there. Meg was now nearly eight months pregnant. Samantha Morton was in a similarly advanced state of pregnancy. Pearl Lowe had given birth to baby Frankie the previous May, and she and Danny Goffey, who had holidayed with Kate many times, were absent too. Each absence was a little tug of reality, a little nudge of inevitable change, a little threat to the group's centre of gravity. Pearl, for one, was certainly trying her damnedest to escape its gravitational pull.

On 7 November 1999 she had been admitted to the Charter Nightingale Hospital in Lisson Grove, north London, ostensibly for post-natal depression, but it rapidly became apparent that treating her for that alone would not touch the root of her problems: Pearl's addiction to heroin. Like Kate at the Priory, Pearl was treated as an inpatient, though her stay at the Charter Nightingale lasted just two weeks. When she left, she had support in the form of counselling and therapy and was advised to be wary about who she mixed with once she was clean. She was told to tear up her address book, clear her SIM card, change her playmates and her playground. It can't have helped that her partner Danny was still using drugs, but he was considerate enough to at least not do so in her presence. Danny, by his own admission, had been shocked by the extent of the drug use by some in this circle, recalling that 'there were really scary times'.

So that New Year he and Pearl absented themselves from the predictable round of parties, staying far away from the usual gang of partygoers and friends. Pearl, Danny and their family travelled to St Lucia instead, and when the fireworks exploded at the dawn of the New Millennium Pearl was tucked up in bed. The only way the still vulnerable Pearl could remain resolute was to be thousands of miles from her regular playmates. Except that when they returned home, they were all – save for the Buckinghamshire-dwelling Gallaghers – still within a square mile of each other in north London. Relapse was inevitable.

Back in London Kate was among the first to visit Meg at the private Portland Hospital following the birth of her daughter Anais on 27 January 2000. The following month Samantha (Morton) gave birth to a daughter, Esme, and asked a thrilled Kate to be godmother. Soon after, Sadie Frost announced that she was expecting her second child with Jude. It should have been the beginning of a golden new chapter in all of their lives – growing up, moving on and getting clean, but sadly it was not; not for everyone at least.

Four months into the New Year, Danny threw a birthday party for Pearl. It was well meaning of course, but in retrospect it wasn't the wisest of gestures, given her struggle to remain clean. With painful predictability, Pearl succumbed to old temptations: this time to the cocaine offered by a 'friend' in the loos of the private members club in Soho that Danny had booked out for the bash. Soon Pearl was shovelling it up her nose with gusto almost every day of the week.

At the same time, new mother Meg was feeling abandoned and disillusioned. Two months after Anais's birth, Noel had taken off on a European tour with Oasis that wouldn't see him play in Britain until the Reading Festival in August. It was just before that, according to Noel, that he and Meg called time on their marriage, and almost exactly a year after Anais Gallagher was born her parents divorced. Meg complained of feeling isolated, stuck in her Buckinghamshire pile miles from her friends. If Noel had hoped that motherhood would take the edge off Meg's desire to party and hang out with friends Kate, Stella, Sadie, Jade and so on, then he was sadly disappointed.

In a fit of pique, Noel branded the lot of them 'the bitches of Primrose Hill', though later his anger softened and he took a more philosophical view. Life with Meg had been, he said, '. . . getting back to the way it was years ago, the constant partying. In the end, I just couldn't be doing with it any more.'

Professionally, the year began positively for Kate with a collaboration that appealed to her desire to be heard rather than simply pictured in a project that underscored the extent to which she had shifted gear from 'model' to 'icon'. Tate Modern opened in London on 12 May 2000, and to mark the event, British *Vogue* decided to celebrate the union of art and fashion. They commissioned seven of the most prevalent and, in *Vogue*'s assessment, 'challenging' artists of the day – Marc Quinn, Jake and Dinos Chapman, Sarah Morris, Tracey Emin, Gary Hume and Sam Taylor-Wood – to portray Kate in any way they wanted. For Kate, whose interest in and fledgling knowledge of art was quite genuine, it was a flattering and thrilling prospect. Of course it helped that four of the seven artists invited to take part in the project were friends of hers – that alone hammered home the truth of the premise that Britart and fashion were overlapping worlds that, to some extent, fed off each other for inspiration.

The fortunes of this particular peer group of artists had risen parallel with Kate's. These artists not only understood celebrity, they had become celebrities themselves, going to the same fashion shows, parties and dinners as models, musicians and film stars. Work began on the artwork at the end of January, on the portico of St George's Church in Mayfair, near Vogue House and across the road from Sotheby's – a pleasing location that sat square between the worlds of fashion and art. Sam Taylor-Wood had chosen the spot to photograph Kate in the first of the series of portraits. Through her videos and remarkable photography, Sam Taylor-Wood has often reworked traditional religious images, so she pictured Kate as the Virgin Mary – blasphemy to some, but one that resulted in a captivating image.

'Kate Moss is the cultural icon of our age,' she explained, 'being represented as the ultimate icon.' True to the blending of fashion and art, Kate wore the new season Boudicca leather jacket as she looked tearfully to the heavens, a length of material draped over her head like a veil. During the shoot a small crowd of Sotheby's staff, passers-by, shop assistants and tourists gathered to watch from pavement opposite. One man blushingly presented Kate with a pink rose, while a tramp waved his filthy bandaged fists and called for 'the beautiful lady', to kiss them better. It wasn't clear whether he recognized Kate or believed he was witnessing some miraculous apparition.

Later, in Marc Quinn's studio in Clerkenwell, Kate stripped to her underwear and patiently waited as a plaster cast of her body was made. It was the first, but not the last, time that Quinn would sculpt Kate. In 2006 he depicted her in a yoga pose – her legs wrapped behind her head – in *Sphinx*. The work was meant, he said, 'to show us a mirror of ourselves,' and cast Kate as 'a contorted Venus of our age'. For the *Vogue* project, Quinn chose to make an ice sculpture that would, he said, 'evaporate rather than melt.' 'It's a perfect metaphor for our consumption of your beauty,' he explained to Kate. 'As the ice evaporates, it will be released as vapour into the art gallery and people will literally breathe you in. There's something Eucharistic about it.'

Kate thought it a beautiful notion, though anybody less used to being 'consumed' might find it vaguely disturbing. Later she strolled through the frozen garden Quinn had preserved in his basement studio: grass, roses, lily of the valley, irises . . . all still seemingly fresh, frozen in full bloom three years earlier – dead, beautiful echoes of the flowers they once were and still seemed.

The initial stages of Sarah Morris's piece must have seemed more familiar territory for Kate. Photographs were taken of Kate in an old bathing suit that belonged to the artist, who had told her to wear the diamond necklace Depp had given her all those years ago. Her make-up was done like a Roxy Music cover – one eyelid yellow, one bright green – a wind machine blew in front of a bright-pink background and Kate sucked Coca-Cola through a straw. Later Morris separated the photographs she'd taken into tiny blocks of colour, and the end result was a high-voltage, disorientating image: the unmistakable face of Kate was nothing but an assembly of pixels.

Gary Hume also began with a photograph only, rather than deconstructing that image, he created another and projected it over the top. He drew sketches of Kate from pictures in magazines – strong, confident, basic lines – then he made slides of the drawings, projected those images onto Kate when she came to pose in his studio, and took photographs of the end result. The rationale behind the process was, according to Hume, that Kate as seen by millions was no more than the infinitessimal width of a glossy piece of paper. He wanted to 'add another layer'. He photographed Kate, naked save a pair of substantial and sensible knickers, then projected his drawings to 'complete the circle of looking'.

At the end of her sitting for him, Hume gave Kate a silkscreen of herself that he had made long before seeing her in the flesh.

Tracey Emin, infamous for putting her own life experience on display – her bed or the names of everybody she had ever slept with stitched on to the fabric of a tent – took the most conventional route when it came to picturing her friend Kate. She invited Kate to her home for a sitting that began in the afternoon and stretched on late into the night. 'We had a cup of tea and a chat,' Emin recalled, 'and then she took off her clothes and sat on my bed. She's really beautiful, exquisite – even her toes are pretty, there's not a blemish on her, like an angel – but somehow I managed to make her look absolutely monstrous, demonic, with these little horns on her head like the devil. Then, after about thirty goes at it, I finally did a drawing that worked. Afterwards, we had an Indian takeaway and sat on my bed again for hours, drinking and talking and smoking. The whole thing was really nice, really pleasant. In between drawing Kate, I took Polaroids of her, then my boyfriend Mat Colinshaw came over and took some Polaroids of both of us.'

Kate loved the simple sketch that Emin finally settled on so much that she hung it on the wall by her bed.

Jake and Dinos Chapman required a more active involvement from their subject. Their studio on the Old Kent Road was dominated by the work they were in the midst of preparing for the Royal Academy that year, *Hell*. On first glance it looked as if the brothers had devoted their hours to creating a sort of dinky-toy village, a *Boys' Own*-style adventure scene, but a closer look revealed the horror of the scenes: concentration camps depicted in grizzly detail, tiny toy soldiers mutilated and hacking each other to death, screaming, suffering and dying in tortured anguish.

Jake and Dinos had been working on it for two years. Kate took one look and declared with characteristic enthusiasm, 'It's *amazing*. I *love* it. It's like Charlie's Angels taking on the Nazis.' No wonder the brothers loved her. Their portrait featured as its centrepiece a self-portrait by Kate, and she greeted the news that she would have to draw herself with horror. Around the edges of her hesitantly sketched work, the brothers filled in Kate's idea of hell. 'Hell . . .' she mused. 'Hell is being chased by a load of paparazzi, or having my picture taken in a room full of people who only notice whether my hair looks right or my make-up is perfect, who never bother to talk to me or see who I am. But this is heaven, sort of, working with people who include me, who ask me what I think . . .' Kate loved working with the Chapman brothers, she explained, because 'it feels like I've been involved in the whole process, instead of just having some nightmare photographer sticking his lens in my face'.

The very month that Kate's image was featured in *Vogue* seven-fold, she acted on that obvious frustration. She was fed up and run down, and in March she was taken into hospital having collapsed with a kidney infection. It's remarkable how many young musicians, dancers, popstars, models, artists and actors have been taken to hospital having succumbed to a kidney infection, and how it often happens during a night out. This was not the case with Kate, nevertheless. Sarah was forced to state that Kate's treatment was not indicative of anything more sinister than the model's failure to complete a course of antibiotics prescribed for a urinary tract infection. Still, Kate was showing signs of rebellion, or at the very least of frustration.

As she recuperated in hospital she called on the services of James Brown and had him dye her hair platinum blonde. For a woman, never mind a model, a drastic change of hair style or colour is never without significance, even if all it signifies is boredom.

As *Vogue* hit the shelves Kate made her decision. She telephoned Sarah Doukas and told her that she quit. She had had enough of modelling. It was over. She had had her fill of the mind-numbing, Groundhog Day existence her modelling life had become. She was sick of the London-Milan-Paris-New York cycle and tired of being a rootless creature whose friendships were, in large part, dictated by the limited group of people who could drop everything – or had nothing much to drop – and join her wherever in the world her work had taken her. She had tried meditation, rehab and therapy, but the simple fact remained: she never again wanted to say to anybody, 'I'm a model.'

It was not a conversation Sarah wanted to be having with her most successful, high-profile and lucrative signing, but she is a sensible and sensitive woman and knew Kate well enough to know that she would not be marshalled into doing anything against her will. Lecturing Kate, as friends will testify, is only likely to be counterproductive. So what could Sarah do but acquiesce? Still there was, notably, no official announcement that Kate's days as a model were over. Sarah was quietly confident that Kate's decision to end her modelling career was reversible; it was just a question of patience and waiting.

Kate headed to Ibiza with Stella and Meg. She had her long hair cropped short and she danced and sunbathed and partied the summer away. She was back on the catwalk by August by which time the seeds had been sown for a torrid argument with one of her oldest, dearest friends.

Depp once remarked that Kate was the closest a human being could be to a cat, and there was a time when Jade Jagger would have agreed that Kate's behaviour owed more to the alley than the runway. The reason for the friends' argument that summer was one of the oldest known to man: they fell out over a man. Jade was dating Dan Macmillan and there was no sense of three being a crowd as they enjoyed a flirtatious friendship.

Jade has always enjoyed a wild reputation. Expelled from school at seventeen, pregnant at nineteen by artist Piers Jackson, she had their daughter Assisi at the age of twenty and three years later gave birth to Amba. She remained with Piers for eight years before leaving him for another artist, Euan Macdonald, and taking the children to live with him in Ibiza. Before long she was partying hard, her relationship with Euan came to an end and a romance with Dan Macmillan followed . . . and so did Kate.

Jade has never seemed to set much store by conventional notions of monogamy and fidelity. 'I do wonder,' she once mused, 'why modern society has made monogamy the one and only option. In England, it's always, "Are you with him, or him?" Perish the thought it might be both.' Still, it seemed that while Jade liked to think of herself as a single adventuress, she was not best pleased when her liberal approach to monogamy found its match in the views held by her man-of-the-moment.

When, some months later, she discovered that Kate and Dan had gone on a trip to Venice *à deux*, the three came to blows. Jade had relished the thought that she, Kate and Dan were three bohemian friends, kindred spirits, playing by their own set of rules. It was something of a shock to discover that she was mistaken. They were nothing of the sort. Kate was playing according to *her* rules, and making them up as she went along.

Such was Jade's fury at her friend's perceived betrayal, and such was Kate's disbelief in the face of Jade's anger, that for close to four years the women did not speak and avoided attending the same social gatherings – not an easy task given the overlapping nature of their tight social circle. It's also worth mentioning that within months of splitting from Jade, Macmillan had been 'linked' with her half-sister Elizabeth.

Kate had complained that her life as a model was a Groundhog Day existence, where every tomorrow is today all over again and every today is yesterday replayed. How strange it must have felt then, in October 2000, to be back in a flat on an unmade bed, working once more with Corinne Day. Even stranger that the reason for their professional rapprochment was a commission from the very magazine that had, however accidentally, brought about their split.

It was seven years since Kate had told Corinne she could no longer work with her; seven years since the pictures of her modelling underwear in her Shepherd's Bush flat appeared in *Vogue* and saw Kate lambasted as a pin-up for anorexia and paedophilia and later berated for glamorizing drug addiction. Now *Vogue* had asked Corinne back to take pictures of Kate for their December issue.

'It was like we had only seen each other yesterday,' Corinne recalls. 'She sat down in her glamorous underwear, said, "Oh, I'm starving," and started eating a sandwich. I took a shot of her in her lunch hour and they published it. You can see in the pictures that there is a friendship.' It must have appealed to Corinne that the pictures were so natural, giving her a certain vindication. 'Fashion', as Corinne put it, had 'come full circle'. But then, doesn't it always?

Corinne too had come full circle, through life-threatening illness back to health. Towards the end of 1996 Corinne had been diagnosed with a brain tumour, news that felt, she said, 'like a bungee jump into hell'. The tumour was operable and needed to be removed, so Corinne asked her partner, Mark Szaszy, to photograph and film her treatment. It helped her to focus on what *he* was doing rather than on what *she* was going through. He filmed her being wheeled into the operating theatre, pale and frightened on the hospital trolley. He even filmed as a needle was plunged into her head. She wondered if she would ever wake up.

Four days later Day was out of hospital, and the film footage went on to form a central part of the documentary, *Corinne Day Diary*, broadcast three years later on BBC Four. The year that Kate walked back into Corinne's working life she had her first solo exhibition, entitled simply 'Diary', and documenting in photos the past decade of her life and the lives of her friends. Now, with Kate's return, the completion of a personal and professional loop seemed too perfect to ignore. Mark had filmed those first photoshoots that Corinne had worked on with Kate at Camber Sands, back in the third summer of love. There had been no grand plan at that stage. 'I was just shooting for the love of filming,' he explains. 'Over ten years passed before that accidental archive fitted into the jigsaw puzzle of Corinne's career in the Nineties.'

For both Mark and Corinne, working with Kate once more was a comfortable and enjoyable time. At one point Corinne took Kate, Rosemary Ferguson and George Clements – all of whom had started out with her at *The Face* back in the Nineties – on a photoshoot destined to appear in *Dutch* magazine in May 2001. The shoot would take place over a couple of days in Blackpool. It was a reunion of friends, and that would show through in the resultant footage, as the three models kicked along the cold sands and relaxed over lunch-on-a-tray back in their hotel rooms.

But however genuine the bonhomie, there was no avoiding the extent to which Kate had moved into another stratosphere since last working with Corinne. When they drifted apart all those years ago, Corinne recognized that Kate had started hanging out in an environment in which she did not belong. 'I didn't want to be there,' she recalls. 'Our relationship, I knew, was over. It's always like that when you lose someone you care for and you're going in separate directions, but I was difficult to work with, and in the end people decided not to work with me.'

Seven years on, Corinne was no more prepared to compromise than she had been back then. She wanted part of the shoot to take place in a 'horrible old bedsit place'. There was a swirly, stained carpet, a bar fire fixed to the wall, flock wallpaper and a pervasive smell of damp. 'I just looked at Kate's face,' Corinne remembers, 'and it said it all. She was quite horrified to go into this tatty old smelly room. She'd definitely gone into another world.' By comparison, Kate appeared far happier in another series of shots, messing around on a bed, stark naked save for a Royal Horseguards' helmet.

Perhaps it was the reunion with Corinne and witnessing the reinvigorated approach to life that her brush with death had given her. Perhaps it was the evident joy her father's baby Charlotte had brought into his life, and that her friends' children had brought into theirs. *All* of them, it seemed to

Kate, were having babies. Perhaps it was just a natural desire. Kate had always imagined that her future would include children – lots of them – but by late autumn 2000 she felt that want more strongly than ever.

Kate made no secret of it. She wanted a baby. When she first spoke of her longing there was one obvious problem – no man – but Kate wasn't going to be stopped by such a minor detail. She was used to getting her own way these days. She joked with her friends that if she didn't find Mr Right, she would just 'do it anyway'. However many reasons there might be for now *not* being a good time – mostly in the form of the assignments that filled the pages of Kate's book at Storm – Kate it seemed had made up her mind. Having a child may have seemed to be the solution to everything: to the rootlessness she felt, the lack of stability that apparently troubled her, the lack of purpose that hung upon her and the possible loneliness that dogged her, however many friends she surrounded herself with.

In November 2000, while she was in America, Kate's house in St John's Wood was broken into by burglars. They took £300,000 worth of property, of which a remarkable £50,000 worth was in travellers cheques, as well as some valuable, in sentimental as well as monetary terms, jewellery: a diamond ring that had been handed down through the family and the £20,000 diamond necklace Depp had given her many years ago. Its loss must have seemed symbolic. It was six years since Depp had given Kate that string of diamonds and she still believed he was the love of her life, but Kate was twenty-six years old; it was time to move on.

As 2000 drew to a close, it became more apparent to Kate that she had already met her Mr Right, or at least a close enough approximation. Certainly *he* was smitten. Jefferson

Hack had remained in touch with Kate since their meeting at the beginning of the previous year. His number was keyed into her mobile phone and they had texted each other and spoken regularly. Their social circles and the sort of cool, urban events to which they were invited overlapped and where once Kate might have registered his presence at a gallery opening or club with little more than a passing smile, she increasingly met him with genuine delight.

Kate liked talking to Jefferson and started inviting him join her at her house, or those of her friends when they wanted to kick back and relax. Jefferson was sweet, witty, well connected and, to Kate's mind, well informed.

By the spring of 2001, as work on Kate's photographic rapprochment with Corinne was coming to an end, her relationship with Jefferson was becoming well and truly established. It may have lacked the drama of a whirlwind affair, but Kate had 'done the whirlwind thing' and it only left her tired. Besides, there was a spark between them. As Corinne took pictures of Kate, naked save for that officer's helmet, she teased her that her nipples had grown since they'd last worked together. Kate was unabashed: 'I know. They're like fighter pilots' thumbs. Jefferson likes them like that. Boys like them like that.' With Jefferson, Kate could and did have fun, but many of her intimates struggled to comprehend quite what Kate saw in him, biddable though he was. The truth was simple: in Jefferson Kate saw a future, and more particularly maybe, a future father for her child.

14

The Savoy Grill was crowded with diners that Saturday evening, all well dressed and well heeled and far too well mannered to stare. Even so this called for discretion. Smiling, Kate asked 'the boys' to excuse her, took her female companion by the hand and led her to the Ladies. She took an envelope from her handbag and, for a moment, the two women stood, heads bowed, over the contents.

It was mid March 2002 and Kate and Jefferson were dining with his parents, Teresa and Douglas Hack, before going on to see the West End musical *Chicago*. Earlier that day Kate had had the first scan of her pregnancy. Confirmation of this much-wanted event had come from Kate's doctor in February and she was thrilled; they all were, and as Kate showed the first blurry images of her child to Jefferson's mother, she giggled with sheer delight. It was still early days, though, and there would be no official announcement for another month. Like any couple, she and Jefferson were keen to keep the news quiet for just a little while longer, but back at the table, Kate could contain herself no longer. 'Oh, Douglas, you haven't seen the picture yet,' she exclaimed, pulling it out once more from her bag and offering it to him across the table.

Kate had wanted, and got, a baby. She had wanted a

purpose in life and now, with this pregnancy, it seemed she would never lack purpose again. Kate's own parents were delighted. For Linda the news was a source of undiluted joy, but for Peter that joy was accompanied by a palpable sense of relief.

It had been more than a year since Kate's relationship with Jefferson, whom she playfully called Jeffo, had become public. They had first emerged as a couple in January 2001 when they attended the premiere of Jude Law's film *Enemy at the Gates* in Berlin. The following month Jefferson beamed with pride as Kate was named Model of the Year at the Rover British Fashion Awards. She already had a clutch of similar accolades, each presented under the banner of a different sponsor. It was an honour, of course, but there was hardly much meaning or import in it.

As far as Linda was concerned, she enjoyed dipping in and out of the circus that spun around her daughter wherever she went, but Peter's take on it all was rather more tepid. He once said, 'Welcome to our nightmare,' by way of an introduction to a new acquaintance of his daughter. It was only half in jest. The 'nightmare' was not Kate, but a lifestyle that was both feckless, demanding and beyond any experience of life for which he, or Linda for that matter, had ever been prepared.

It worried her father that success had come so young to Kate. 'When that happens,' he said, 'there's not a lot to shoot for later in life.' Pregnancy meant purpose, and, he hoped, stability; that had to be better than travelling round the world from shoot to shoot and never truly having anywhere to call home. According to Peter, 'It is something she really wanted. Kate called to tell me she was going to be making an announcement. I knew straight away it would be one of either two things – either she was getting married or she was pregnant.

She sees getting pregnant as one of the best things that has ever happened to her.' He was inclined to agree. After all, pregnancy was the most normal thing that had happened to Kate in a long time.

'Normal? What's normal,' she once mused when the extraordinary nature of her life was pointed out to her, set against that of a normal Croydon girl. '"You're not normal!" That's what Leslie Ash says to Phil Daniels in *Quadrophenia*. I love that film. "You're not normal!"'

A side effect of Kate's relationship with Jefferson had been that, with her introduction to his parents, the utter lunacy of some aspects of her world was cast into sharp relief. Seen through the prism of these 'outsiders', the excess and indulgence became more apparent than ever, and it wasn't an altogether welcome sense of perspective. Jefferson had explained to his parents that his relationship with Kate might be the focus of some press attention, and they were bemused. 'I thought she was just a model,' his father admitted with devastating candour.

When Jefferson explained the extent of Kate's wealth and status, it left his parents even more perplexed by the fact that a woman with so much could do so little with it. Aside from buying art and jewels she seemed to have no discernible hobbies or interests other than partying. There was no judgement in their observation. What Kate did with her time and money was entirely her business of course, and both Teresa and Douglas Hack thought Kate perfectly charming, easy-going and laid back.

'Normality' for Kate was going to Mustique, Jamaica or Ibiza at the drop of a hat. It was being fast-tracked through airports. It was having your life organized by bookers and assistants. It was being a member of Quintessentially, the 'life management company' set up by the Duchess of Cornwall's nephew Ben Elliot, which promises to 'access the inaccessible'. It was having three cars within months of passing her driving test. It was having telephones, apartments and staff in different continents – parallel lives ready to kick into action when Kate was in town. It was having jewels too valuable and foreign currency too excessive to keep in her home – since her burglary she had taken to keeping certain items in a safety deposit box in a bank.

Still, all Teresa and Douglas needed to know was that their son really loved this woman, and he did. He told them so without hesitation. He would need to.

According to businessman, restaurateur and socialite David Tang, who first met Kate in 1997 on a trip to India with integrated health-guru Dr Ali, 'She's like the neutrons and protons sleeping in the centre of the atom with all these electrons spinning around her. She's in the middle and every-body's going fucking *mad* on the periphery pandering to her.'

Yet however demanding Kate could be she *did* love Jefferson. There was a certain appeal in his pale, delicate features and his refusal to flatter her piqued her interest. She was terribly fond of him and thought him exciting and knowledge-able; she has long had a tendency to award 'college people' rather more importance than they perhaps merit.

Kate *wanted* a baby. She had made no secret of the fact. And it would prompt some among Kate's circle to make an unchari-table assessment of their relationship and label Jefferson 'the sperm donor'. It was as unkind as it was unfair and truth be told Jefferson's role was far from as perfunctory as that sug-gests. There would be many times when Kate turned to Jeffer-son for support though she could not have anticipated them back then. His constant willingness to offer it is testament to his decency, his love for his child and his enduring love for Kate. Solid, reliable Jefferson: when it came to the man who would be the father of her child some would consider Kate's relationship with Jefferson the most sensible choice of her life.

In Easter 2001 Jefferson and Kate took a lease on a cottage in the country. It would be a retreat, a bolthole, another step towards that idyllic existence – children, a dog, a house in the country – Kate had spoken of. The location was perfect – Fyfield in Oxfordshire – a couple of hours' drive from London and a similarly easy distance from the country house in which Meg was spending an increasing amount of time since the birth of Anais. An agent viewed Walnut Tree Cottage on Kate's behalf and contacted its owners, Sir Rowland and Lady Isa Whitehead. Sir Rowland, a retired merchant banker who was educated at Radley, a private school just south of Oxford and Trinity College, Cambridge, met first with Jefferson who, with his private school background, impressed the baronet as a polite, well-bred sort of chap.

Later he visited Kate in London. She was just back from a job in America and was simply dressed in a T-shirt and jeans, her face scrubbed free of make-up. She offered him tea and chatted excitedly about the wonderful cottage he and his wife owned. It was indeed a lovely home. Three hundred years old; built from honey-coloured Cotswold stone; beeswax polish and chintzy comfort within and a swimming pool and carefully nurtured garden without. The couple were particularly proud of the trees they had planted and watched grow to maturity: there was a rare tulip tree, mulberries, acacia, copper beech and a dozen rare apple trees.

Sir Rowland and his wife had owned the three-bedroom property for forty years and only rented it out twice, once to friends and once to another couple. Experienced landlords

Right Kate and Helena
Christensen, London
Fashion Week, 1997.
The strain of a life
that is all work, all play
is beginning to show.

Below Kate and Johnny
attend the disastrous
premiere of his film,
The Brave, Cannes, May
1997. As unthinkable as it
seems, their relationship
is about to unravel.

Left Marianne Faithfull with her 'naughty little girl' at Ronnie Wood's fiftieth birthday party at his home in Kingston-upon-Thames, Surrey, 1997.

Below, left The CFDA Fashion Awards, New York, 1998. A kiss for John Galliano, the designer who took a risk on an unknown Kate, sparking their lasting friendship and her catwalk career.

Below Kate with the woman who discovered her, 5 May 1998. Sarah Doukas celebrates ten years of Storm – and ten years of Kate – at the Kensington Roof Gardens, London.

The 'Dynamic Duo': Kate and Jade, 1999. In the background is Dan Macmillan, the man over whom the girls would briefly fall out.

Vogue magazine's party at the Lisson Gallery, 20 May 1998, sees Kate at the heart of a hedonistic scene with friends Meg Mathews and Fran Cutler.

Post-Priory, Kate celebrates her twenty-fifth birthday with a party in Paris thrown by Donatella Versace. That night her mother watches her 'like a hawk'.

Left With Jefferson Hack, March 2001, three months after their relationship became public, and already Kate has decided he will be the father of her child.

Below Kate and Jefferson with Sadie Frost and Jude Law at the New York premiere of *A.I.* Their romances would both founder but the women's friendship would endure.

Above Kate with her mother, Linda, April 2003 – the 'cool mother' on whom she can always depend.

Right New mother Kate takes daughter Lila Grace for a stroll along Portobello Road, Notting Hill.

The Beautiful and Damned:
Kate with James Brown,
her childhood friend and
hairdresser, transformed into
their glamorous F. Scott Fitzgerald
alter-egos for Kate's thirtieth
birthday party at Claridge's.

With Pete Doherty, the rockstar
with whom she was besotted,
(*left*) at Glastonbury, June 2005,
and (*above*) sharing a kiss in
New York just days before the
'Cocaine Kate' scandal broke
and threatened everything.

Kate makes a brief appearance
in the window of Topshop's
Oxford Street store as her first
collection of clothing launches
to frenzied anticipation,
30 April 2007.

Kate arrives at London's
Victoria and Albert Museum
for the Golden Age of Couture
exhibition opening, September 2007.
In vintage gold satin, accompanied
by photographer Mario Testino
– who calls her his 'favourite girl' –
she approaches twenty years in the
business, and is still relevant,
mesmeric and compelling.

Annabel's nightclub, October 2007: Kate celebrates her second Topshop collection with the fashion and art scene elite. At her side, safe date for the night, is singer Jamie Hince. On the far left is Jade Jagger, while Jake Chapman is on the far right.

On a weekend at her country house in the Cotswolds, Kate and The Kills's Jamie Hince chat and smoke after Sunday lunch at the local pub.

they were not. Still, Sir Rowland thought it might be interesting for Kate to have the house; he knew she was a model and wasn't immune to the sheen of glamour that hung about her. Lady Isa told him not to let the house to Kate, but his mind was made up. It was a decision he would live to regret.

But then, how could the elderly baronet and his charming wife have begun to have imagine the lifestyle that this 'nice couple', in his estimation, or at least one half of it, and some of her friends led? How could they have dreamed of the boundaries transgressed, the relationships compromised, the hostilities harboured? How could they have known just how messy their home, and Kate's life, would become at the very time when she seemed to be preparing to settle for something, well, more settled? How could they know that what was acceptable – normal even – to Kate could be so far removed from their own sense of what was and was not tolerable?

By the time Kate and Jefferson rented Walnut Tree Cottage, the rarefied air of Primrose Hill was becoming, in parts, more fetid and unhealthy. Relationships suffered and friendships were compromised. Kate was not always at the centre of the action. Still, these were her friends and this was her world. Tabloid accusations relate how, during the summer of 2001, Pearl Lowe and Danny Goffey holidayed in Greece with a group of friends that included Sadie Frost and Jude Law. It had all the makings of a far from memorable holiday – fun in the sun, something with which this crowd were achingly familiar. Which is, as the reports have it, precisely why it got out of control. Boredom was the poison that dripped into this foursome that summer, helped along by liberal lashings of tequila.

The claim is that one evening, after a night out, the four were drinking back at their shared villa. Liberated by alcohol, Sadie, who had been friends with Pearl since they were sixteen, slipped out of her clothes, sat on Danny Goffey's knee and said the four words that nearly destroyed two relationships: 'Why don't we swap?' According to Pearl, they thought it would be fun, but 'in fact it turned out to have some unpleasant repercussions'. Jude has vehemently denied that any wife-swapping ever took place. Certainly his marriage with Sadie appeared solid enough in the short term, though ironically it was this union that ultimately crumbled.

Pearl has insisted that the tales of wife-swapping during that Greek holiday are true and that they carried on in the form of emails and flirtatious texts on the group's return to London. It had happened, however much she would later wish that it had not. Her friendship with Sadie endured and her relationship with Danny suffered but was, ultimately, she believes, strengthened by having survived the complexities of jealousy and insecurity that followed in the wake of that summer's experimentation. She felt they had blundered, blind drunk, into something more corrosive than any of them realized at the time – and it would be something of a recurring theme, bleeding through the dynamics of the wider group. Having fun all the time, Kate once observed, can actually 'make you miserable'. It was a lesson many of her friends seemed doomed to learn and forget with alarming regularity.

As summer gave way to autumn 2001, Kate landed two major contracts that showed by their sheer diversity the omniscience of her selling abilities. In October she was announced as the first face of Rimmel cosmetics, a company established in 1834 but which had never felt the need to have a 'spokesmodel' before. For their 'London' line Kate was, according to marketing director Emmanuelle Bonte, the natural choice. She was, she explained, 'the ultimate London girl'. She was also an intriguing choice and one who, Bonte correctly recognized, could only add value to the brand. She would be worth every penny of the £2 million they offered her.

Rimmel's reputation when Kate signed was thoroughly high street, the reserve of teenage girls buying make-up for the first time. Kate grew up wearing Rimmel, she said, her favourite lipstick being pale frosted pink. That pretty much summed up the place Rimmel had in many young women's lives: nostalgic, not at all bad, but relegated to teenage years (or younger). In signing Kate, Rimmel moved up a gear in the breadth of their sales demographics. Kate was then twenty-seven years old, yet she managed with extraordinary, apparently artless, grace to be both girl and woman when it came to the serious business of selling. She brought credibility to the product; with Kate championing Rimmel it suddenly seemed a cool choice for women who would previously have blushed should a Rimmel mascara be found at the bottom of their make-up bag.

Cool Kate was old enough to appeal to women her age and above and eternally youthful enough to hold and expand on the existing teen market. The move certainly paid off: Rimmel's sales rose an incredible 20 per cent within the first year of Kate's signing and each year thereafter.

The same month as Rimmel announced their new face, another contract, one actually signed two months earlier, became public with the European launch of a new perfume. In August Kate had signed with a name that sat at the opposite end of the fashion – and age – spectrum when she became the face of Chanel's Coco Mademoiselle. Where Rimmel had wanted to get credible and 'age up', Chanel's market expansion was heading in the opposite direction.

The new scent was aimed at a customer every bit as stylish

as Chanel's established clientele, but more youthful and, perhaps, a tad more playful and sexy. Jacques Polge, creator of the original Coco perfume in 1984 and resident 'nose' at Chanel, explained the difference between the two. For Coco he had been inspired by the baroque interiors of Mademoiselle Chanel's private Paris apartment above the shop in rue Cambon. Coco Mademoiselle was, he said, 'more Tate Modern. There is a purity in Coco Mademoiselle that contrasts with the opulence of Coco. The notes are more or less those that are present in Coco, but I used the fresh aspect of every ingredient and got rid of all the heavy, animal-like notes. The jasmine, for example, is much lighter, so are the woods, and all the spices are fresh. The musk is white musk.'

The advertising campaign was shot by Michael Thompson and featured an elfin-cropped Kate, her eyeshadow smoky, her eyeliner thick and her lashes plump and sensual. She wore a little black dress from Chanel's spring/summer 2001 *prêt-à-porter* rather than haute couture. This was young and sexy; classy and sassy. According to Jacques Helleu, Chanel's artistic director and the man responsible for casting Kate, 'she truly embodied the Coco Mademoiselle fragrance'.

It was true that, however wild Kate's life may have become, on set she still possessed something approaching innocence, the purity of which Jacques Polge spoke. She appeared simultaneously accessible and unobtainable; whatever she had, people wanted it, and that was a compelling commercial imperative. Little wonder then that when she looked at the images others saw of her – those moments when she 'embodied' whatever product she was selling, or whatever product was selling her – she no longer recognized herself. 'I just see an image of what someone's trying to advertise,' she admitted. 'And that's sad.' It was also not enough.

The previous year's experience posing for artists for *Vogue* had piqued the second hunger burning in Kate that summer. Her apparent desire for a child would soon be sated, and so too would her desire to be a muse. In fact, in what could be seen as a sort of double validation, the most famous portrait of her would be one of Kate naked and pregnant; canvas proof that she was more than 'just a model'.

Kate had mentioned when interviewed by Jefferson that she would love to meet and be painted by Lucian Freud. She was not the first celebrity, nor will she be the last, to casually drop a desire into an interview in the hope that someone, somewhere takes the hint. It's a convenient way of asking for a meeting without going through the potential embarrassment of having a direct request rebutted. Someone, somewhere did take the hint. In fact, Freud himself read the article and invited Kate to dine with him at the Ivy. Then he invited her to sit for him. Freud has said that he chooses his subjects 'on impulse', but in some ways it was a surprising development. Freud has often said that he enjoys finding and painting 'real people' – the last thing he looks for is a professional model – yet it would be hard to imagine a more practised holder of poses than Kate. Still, he made up his mind to paint Kate, and she looked forward to what both anticipated would be a long drawn-out process, as Freud is renowned for taking his time over his work.

In December 2001, Kate embarked on a series of predominantly nocturnal sessions sitting for Freud. Kate would look back on those occasions with particular pride. There was something vindicating about the time it took, a world away from the blink of the camera lens. Only their time together was not quite as languorous as either would have chosen. Less than three months into their collaboration, life would impose an inescapable natural deadline on the sessions. Kate was only late once for her evening sessions with Freud – the day in February when she received official confirmation of her pregnancy. Freud, rather pragmatically, chose to focus his attentions on fixing Kate's midriff on canvas before finessing the rest of her.

Kate had been feeling a little under the weather as the New Year began, but it didn't stop her fulfilling her commitments, both work and social. For much of January she had been out of the country shooting as far afield as China. She was tired and it didn't help that, having decided to redecorate her home in Melina Place, she had been forced to decamp. The refurbishment of Kate's Georgian cottage was taking longer than anyone had hoped. Kate, like many wealthy people, would undoubtedly wonder if there was an elevated 'Kate Rate' when she was quoted for any work she need doing. This anxiety, rather than an inherently 'difficult' personality, accounted for often protracted negotiations and it certainly didn't help when Kate was impatient, as she was that winter, for work to be completed. Until it was ready, many of her belongings were in storage and she was stuck in a rented apartment nearby that she was far from thrilled with. It may have been stylishly revamped, but the only really convenient aspect of the ex-local authority, one-bedroom flat in question was that it was in St John's Wood.

At the beginning of February, Mario Testino's work was celebrated with an exhibition of 120 of his portraits at the National Portrait Gallery. It was the first time his work had been displayed in a museum and his celebrity friends turned out in force to support and celebrate him. Kate, his 'favourite girl', was among them. She invited her mother to join her that evening and Linda stayed over with Kate in London that night. The following day Kate nursed what she thought was the beginning of a cold. She was glad her mother was there to keep her company. Unbeknown to Kate or her mother, Kate was already carrying Jefferson's child.

As far as Kate was concerned the timing could hardly have been better, save for the domestic upheavals. Less than a month before her own good news, Sadie had learned that she too was expecting. This would be her fourth child – her third by Jude. For first-time-mother-to-be Kate, the comfort of going through her pregnancy with such a close friend was immeasurable, though ultimately their approach to motherhood would prove very different.

As Pearl put it, 'A mother can do two out of three things: motherhood, work and socializing.' With Pearl, by her own admission, it was 'always the work' that went. With Sadie it would take a couple of years – years that were frantic by any standards – but ultimately socializing dimmed in favour of spending time caring for her children. With Kate, well, she was back at work within four months of giving birth and, with a live-in nanny, Sadie's sister Jade Davidson, she showed little inclination for swapping nights out for night feeds.

Kate enjoyed her pregnancy, loved putting on weight and wasn't particularly troubled by morning sickness. Well known within her group of friends for two culinary feats – rustling up a 'greasy spoon' breakfast and doing a mean Sunday roast – Kate indulged in French toast in the morning. It was true when she said that she had never had to diet, but while she had eaten well, she had increasingly eaten little as the ferocious metabolism of her teenage years inevitably slowed. Now, however, she didn't have to worry about the pounds piling on; quite the opposite.

The one thing she really struggled with was giving up drinking and smoking, neither of which she succeeded in doing completely. She dramatically cut back on both, but still there were times when she struggled and when others simply had to bite back their disapproval. When she went to support Gwyneth Paltrow in her London stage début, *Proof*, at the Donmar Warehouse, she unapologetically knocked back shots of vodka and enjoyed a cigarette. But there was no point in taking the moral high ground with Kate.

In August, Lucian Freud put the finishing touches to his portrait, and Kate declared it her favourite piece of art featuring her. Not all of Kate's friends were keen on the end result, though Kate liked it enough to bid for it that year. She was unsuccessful, though three years later she got a second chance when the painting was auctioned at Christie's. It fetched £3.9 million, the second highest price paid for a Lucian Freud. Tracey Emin didn't like it because, she said, 'It doesn't look like Kate. For me, Kate is delicate and beautiful.' The phrase was revealing: 'For me . . .'

Kate Moss was all things to all men and women. To Tracey she was 'delicate and beautiful'. To Sadie, Pearl, Davinia and Meg she was best friend and bad influence. To their lovers and husbands she was both bait and one of the lads. To Jacques Helleu she was the spirit of Coco Mademoiselle. To Marianne Faithfull she was her 'naughty little girl'. To Sarah Doukas she was the unknown she had 'made' and the making of Storm – a fraught combination if ever there was one. To Jefferson she was a lover and, unbelievably, soon to be the mother of his child – a woman to whom he would be forever bound, for better and for worse.

To Lucian Freud she was something other than 'Kate Moss' – the sum of all these parts and then some. Freud ignored the lucrative personal mystique that hung around Kate. Her face seemed hardly to matter in his portrait and her body, pregnant and a blur of colours and textures unlike the glossy image of so many fashion pictures, was, in its sheer voluptuousness, unrecognizable as that of the famous waif. He was interested in Kate not as an icon, model, celebrity or any of those intangible notions. He was, he said, interested in her in the same way that he was interested in all of his sitters, 'merely as an animal'. When it came to giving the picture a title he did not even identify her. Perhaps recognizing that nobody could come to an image of Kate and see it for the first time, he called the painting simply *Naked Portait 2002*.

The following month, Kate gave birth to a daughter in the early hours of Sunday, 29 September. She had been lunching at a Greek restaurant with Jefferson, Sadie and Jude when her contractions started and went straight from there to the maternity ward of St John & St Elizabeth Hospital in St John's Wood. Scented candles burned and the room was softly lit for the natural birth. Jefferson, Kate and Sadie were in the birthing pool when her little girl arrived, all 6lb 8oz of her. Later the moment was toasted with champagne and it was, according to Kate, 'the best'. Kate named her little girl Lila Grace. Grace was simply a name that both she and Jefferson loved, while Lila was Kate's suggestion, inspired by a book she had read some years earlier called *Lila Says*.

As pretty as the title may seem, it was an odd source of inspiration when it came to naming a child. The book became a cult sensation when it was originally published in France during the mid-Nineties, and it was first translated into English in 1997 where it came complete with its own myth. The French publishers claimed that the manuscript had come to them via a lawyer who had mysteriously received a bundle of notebooks. The books contained a story scrawled by 'Chimo', the pen name of the young half-Arab immigrant who narrates the tale but wishes to remain anonymous. Not even the publishers who went on to print his words claimed to know his true identity.

The story itself is shocking, violent and ultimately tragic. The Lila of the title is sixteen years old, blonde, beautiful and growing up on the same sink estate as Chimo. What Lila says, and shows, to Chimo is effectively a pornographic litany of supposed sexual adventures and experiences in a brutal environment. It's a shocking, punchy, sexy, little book in which Lila – blonde, tinkly voiced and sexually precocious – is brutalized, broken and cast aside.

It's not difficult to see what Kate might have related to in this story of a sexual young beauty, used, abused and consumed by the men she attempts to control through her brazen sexuality and fearless, shameless powers of attraction, but it's difficult to reconcile Kate's decision to name her daughter after such a character with her assertion that 'when you're a mother it definitely changes the way you feel about life in general'.

Certainly the news was not a perspective-imbuing event as far as Jade Jagger was concerned. The thought of Kate blissfully cradling her daughter did not lead to a rush of forgiveness over her betrayal. It was rumoured that among the many gifts that Kate and Jefferson received, one of the most exquisitely fashioned was one of the least welcome: a gold necklace made by Jade, who was by then employed as a designer for the revamped former Crown jewellers Garrard – studded with diamonds and bearing the letters 'SLAG'. Jade would later laughingly dismiss this tale as apocryphal but so good that it seemed a shame to deny it. Certainly there would have been a touch of irony in the fact that, just before supposedly receiving the trinket, Jefferson had been in Garrard discussing the possibility of having a ring made for Kate to celebrate their daughter's birth.

There was no question of it being an engagement ring. In later months it would be speculated many times over that Jefferson had proposed, was about to propose or would most certainly propose once he was assured of a positive response from Kate. In reality, though, as Jefferson had already told his parents, however much in love he was with Kate, he believed that neither he, nor she, 'were the marrying kind'. It's true that many months later, when joking with friends about the state of her romantic life, Kate responded to an enquiry about whether she would marry Jefferson with an expression of faux horror and the words, 'God no!' But whether this was out of self-preservation as much as a cynical take on the institution of marriage, the dilemma never truly presented itself since Jefferson never asked.

A glance at the fortunes of some of her closest friends' unions – not to mention her own parents' – had given Kate a less than rosy impression of marital bliss. Nothing seemed to last. Meg and Noel's marriage had ended in acrimony. Jade was no longer with the father of her children. Samantha Morton saw no need to marry the father of her daughter, Esme, and later they drifted apart. In fact, the most enduring relationship among their set was that of Pearl Lowe and Danny Goffey – hardly conventional, riddled with substance abuse and difficulties and not sealed with a wedding ring but still, at the bottom of it all, sound. The same could not be said for Sadie and Jude. As a couple, Kate and Jefferson had hoped that the Laws would be godparents to Lila. It seemed a natural choice. They had been friends for a long, long time. Kate had shared many intimacies with both and had been supportive of Jude in the years before his acting career took off, and he and Sadie were loving and devoted parents to their own children. But barely a month after Lila's birth, something so devastating happened that it proved the blow from which Sadie and Jude's marriage never seemed to recover.

Jude was in Romania filming *Cold Mountain*, the American Civil War drama in which he starred alongside Nicole Kidman in a performance that earned him an Oscar nomination, when it happened. Inspired by a birthday party at private members' club Soho House, which Sadie had held for her son, Finlay, Pearl Lowe had arranged for a similar event for her son Alfie. It was his fifth birthday. The club would show the film of his choice – *Lilo & Stitch* – and for £1,000 there would be food for the children, waitress service and a pleasingly grown-up environment for the adults to relax in while the children had fun.

Most of the children were settled in front of the cinema screen when Pearl sat down to have a chat with Sadie on one of the club's vast leather sofas. Sadie had two-year-old Iris on her knee, and as the women chatted Iris began to fidget and rummage around down the back of the sofa. She put her hand in her mouth. Sadie took her hand away and pulled out the object that Iris was about to swallow. It was a small white pill. Both women recognized with horror that they were looking at an Ecstasy tablet.

According to Pearl they were calm, in spite of the shock. They hadn't been drinking and they didn't want to alarm Iris, who was by now wailing about having the 'sweet' removed from her mouth. They took Iris to hospital where she was given charcoal to get rid of any poison she may have ingested. She was kept in hospital overnight and returned home, safe and well, the following morning. The damage to Sadie and

Jude's relationship was not so easily fixed. Thousands of miles away, helpless and understandably horrified by what he was told, Jude was livid. Pearl wanted to speak to Jude herself but her calls went unanswered. She felt certain that, in his anger, Jude was blaming Sadie, and also blaming her and Danny.

It's worth remembering just how close Kate and Sadie had become through their recent pregnancies and childbirth. There had been times when it seemed that Kate was practically living at Sadie's home. If it were to come down to taking sides – and it did – Kate's loyalties would lie with Sadie rather than her friend's disapproving, disgruntled husband. Two months after the Soho House scare, Sadie and Jude joined Kate, Jefferson and Lila on holiday in Phuket, Thailand. In hindsight, perhaps a holiday away from others might have been preferable. Of course Sadie and Jude's relationship problems could not be attributed to one simple cause, nor could they be fixed with a beach holiday. So while *their* marriage limped to an end, Kate focused her attentions on something that *could* be. She was keen to return to her pre-pregnancy physique, and for the first time in her life she had to put some serious work into being 'Kate Moss'.

She had practised yoga for some time – an instructor came to her home each week when she was in Britain – and she continued to do so after Lila's birth, as well as working out, though not with great enthusiasm, with fitness instructor David Marshall. In Thailand a chef provided low-fat meals for the group. Back in London, she and Sadie found a more entertaining way to get back in shape when they took pole-dancing lessons at Astal strip club. The following summer Kate showed what she had learned when she appeared in knickers and bra, dancing round a pole for the video of The White Stripes' cover of 'I just don't know what to do with myself.' (Coincidentally, the band's singer, Jack White, had acted alongside Jude in *Cold Mountain*.) But the results of Kate's exercise regime, and determination, were on display much sooner than that. Barely four months after giving birth, Kate appeared in her first photoshoot, modelling a leather frockcoat and matching miniskirt by Alexander McQueen for *Harpers & Queen*. She looked phenomenal. She was, McQueen declared, 'the perfect sex-kitten'. Motherhood may have changed the way that Kate felt about the world, but it did nothing to change the way the world felt about her.

15

It would be hard to imagine a more picture-perfect setting. When it came to choosing a place for Lila Grace to be christened, Kate and Jefferson opted not for some fashionable London church, but for the 12th-century parish of St Peter's in Southrop near Walnut Tree Cottage, the country home they continued to rent. In summer, wisteria blooms on the Cotswold stone of the buildings in the pretty village that has grown up along and around what was once little more than a crossroad. There's a school, a post office, a bus shelter, a rather smart bar and restaurant – Southrop may be small but it's decidedly well heeled – and the church; each a healthy thump of the heart of this traditional village.

It would be easy to attribute the more 'conventional' elements of Kate, Jefferson and Lila's 'family' life to his influence rather than Kate's, but the reality was always more complicated than that. A house, family and life in the country had always been *Kate's* dream, not Jefferson's, though he was happy to go along with her desires. Lila's christening gown was a vintage piece made personal with some delicate hand embroidery by Stella McCartney. The notion of a country christening, of being a mother in an old-fashioned floaty frock, of making cupcakes and playing at dressing up and reading bedtime stories seemed to hold an enormous appeal to Kate, but somehow it lost something in the translation from fond fantasy to reality.

There were eighty or so guests invited to the christening at the morning service on Sunday, 3 August. Lila Grace's was the first of two ceremonies scheduled to be conducted by Canon Tony Ross, a fact that made the tardiness of the guests and immediate family something of a worry. Sadie was godmother. Jude's role as godfather, pencilled in the previous autumn, had been unceremoniously erased as his and Sadie's marriage collapsed early in 2003.

By August, Jude had become so tired of the scene he used to be part of that Sadie attended the christening without him or the children. Kate's family was there, as was Jefferson's, but save for their immediate relatives, the congregation was decidedly rock 'n' roll: Marianne Faithfull; Anita Pallenberg; Meg Mathews; Rhys Ifans; Corinne Day's discovery, model Rosemary Ferguson, and artist Jake Chapman (who would go on to marry each other the following year); Bobby Gillespie and his girlfriend, stylist Katy England . . . the list went on – and so did the 'after party'.

A marquee had been erected in the field behind Walnut Tree Cottage. Kate and Jefferson had done this before for his thirtieth and there had been no trouble, but this time no permission was sought and the fallout was rather messy. After lunch, Lila was taken away by her nanny while the adults relaxed into the party spirit. And it was some party. At one point Kate fell, giggling, into Sir Rowland and Lady Isa Whitehead's well-tended herbaceous border, covering herself not so much in shame as scratches. Godmother Sadie's mood took an understandable turn for the gloomy and Marianne Faithfull was spotted weaving through Southrop.

For some the party went on until 5a.m., then started up

again the following afternoon, once guests had slept off the excesses of the previous day and strays had been retrieved. More than one villager awoke on Monday morning to find a discombobulated christening guest asleep in their front garden. In all, the partying lasted more than two days, and by the time the final car had taken the last guest back to London, Walnut Tree Cottage's septic tank had overflowed and the lane that led up to the house was lined with bin liners of rubbish, rapidly turning putrid in the late summer sun, attracting crows, foxes and rats from the neighbouring farm.

There seemed little evidence from the revelries of the change of perspective that motherhood had supposedly brought to Kate's life. Soon after Lila Grace's birth, Kate spoke of her intention of easing up on life as she had been enjoying it. Once she had been 'bang into drugs', but, she announced, she would no longer do them, though drinking was fine and back in the equation. Cutting back on work was also supposedly on the cards, and it is true that Kate reviewed her career and started to rethink elements of it. She began to move in a different direction, but the direction she took ironically made her more visible than ever.

Kate continued to do runway work, though she no longer 'did' the seasons as she had before – the days of nine shows a day, back to back for a week in New York, Milan, London and Paris were consigned to history, and instead she focused on a few favoured lucrative labels – Versace, Missoni, Burberry, Chanel and the like. Her work still took her all over Europe and America, but the intensity had dimmed. Kate could pick and choose magazine editorials that interested her and, increasingly, she did. As a result the shoots became rather more iconic in nature, with the magazine often being the only discernible product that Kate was actually selling.

In September pictures of Kate graced no fewer than nine alternative covers for that month's edition of American style magazine *W*. She had already been a *W* cover girl fifteen times before. One year after the birth of her daughter, Kate's appearance in *W* was billed as 'The Triumphant Return of a Superstar'. The magazine's creative director Dennis Freedman had been inspired, in part, by Kate's posing for Lucian Freud. He invited fashion photographers and artists to create images of Kate that would run over a forty-page portfolio. The result was remarkable.

Freedman explained, 'We [at *W*] are far less interested in appearances. We look for character, and Kate has character. Kate has been our muse – ours and our photographers' – for the simple reason that there are so many aspects to Kate's personality. She's a woman, she's a child, she's a tomboy, she's very sexual, she's smart, she's funny, she's good, she's bad.' Craig McDean photographed her in black and white, her hair tousled, her lips open in a sex-kitten moue. 'She's kind of off-beauty,' he observed. 'She's not a little cookie, but she's probably the most beautiful girl in the world.' Painter Alex Katz, whose image of Kate was simple, clean and very, very blonde, was struck by the fact that she is 'completely ordinary. That's what makes her so extraordinary'.

She was also – unusually for any woman, never mind model – seemingly without vanity. She wanted each of the photographers' and artists' visions to work – Mario Testino had commented on this energy in the past. Her desire was not diluted by any concerns about how 'good' or otherwise she would look as a result; quite the opposite. At the time, artist Chuck Close had been perversely toying with the notion of not showing Kate's face at all – it was so recognizable that he considered eliminating it entirely and making, instead, a daguerreotype of her nude, headless torso front and back. He had taken a similar approach to dozens of lesser-known subjects. Kate no longer had the waiflike body for which she was remembered and with which she will forever be associated. She and Close spent some time talking about her pregnancy and delivery and the changes the process had brought to her body. 'She seemed to be very happy with them,' Chuck recalled. 'She'd become a woman, broadened slightly.' Albeit very slightly – Inez van Lamsweerde and Vinoodh Matadin's photographs of Kate as a bride, her veil back and naked save a strategically positioned bridal bouquet, showed just how sleekly feminine her frame now was.

After five hours of photographing her torso, Close shot several tightly cropped pictures of her face. She wore no makeup and she hadn't combed her hair. She did not so much as glance in a mirror before the camera shutter flicked open and shut. Close was amazed by Kate's willingness to allow him to do this: 'My daguerreotypes are not flattering – any flaws on one's complexion are exaggerated wildly – and I thought she might be upset. But she said, "I've had enough pretty pictures of me." She understood what it is that I do, and she was perfectly willing to provide it.' It's an irresistible trait in a model, and one which comes up again and again in photographers' and artists' testimony of working with Kate.

The month after *W*'s homage to Kate it was music magazine *Q*'s turn. The shoot had actually taken place in New York in May, but it was cover of the October issue that Kate appeared on, wrapped around David Bowie. The feature was billed as the 'clash of the titans'. Senior editor Gareth Grundy explained, 'As power summits go, it's an all-time great – two of the world's top-drawer icons brought together to bond over fast times and a mutual fascination with each other's mythical status. David Bowie is rock'n'roll's great shape-shifter, a peerless, eternally relevant figure who still towers over any musician who thinks they're a bit clever. Kate Moss is the most rock'n'roll of all supermodels.'

Kate may have got a bit short-changed on the description, but pretty much everything that Grundy observed of Bowie's status could be happily applied to Kate – she was a shape-shifter, peerless and, in the notoriously transient world of fashions, 'eternally relevant'. Interestingly, the article also revealed the extent to which Kate still felt – indeed would always feel – something of an imposter in her own world, an unworthy adjunct to those whom she regarded with awe. Kate may have been an icon, but she was also a fan when it came to Bowie, and one not entirely prepared for some of the questions he asked on the day they met in room 606 of the Mercer Hotel in New York.

'When I walk on set,' she told him, 'I feel . . . When they can put anything onto me and I can become that image, I feel I've accomplished being a chameleon . . . being whoever they want me to be.' Bowie was perplexed and asked, 'Why would you feel that you can take on the identity that someone is dictating to you? Do you feel you're earning their affection or their love in some way?'

Suddenly Kate seemed on uncertain ground. She was disconcerted, surprised. The rationale that allowed her to 'enjoy' modelling and to find it in some way fulfilling, an achievement she could respect at least a little had been questioned – it looked thin in the light of Bowie's gaze. 'Oh . . . !' came Kate's response. 'I dunno. Maybe.'

That year, Kate took a second significant step towards ensuring that her market supremacy would remain unequivocal. Kate was well aware that to survive in her game you had to stay ahead, and she had an uncanny knack of doing just that. In 2001 she had signed with Rimmel; now she continued the move towards the high street and a career pinned increasingly on lucrative brand endorsements. Product and label endorsements meant a defined number of working days per year, per label, and they meant serious exposure and money. Nice work for a working mother if she could get it and, of course, Kate could.

In September 2003 Kate signed a £2 million deal to be the face of Zara. It was the first UK advertising campaign for the Spanish-owned chain that specializes in producing the newest fashions for high-street prices. It went on to do so with such rapidity and affordability that the brand arguably changed the rhythm of British high-street fashion, setting a pace that other stores were compelled to keep up with. First, however, Zara needed a foothold in the market, and for that they turned to Kate. By this point the balance of power had changed as far as Kate's relationship with a label was concerned. Eleven years earlier, Calvin Klein's pay cheque had come on the condition of Kate's exclusivity. Now, if advertisers wanted Kate they would have to share her. And they did, because she was worth it.

Jefferson too was learning that having Kate meant sharing her – with work, friends and a schedule so unpredictable that separation, at first physical then latterly emotional, was an inevitable feature of their being together. She went to Glastonbury, she went to St Tropez, she went to Ibiza, she went to Sadie's son Rudy's first birthday party – all without Jefferson and in part because of his commitments. That summer Kate checked into a London sleep clinic to have her sleep patterns monitored. Like many new mothers her nights were disturbed and her sleep broken, though it would be fair to say that the cause of Kate's restless nights was not always her crying child in the nursery above Kate and Jefferson's vast master suite. Travel, drink, nicotine and an almost complete absence of routine all played their part.

Kate loved to be spontaneous and she could afford to be – travelling to France, Spain, Jamaica or Thailand at the drop of a hat – but Jefferson was yet to make his millions. He had a business to run, and tending to that, Kate and the new experience of fatherhood would be a pretty tall order for any man. According to Kate, Jefferson proved a good father – that was 'Mother Nature's intervention'. But however joyous the experience, life with Kate proved draining, both emotionally and financially. For all her considerable wealth, it was often Jefferson who footed the bill for Kate's impromptu trips abroad. When Kate and Depp had argued, they had done so passionately. They yelled at each other, threw objects, then made up and went out to dinner. When Kate and Jefferson argued, they bickered and sulked, then he tidied up and she went out to dinner. It was a telling distinction.

Kate is a tactile, physical creature who it seems would rather be *with* a man than without one. To that extent she has always *needed* a man, but less than a year after Lila's birth it seemed to be already becoming apparent that the man in question did not necessarily need to be Jefferson.

Perhaps it was inevitable that Kate should re-evaluate her relationship with Jefferson that summer, since it was a significant one, romantically speaking, for two of her closest friends. On 30 July, Stella McCartney married magazine publisher Alasdhair Willis. The ceremony took place in Scotland, in the chapel in the grounds of Mount Stuart, the spectacular Victorian Gothic house owned by former Formula 1 driver Johnny Dumfries, the Marquess of Bute. It was a location laden with nostalgia and emotional ties for Stella. She had spent many a childhood holiday scrambling around the beaches and coves of Mull, an hour's boat trip or a hiccup of a helicopter flight west of the Isle of Bute. Kate and Jefferson were among the 100 guests who travelled north for the occasion, together with Liv Tyler, Chrissie Hynde, Rod Stewart, Chris Martin and Gwyneth Paltrow, Madonna and Guy Ritchie, Sting and Trudi Styler, Marianne Faithfull and Anita Pallenberg . . . the list went on.

They flew to Glasgow, loading into the blacked-out Range Rovers that seethed between the airport and Wemyss Bay, the dot on the map where the ferry leaves the mainland for Rothesay, the only town on the Isle of Bute. Kate, Jefferson, Marianne, Chrissie and Anita were late and missed their allotted ferry, so they wiled away the forty-five minutes until the next one by knocking back drinks at the local Station Bar. They made a shambolically happy group. And why not? It was a wonderfully happy occasion. However long the list of failed marriages and high-profile infidelities shared by members of the congregation in the chapel in Mount Stuart that day, it was impossible not to be caught up in the romance of the occasion. It was just unfortunate that, as Stella was plighting her troth to Alasdhair, Sadie and Jude were unravelling their marriage, hammering out a divorce settlement in what had become an increasingly acrimonious split.

The Laws' divorce papers were filed barely two weeks after Stella's wedding. Kate was not immune to the piquancy of the timing. When Sadie walked down the aisle in 1997 she had done so in a dress loaned to her by Kate – a beautiful, classic, cream design with an extravagant fishtail by John Galliano. Now, as Sadie's marriage careered towards the car crash of divorce, Kate was once more on hand to help. Somebody once said that the only way to get over somebody was to get under somebody else. As life philosophies go, Kate certainly seemed to think it was worth a punt to help her friend mend her broken heart.

By the time Stella was walking down the aisle towards a lifetime of commitment, Sadie, with Kate's encouragement, was starting to believe in life after marriage, and that she could find that life in a much younger man. The pain of divorce could not be simply dissolved with this discovery, but it could certainly be punctuated with something more pleasurable.

A couple of weeks before Stella's wedding, Kate suggested to Sadie that they get out of London, away from the headaches and heartaches, and head to a beautiful Spanish retreat she'd been going to for years. Sadie's spirits must have lifted the moment their car turned into the cedar-lined driveway that leads to Trasierra, the ravishingly beautiful renovated finca one hour north of Seville, set high in the Sierra Morena in 1,000 acres of olive groves.

There are only a handful of rooms at Trasierra and mobile phones are forbidden. By night, fairylights twinkle in the cobbled courtyard and candles burn in Moorish lanterns by the poolside. By day, light bounces off the whitewashed walls of the barns and stables, converted by owner Charlotte Scott into a porch-fronted guesthouse. As well as its obvious charms, Trassiera was an appropriate place for Kate to take Sadie that summer. For Charlotte Scott, the guesthouse itself was akin to a bricks-and-mortar rendition of 'I Will Survive'.

She had lived there for six years with her husband in what was little more than an abandoned ruin, having four babies and living by gas and candlelight. Then he left and Charlotte, who had worked as an interior designer in a previous life in London, decided to make something of Trasierra. The result was just the sort of bohemian blend that appeals to Kate.

Charlotte's motto, inscribed in a note left in her guests' bedrooms, was 'Feel free' – that appealed too. Her children,
Charlotte added, were friendly and bilingual, 'so feel free to
call on them'. When it came to Charlotte's then twenty-two-
year-old son, Jackson, Kate and Sadie would need little encouragement.

Whippet thin, with hair that kicked over his collar falling
in a heavy fringe over his pale hazel eyes, Jackson Scott was
exactly the sort of 'off-balance' handsome that both Kate and
Sadie favoured – post Jude and his thoroughly centred Hollywood handsome charms, that is. Jackson had been living in
Seville, studying flamenco guitar at the Cristina Heeren Foundation, one of Spain's most prestigious music academies, but
he had developed tendonitis, which required treatment and
rest, leaving him downcast and unable to play that summer.

His mother suggested he leave the heat of his rented flat in
Seville in high summer and come home. His sister Giocanda
cooked at Trasierra, so Jackson could help out in some fashion
until he was fit to play again. During the days Jackson painted
walls, skimmed the pool and kept the place in suitably idyllic
shape, while in the evenings he joined Kate and Sadie, talking,
drinking, smoking and flirting. By the time Sadie and Kate
were packing their bags to go home, he and Sadie were lovers
and he was planning his own trip to London. Jackson was
fifteen years Sadie's junior.

Back in the cold light of London, when she asked her
friends what they thought of him, Kate, Pearl, Rosemary (Ferguson), Fran (Cutler) and Samantha (Morton) were united.
'He's gorgeous, darling,' they told her. 'Totally gorge.' On paper
the relationship hardly seemed one of much substance – the
age gap was large and the gulf between their drastically different life experiences vast – but Jackson seemed to make Sadie

happy and that, in turn, pleased Kate. Jackson had brought a morale-boosting injection of fun into Sadie's life at a time when it was sorely needed. Sadly, it seemed Kate's relationship with Jefferson was proving less satisfying by the day.

Jefferson's parents certainly began to notice the tension that all too often hung in the air when Kate and Jefferson were together. The couple were still renting Walnut Tree Cottage, but Kate's thoughts were turning towards making a more permanent country home. She wanted to buy a place, but there seemed no question of any such purchase being made in conjunction with Jefferson. Given that the couple were now parents and living together, it was a pretty clear indication that Kate wasn't prepared to make the relationship any more binding than the act of having a child together had already.

Shortly before Christmas, Jefferson invited his parents to have Sunday lunch with them in the country. Teresa and Douglas Hack naturally assumed that Kate would be joining them, but from the moment they stepped through the door it was clear that she had no such plans. If anything, they got the distinct impression that she didn't want them there any more than she wanted to be there herself. Kate is rather good at cooking a roast, but on this particular winter afternoon, the cooking, organizing and looking after of guests and daughter was left entirely to Jefferson. Instead of chatting with her putative in-laws, Kate fussed about what outfit to wear. Again and again she came downstairs to the kitchen, where Jefferson and his parents were talking, asking his opinion on the outfit she was wearing to a party for which he had little interest.

He became exasperated, telling Kate, 'Don't ask me. I haven't a clue.' She left soon after, making polite but cool goodbyes to Lila's grandparents. Their instincts told them the relationship was in dire trouble, and they were right.

They were not alone in their assessment. Kate shared her concerns and frustration with Marianne Faithfull. Their friendship had been cemented during Kate's time in the Priory, when Marianne had provided the sort of support only possible from somebody who has gone through a similar crisis themselves. Marianne thought Jefferson a good man; more than that, she thought him good for Kate. He was kind, loyal, thoughtful and loving. He has been painted as a dull, weak presence in her shadow, but that is unfair and inaccurate.

Many moons earlier, Ronnie Wood had come to the conclusion that very few men would stand a chance of having something permanent with Kate. Jefferson had the peculiar, quiet strength that saw him come very close.

Marianne reflected how, at a time in her life when she could have done with somebody to say, 'Stop! Enough!' there had been no such voice of reason. Now, as she saw Kate on the verge of throwing away any notion of a romantic future with Jefferson, it was she who tried, gently, to be that voice. Admittedly she may not have been the most consistent of moral mentors, but Marianne was certainly genuine in her desire to help Kate be Kate and be happy in the process.

It's hard to escape the notion that Marianne's quiet championing of Jefferson was influenced by a keen awareness of her own personal regrets, or that hers was, in part, an attempt to coax Kate away from choosing a path similar to the one she had taken many years earlier, one which had proved a profound mistake.

Kate's relationship with Jefferson bore more than a passing resemblance to Marianne's relationship with John Dunbar. He was nineteen years old and a student at Cambridge University when he met seventeen-year-old Marianne at a party. They fell in love and she fell pregnant. They married in 1965. Dunbar was neither straight-laced nor prim. He was friends with Allen Ginsberg, he took acid and he was a great facilitator. It was he who, fatefully, introduced Marianne to Rolling Stones manager Andrew Loog Oldham. But what life with him *did* offer was something more solid than the glamorous haze of which both he and Marianne were aware and to which she, to her cost, turned. The marriage lasted two years then fell apart. 'John was perfect for me,' Marianne later admitted. 'And if the Sixties hadn't thrown up so much dust, we would have stayed together. I think for both of us there was the allure of another life ... then this glamorous, dangerous figure called Mick Jagger turned up and swept me off my feet.'

Marianne's life, never mind career, nearly ended as a result of the excess and heartbreak into which her relationship with the romantic, dangerous, talented Jagger and, equally pertinantly, her relationship with heroin, plunged her. She lost custody of her child because of it all. In later years Marianne managed to establish a relationship with her son Nicholas, and John, remarkably, remained a true and loving friend. Kate herself knew John well. They'd been introduced by Keith Richards at a wedding some years earlier and Kate would go on to invite John to her thirtieth birthday party.

Marianne was wise enough to know that it's almost impossible to convince others to learn by your mistakes, rather than their own. Perhaps some patterns are doomed to be played out again and again. Certainly nobody could have anticipated just how close the parallel between Kate and Marianne's love lives would run. For Marianne there was Dunbar, a man who moved in the world of musicians, poets and writers, but was not quite of that world. With him there might have been security and certainly there was family. Then there was Jagger – a wild, seductive, talented figure in his youthful prime. For Kate there was Jefferson. And then there would be Pete Doherty.

Marianne's friendship with Kate has always been complex and close, and it has always been guided by a genuine love for Kate. As a result of their shared interest in Kate's welfare, she and Linda have always got on pretty well too.

In 2001 Marianne was cast by French director Patrice Chéreau in one of his rare English-language films *Intimacy*. She had long been an admirer of his work, and the role in *Intimacy* only came about because she had seen him in a restaurant in Paris, told him how much she had loved his film *La Reine Margot* and asked, 'Can I be in your next film?' He said, 'Yes,' and began writing a part for her that night. The film starred Kerry Fox and Mark Rylance as the central pair and the focus of the troubled notion of *Intimacy* on which the film turns. They are, to all intents and purposes, strangers who meet for sex, not in some luxurious hotel room but in the squalid shared house in which Rylance's character has lived since the demise of his marriage.

The sex scenes provoked controversy for their unflinching realism. These are not well-lit, well-toned lovers with well-thought-out lingerie and expert caresses. Tights get tangled, socks stay on, passion is killed for the application of a condom and the room is illuminated by the unforgiving glare of a naked bulb. Marianne's part is a minor one, though she approached it with all the seriousness of a leading lady undertaking a pivotal role. She was nervous. It was, she said, 'the first important part of my acting career.'

The part written for her was of a working-class woman called Betty, but Marianne's own background was exotically aristocratic. She has always made sure that everybody knows her schoolteacher mother was an Austro-Hungarian Baroness by birth, so to 'do' working class she turned to Kate, or more accurately to Kate's mother.

She explains, 'I based my character on Linda, Croydon accent and all. I had a voice coach and everything, but her character, her type, was based on Linda.' Given that Betty is essentially an unglamorous, rather loopy bag lady, this could be considered something of a back-handed compliment, but evidently Linda harboured no ill feelings and took Marianne's 'homage' to her in the spirit in which it was intended. In fact, Marianne's participation in the film inspired her to write a song that led to *Intimacy* being even more of a Moss family affair.

Intimacy was about having sex with strangers, so Marianne wrote a song called, 'Sex With Strangers'. It was released in March 2003 and Kate appeared in the frankly bizarre video that accompanied it. In a string of strange, dreamlike sequences, Kate is shown getting out of bed in what appears to be the middle of the night, driving to a remote house where she is met by a smiling Marianne, who leads her by the hand while singing that it's time 'to have sex with strangers'. It's all very odd.

As 2003 drew to a close it was clear that Kate and Jefferson's relationship was under threat from all the issues their lives were throwing up. Still, if Marianne were to give any advice, she would have to do so carefully and tread the precarious line between guiding and meddling. That Christmas presented her with ample opportunity to do so. Kate invited Marianne and her lover – her manager François – to spend Christmas with her, her mother, brother Nick, Jefferson and Lila. She had rented a cottage in the coastal town of Falmouth in Cornwall. Snug against the buffeting wind that whipped off the English

Channel, blustering up the sandy beaches and rousing the ships in the town's harbour, it was an ideal spot.

On Marianne's suggestion, Kate and Jefferson were going away for the first couple of weeks of 2004 to Jamaica. There they would be guests at Island Records' owner Chris Blackwell's GoldenEye estate. Once home to James Bond creator Ian Fleming, it's an exquisite resort a couple of hours' drive east of Montego Bay and just outside Orocabessa. Naomi Campbell owns a house nearby. Marianne had suggested the trip, thinking that some time away from the exigencies of London life might help Kate and Jefferson's ailing relationship. Kate's response was to embrace the notion with great enthusiasm, then fly Marianne and François out to join them – first class of course. It was hardly the act of a woman intent on spending anything but the bare minimum of 'alone time' with Jefferson.

The sad truth was that Jefferson had apparently lost what interest he once held for Kate. Something in Kate's feelings for Jefferson seemed to have changed with Lila's birth. She would not be the first woman to find her feelings for her partner or husband different following the birth of a child, but where some relationships are strengthened by such an event, the impact of Lila's arrival on Jefferson and Kate's romance did not seem so positive. With her birth, something ended between them. Kate had recognized from the very beginning that Jefferson would make a wonderful father but seemed to be questioning their future.

Time was running out for Jefferson and Kate, but there was one final distraction that would prolong their relationship for another few weeks. That January Kate would turn thirty and Jefferson would be there to ensure that her party was everything she had hoped for and more. The celebrations would start at lunchtime and roar on until the following morning. It would be glamorous, decadent and dark. It would be fancy dress and the theme would be taken from Kate's favourite writer, F. Scott Fitzgerald, a man whose writing she loved and whose chaotic and pathos-laden life appealed to a part of Kate that motherhood and age could not touch. The invitations went out: the date, Friday, 16 January 2004; the theme, *The Beautiful and Damned.*

16

It was a brisk January afternoon. Kate left her north London home, with James Brown by her side, and headed for lunch at the Mandarin Oriental in Knightsbridge. She was in a lemon-yellow dress and leopard-skin coat. Just back from Jamaica, her hair seemed very blonde against her honey-tanned skin. She wore sunglasses and a smile – both large. Kate was thirty years old. It was her birthday and she must have been relishing the prospect of the day ahead.

While she ate and drank with her friends, her clothes and make-up were taken to Claridges Hotel, Mayfair, and up to the Brook Street Penthouse into which she was booked. After lunch she would go there to get ready for the second of the triumvirate of birthday celebrations that day. She would run along the narrow seventh-floor corridors, darting in and out of the bedrooms where her closest female friends were staying that night and where they too were getting ready for the evening ahead. The rooms, once relegated to servants' quarters, had long since been transformed into an elegant domain for those with the wealth and the desire to house parties and guests above the footfall of the hotel's other clients.

Kate's blonde hair would be curled into a chaos of loose ringlets and her face would be heavily made up. Blooms of dark navy-blue and graphite shadow would be layered round her eyes, echoing the dark, sequinned sparkle of her long, midnight-blue party frock, cut in a deep V at the neck, scooping low over her tanned back and clinging, with all its shimmering weight, to her slender body. She would also carry a long cigarette holder, though she later chose to ditch this affectation.

All through lunch she must have fizzed with excitement. Kate, the living mannequin, loved dressing up and getting into character. She could hardly wait. That evening she would be the ultimate party girl, playing the ultimate party girl. It was Kate who had chosen the theme *The Beautiful and Damned*. The choice was inspired, in part, by a party Sadie had thrown the previous autumn, where Evelyn Waugh was the theme and to which fancy dress was, of course, compulsory. Later, as lurid details of Kate's party seeped into the public domain, they would be accompanied by a sneer of condescension. It offended a tract of intellectual snobs that Kate and her friends should dare ally themselves with such literature and high art when their own forays into the arts were deemed so terribly low. It was a blinkered and bigoted interpretation.

Kate's love of F. Scott Fitzgerald was genuine and she was every bit as acquainted with his works as many of those who poured scorn upon her – in some cases perhaps better. She knew the emptiness that lurked beneath the glamour of the worlds described, and lived by Fitzgerald and his wife Zelda. Of course it was precarious and could be as bleak as it was glamorous, but it could also be fun, and compellingly so. Trace the outlines and transpose it several decades and Kate's own world was drawn along similar lines: excess, wealth, creativity and folly combined to generate a life that was at once thrilling, tiresome and exquisitely insecure, propped up by some profoundly shallow friendships, yet deeply felt.

On the evening of her birthday, Kate modelled herself on Gloria Patch, the beautiful, spoilt creature who marries Anthony Patch in F. Scott Fitzgerald's book. Patch is a young man who has put his life on hold, filling it with nothing as he marks time, waiting to come into his inheritance. He anticipates his grandfather's death as the event that will sound the starting pistol on his own life. Until then, Patch drinks, dances, fritters away his allowance and talks and thinks about the book he will never write. Physically he is described as 'too thin but his shoulders had widened and his brunette face had lost the frightened look of his freshman year. His friends declared that they had never seen his hair rumpled. His nose was too sharp; his mouth was one of those unfortunate mirrors of mood inclined to droop perceptibly in moments of unhappiness, but his blue eyes were charming . . . he was yet, here and there, considered handsome . . .'

Before he meets Gloria he hears about her from her from her mother: 'Gloria goes, goes, goes . . . She dances all afternoon and all night, until I think she's going to wear herself to a shadow. Her father is very worried about her.' Gloria smokes heavily, sunbathes – a new craze at the time – flirts and dances. She is exquisitely beautiful. When she and Patch first meet, Fitzgerald wrote, 'He saw at length that her eyes were grey, very level and cool, and when they rested upon him he understood . . . she was very young and very old. She talked always about herself as a very charming child might talk, and her comments on her tastes and distastes were unaffected and spontaneous.'

It doesn't require much of a leap of imagination to see how Kate might cast herself and Jefferson as this couple for the sake of an evening's fun . . . however doomed the parallel if followed to its logical conclusion.

Kate's party had been a feat of organization planned by

Fran Cutler, with Jefferson's assistance and the kindness of friends Agent Provocateur co-owner Serena Rees and photographer and artist Sam Taylor-Wood and her husband Jay Jopling. By late afternoon, Kate was at Claridges preening, preparing and giggling upstairs with a cluster of friends that included Naomi, Davinia, Sadie and Samantha Morton. As afternoon gave way to evening, Marianne Faithfull squeezed into the crowded hotel bar six storeys below. She was jostled by the after-work crowd of drinkers as she laid claim to a bar stool and rasped her order: a gin and tonic. Confusion spread over her and the barman as she fumbled in her clutch bag, tipped out a jangle of Jamaican currency and attempted to pay for her drink with it. She squinted at the alien coins in her hand, evidently aware that something wasn't quite right but unable to work out where her error lay. 'God I'm jet-lagged,' she wailed as her mistake was explained. Pointing at a coin she added, 'I'm just back from there, you see.' Moments later Marianne was rescued by an emissary from the seventh floor, who met her with the exclamation, '*There* you are. They're all waiting upstairs.'

A reception was being held upstairs in Kate's suite, but it would soon be time to leave and head over to Serena Rees and Sam Taylor-Wood's adjacent houses in Marylebone, where Act II of the birthday party would be played out. At half past nine a frisson of excitement shimmered through Claridges grand hall. Kate, her girlfriends and Jefferson were on the move. Jefferson took the lead, dressed in a slick white suit, its drainpipe trousers accentuating his slimness. He stood protectively in front of Kate as she and her friends and PA Fiona readied themselves for the inevitable explosion of flashbulbs with which their exit would be met. Sadie Frost wore a vermillion-red flapper dress and clung to Jackson Scott, whose cadaverous appeal was accentuated by the dark pinstripe suit and low-buttoned dress shirt he had chosen to wear for the evening. Kate eyed Jefferson's face and waited for his assurance that the car had pulled up at the front of the building. He spoke into his mobile phone. She held his free hand – as much an act of reflex as affection. It was as close as they would be all evening.

Serena Rees's and Sam Taylor-Wood's homes had been given over to the party girl and her party theme: one was decorated in keeping with 'The Beautiful', the other, 'The Damned'. Bouncers manned the bottom of the four steps up to the front door where a smartly dressed girl stood, clipboard in hand, checking off names against the guest list as people arrived. A grand piano placed at the foot of the elegant curve of the stairs in Serena's grand entrance hall became the focus for some of the impromptu entertainment as the evening wore on. Michael Howells, a production designer and art director who has worked on films such as *Bright Young Things*, provided sets for Galliano and Dior catwalk shows and masterminded parties for Jacob Rothschild and Jimmy Goldsmith, was the man responsible for 'dressing' the houses that evening. Rooms were different colours and an extravagant fantasy was created in each. One was papered with orange flowers and filled with piles of tambourines, another was all in red. The idea was to spin an overwhelming profusion of fabulous colour and intoxicating perfume. Jewel-coloured flowers were wreathed around the banister, scantily clad waiters wove through the guests with silver trays bearing champagne, Cosmopolitan cocktails and shots. There were cigarette girls, too, a reminiscence of a peculiarly smoggy bygone notion of glamour in which starlets and Hollywood heroes' kisses were preceded by plumes of cigarette smoke.

Upstairs a room had been blacked out and given over to dancing. There was a DJ in the corner, and at the beginning of the evening Bella Freud could be found dancing alone and apparently perfectly happy with that state of affairs. Another room had been turned into a bar. The walls of this floor, indeed of most of the house, were hung with paintings and photographs in colour and black and white, most of them the sort of retro, boudoir images associated with Agent Provocateur and all of them sexually graphic. Most parties start with the sort of lull that hosts hope will dissipate as the venue fills, and this evening was no different. But by the time Kate arrived at ten o'clock the hall was buzzing with chatter and jazz.

A heavily pregnant Gwyneth Paltrow was there with her husband, Coldplay lead singer Chris Martin. Gwyneth looked understandably tired and anxious to leave, no easy feat given the frenzy of photographers camped at the front of the Marylebone houses. Each time the front doors opened into the hall, guests were treated to a blitzkrieg of flashbulbs. So when Chris and Gwyneth decided to make a move, they chose to do so out the back door. It made little difference. Chris walked ahead of his wife, having checked that their black Range Rover was there and waiting, but a handful of paparazzi had spotted movement. Gwyneth was wrong-footed as a flash went off and she stumbled and looked stressed and anxious. It was too much for her husband, who lunged forward, scuffling in an attempt to separate the offending photographer from his camera.

Inside, the party continued oblivious to the commotion. Sarah (Doukas) was there, naturally, as was her brother Simon. Jools Holland was there with his wife and was a charming addition to the throng, happy to play the piano while Kate sang and laughed her way through George Gershwin's 'Summertime', and later as Marianne Faithfull performed the Cole Porter classic 'I Get a Kick Out of You', replacing the 'you' of the lyrics with 'Kate'. Ronnie, Jo and Leah Wood were there, Kate's mother Linda and brother Nick, and actor Rhys Ifans, dressed in cream blazer, boater hat and neckerchief, resembling nothing so much as an elegantly dishevelled scarecrow.

Elsewhere the guest list reflected the layers of Kate's personality and interests, layers that were flattened out in the stories that later seeped out, focusing only on the most vacuous end of the celebrity spectrum represented that evening. There were writers, musicians and artists, among them dancer Michael Clark, a friend Kate had met through her many artist friends and a man whose life story had been one of damned beauty and redemption. One of the most luminous dancers of his generation, Clark nearly lost everything to heroin addiction, but was saved by love, quitting London and spending four years rehabilitating back in his mother's care in his native Aberdeen. Kate loved his talent and the dark glamour of his story, and she became patron of his dance company, the Michael Clark Company. She told Michael that she wanted to dance with him, and her wish was granted, not that evening, but some months later when they danced together at an Alexander McQueen fashion event.

There was also a cake, of course – a pyramid of profiteroles, dipped and glistening with honey, toasted almonds and cream rose petals sprinkled over and stuck in its gloss. Kate blew out the candles as her guests applauded, but for much of the party they were not treated to her presence. Instead, Kate spent most of the party at the top of the house, above the civilized milling around on the ground floor and the laughter and dancing on the first floor, tucked away in the bedrooms of the top floor with her closest friends.

The halls and bars of Claridges were all but deserted by the time Kate and her closest friends returned to the hotel for the third and final act. It was half past two. Night cleaners quietly moved through the hotel, discreetly cleaning around the guests who lingered on in the lounge area. Then they arrived, the privileged few invited back to carry on partying in Kate's penthouse suite. Ronnie Wood was one of the first to burst through the doors with wife Jo and daughter Leah by his side. His unmistakable voice resounded round the marble hall: 'We're in fucking Claridges!' before a night porter solicitously guided the trio towards a lift to the seventh floor.

The geography of Claridge's seventh floor is different from every other level as it's the only one that was never intended to be public. Where elsewhere the halls are wide and dotted with hotel-room doors, the seventh-floor corridors are narrow and blank with tight little staircases running up and off into penthouse suites and neat little corridors of rooms, all of which are exquisite. By the time Kate made it back to Claridges there was something of a logjam at the foot of the seventh-floor stairs to her suite. Security men struggled to name-check the shambles of high-spirited guests, eager to carry on partying and impatient at this third security check – nobody could make it through the front door of the hotel and beyond the foyer without having gone through a similar process. Lifts to the seventh floor were manned by porters. Annie Nightingale leaned on a radiator. 'What did you do for Christmas?' some-one asked her. 'Magic Mushrooms. And you?' she deadpanned as she waited her turn at the foot of the final staircase, along with Anita Pallenberg and Marianne Faithfull. Others were less patient, and on one surge upstairs more than one uninvited guest would be carried up and into the inner sanctum.

At the top of the stairs, guests shuffled in to hand over coats and bags, dumped with little ceremony in the cubby hole that had been turned into a cloakroom-cum-bar to the right of the suite's main room. At the very far side of the room, in which no more than forty people gathered, a door stood open to reveal a four-poster bed. As the night wore on, people sprawled and couples rolled around on it, more in fun than serious sexual endeavour. Janet Street-Porter, in a short psychedelic minidress and lurid purple tights, joined in only to roll off as quickly as she had rolled on, landing in a heap on the floor, her legs kicking, helpless with giggles, while Kate screamed with delight, 'Janet Street-Porter's on the fucking floor! Janet's my intellectual friend. You're such a fucking intellectual!'

Queues for the suite's bathrooms were long, and in one at least any hope of privacy had to be abandoned at the door. It was full of people, drunk, sitting on the floor, perched on the sanitary wear, smoking, talking and reluctant to move on or out for anyone other than Kate. Guests chatted in the elegant main drawing room, from Patrick Cox to Marco Pierre White, Jay Joplin to Rhys Ifans, Linda to Nick and, fleetingly, Kate. Ronnie Wood was occupying a sofa pushed up against the back wall, affording him a clear view of the room in full swing. His wife and daughter sat next to him. To his right a heavy drape partially concealed the door to the second of the suite's two bedrooms. This one remained resolutely shut, save for the odd coming and going over the evening. Jefferson, Kate, Sadie and Jackson, Davinia and Ronnie were among the guests to spend time within those four walls. At one point the door opened to reveal Sadie, her dress riding high about her thighs and drooping precariously at her shoulders, straddling Jackson as he lay back on the bed. Later a dark-haired female guest swung wildly around the door and asked, 'Does anyone have any condoms?' before disappearing back inside, her request unanswered.

Kate had changed out of her long sequined gown soon after returning to the hotel suite. She rocketed across the room barefoot, her hair a bundle of curls, her dress a tiny corn-flower-blue flutter of material that revealed a tanned back and limbs. She looked impossibly delicate against the grandly dressed guests around which she moved and danced. Jay Joplin urged guests to go outside onto the roof terrace that ran almost the length of the suite; to take their drinks and head out into the cool morning air; to take in the London skyline and the view across to where the crescent moon hung over the illuminated orb of the London Eye. There were few who showed much interest, and the later it got, the messier the party became.

Naomi Campbell, her hair slicked into pin curls, decorated with an ostrich feather headband and wearing a tiny peach flapper dress, looked like an exotic bird, somehow inhumanly beautiful until she announced in her odd Streatham-meets-LA drawl that she was going to bed before she 'fucking died of hunger'. A member of the hotel staff was ejected with good humour having ditched serving champagne in favour of drink-ing it and mingling with the guests. Stella McCartney and her sister Mary argued as only siblings can, facing each other in a bathroom, their voices pitched in anger as inhibitions dis-solved with alcohol and the lateness of the hour.

Jefferson – well-brought-up, middle-class Jefferson – made sure guests had drinks, fetched vodka for Kate and their friends and, at moments, seemed so suddenly distant from the spin-ning, giggling birthday girl that it was heartbreaking to watch.

In the days that followed, newspapers and magazines would

make much of this party – of the way it rolled on until dawn, of the tangled limbs of guests on the beds, of the substances consumed behind closed doors, of the disarray of the departing guests in stark contrast to the glamour and poise with which they'd arrived. Sadie Frost was one such victim of the paparazzi at the hotel door as she emerged, stumbling and bleary-eyed, into the morning air, the dress that had struggled to remain decent for much of the evening promptly abandoned the fight and exposed her breast to the waiting photographers.

Three years later, *Harper's Bazaar* would rate Kate's thirtieth birthday number three in its top ten of scandalous parties of the past fifty years. The chart described the general vibe as, 'The fall of Babylon, Sodom and Gomorrah, the last days of Rome, etc., etc.'

True, the events of that evening and early morning would cause teacups to rattle on saucers across Middle England, but much would be ignored about the night's events too, perhaps most importantly the generosity and isolation of Kate herself. Truth be told, her reality was uncomfortably close to that of glorious Gloria Patch: she was the centre of attention, beautiful, fizzing with energy, spoilt and demanding, childish and old and supposedly so terribly, totally loved. Yet there were many among the group of intimates that she could not, and did not, know. In one moment of pure Croydon, she yanked at the collar of a dark-haired young man in the bathroom, enquiring, 'Oi, do I know you, darlin'?' before ejecting him from the room but not the party.

At the time that this party was thrown, the received wisdom seemed to be that this would be Kate's ultimate party: the last hurrah; the final big bash; the bookend to a frantic whirling lifestyle that had its opposite number in her twenty-first in the Viper Room. Back then Johnny Depp and Michael Hutchence had sung 'Gloria' to her. Back then she had been closer in age to Gloria Patch as she was in the opening pages of the book. Not any more, though, Kate was thirty years old. She was a mother. She was with kind, sensible Jefferson. She would settle down any time now. That was certainly the general assumption of how her life *should* go, but the reality so visible that night was radically different.

That 'ultimate' party was devoured by others with as much, if not more, gusto than it was by Kate herself. Kate's largesse was boundless. Guests could and did have whatever, and in some cases whomever, they wanted. But the distance between Kate and Jefferson could not have been more evident in the stiff body language and absence of intimacy between them. People remarked that Kate treated Jefferson as a butler rather than a lover, but it was not so straightforward. When a relationship is in tatters in private, often the only thing left propping it up is a nod to propriety in public. Kate was not rude to Jefferson that night, she was civil – a far more devastating stance. That civility, admittedly only a notch on the dial away from hostility, was so icily out of kilter with the tenor of the rest of the evening that neither could have failed to find it a strain.

Among the many extravagant birthday gifts Kate received that year, Jefferson had bought and named a star after her, and given her a telescope with which to view it. It was a tongue-in-cheek thing to do. Certainly there was nothing on earth that he could buy her that she couldn't buy herself many times over or had not already been given. But the truth was that he could have given her the moon and it wouldn't have made any difference. Their romance was over. Kate had accepted that. Now it was Jefferson's turn to do likewise.

He made arrangements to move his belongings out of Kate's

London home and into a flat that he had rented nearby, maybe ostensibly as an office. In reality no one would have raised an eyebrow if it had always been earmarked as a sort of Plan B, a fall-back position, a home near Kate and his daughter should the romance prove beyond resuscitation.

That same month, their lease on Walnut Tree Cottage came to an end and was not renewed, but their connection with the place was not so neatly severed. Sir Rowland and Lady Isa Whitehead got access to their much-loved cottage on 1 February 2004, Lady Isa's birthday as it happened. Early on in Kate and Jefferson's tenancy there had been perhaps a hint that they might not be the ideal tenants of Sir Rowland's early assessment.

In December 2002, when Kate and Jefferson had gone to Thailand, they had forgotten to fill the oil tank, a disastrous turn of events that could be explained away as oversight and accident – certainly there was no hint of wanton destruction. But while they were away there was a cold snap and the pipes burst. 'Our poor little cottage flooded,' Sir Rowland later recalled in dismay. At the time his description was rather more dramatic. The ceiling in the living room had collapsed and water was cascading 'like Niagara Falls'. Kate brought in workmen to have the cottage dried out, rewired and redecorated, but declined to replace the furniture that was damaged and other items destroyed by the flood.

After some quibbling over what was and was not covered by Sir Rowland and Lady Whitehead's household insurance, an out-of-court settlement was reached. It had all been rather a bore, perhaps, but there was no hint of malice. Accidents, Sir Rowland thought with admirable equanimity, do happen after all. Certainly none of this earlier experience could have prepared the couple for the scene of utter devastation that met them when they entered Walnut Tree Cottage once more. Lady Isa walked from room to room and wept. 'Everything was so demeaned, so kicked about,' she said.

The chandelier in the dining room had been pulled from the ceiling and dumped in the hall with a football. Bed heads were broken, mirrors taken from the wall and left face up on tables, china was broken, lampshades burned, chairs soiled and windows smashed, plasterwork was ruined, the place was filthy with bedclothes so dirty that Lady Isa would not touch them, the walls of the house seemed covered with a layer of sweet, cloying scent. In all they were given an estimate of £10,000 to return the cottage to some semblance of its former condition. One year on, the couple were still embroiled in legal correspondence and dispute with Kate's representatives. It was a situation they found 'exasperating', but one ultimately settled out of court.

Some things were, of course, irreplaceable. An Aboriginal boomerang, bought by Sir Rowland's great-grandfather James Whitehead in 1889 during his travels as Lord Mayor of London, was gone forever – tossed away perhaps in the assumption that it would chop its way back through the air. It did not. Among the irritations for the couple was the fact that Kate had had the telephone number for the cottage changed and made ex-directory. Sir Rowland went to the highest authority at BT to have his number returned. The final sheet of the folder of correspondence over this matter is a letter from Sir Rowland's old friend, BT chairman Sir Christopher Bland. A handwritten note at the bottom of the official letter reads, 'Beware the supermodel.'

When life is lived fast and loose, things are bound to get

broken and lost: relationships, objects, hopes, direction. It would take a phenomenal act of will to avoid that.

Nothing is designed to bring a celebrity back down to earth with a bump so much as being handed a name badge on arrival at an event. In March, Kate found just such a badge pinned to her rabbit-fur shrug when she attended Buckingham Palace's first all-women lunch. The event was intended to mark International Women's Day and was hosted by the Queen. One hundred and eight-five women were invited, including politicians, artists, models, clergy, military and lawyers. There was Cherie Blair, Zadie Smith, Heather McCartney, Baroness Margaret Thatcher, J.K. Rowling, Kate Adie, Commander Cressida Dick (head of Metropolitan Police's Operation Trident), Dr Nancy Lane, a researcher in cellular and neurobiology, restaurateur Ruth Rogers, *Vogue* Editor Alexandra Schulman, Professor Jocelyn Bell Burnell, who had discovered a new type of star (the pulsar), Vivienne Westwood, Twiggy . . . the list went on and on. And among all these remarkable women of intellect, culture, art and beyond, the one unifying factor was that each and every one had agonized over what on earth to wear.

Kate was no different, and nor was her friend and fellow invitee Sam Taylor-Wood. Sam telephoned Kate on the morning of the lunch and asked her to come over with a suitcase of clothes. Sam had planned to wear something by Alexander McQueen, but decided it was 'too tits and bum' for the palace. In the end she wore a silver satin Chanel dress and black Chanel jacket, both lent to her by Kate – though, horror of horrors, Jemima Khan turned up in the same jacket. Their departure was delayed when Sam confessed that she had forgotten her knickers. Kate told her she could not go to Buckingham Palace without them. Kate wore a vintage blue tea dress, which turned out to be exactly the same shade of blue as the Queen's dress that day, and completed her regal ensemble with a white rabbit fur shrug. They ate salmon and monkfish casserole, loin of lamb and passion fruit cheesecake, they drank wine and gin and tonics and marvelled at the fact that they had been invited to such an event.

Being there that day must have been both thrilling and disconcerting for Kate. It wasn't hard to see the achievements of some of the women who gathered that day – among them were women who had made key scientific discoveries, championed human rights, opened people's eyes to injustices or opportunities and established businesses. But how could Kate's contribution to this great amorphous mass of women achievers be quantified? In money? In exposure? In cultural influence? Certainly she could be judged deserving on all such scales. But when the foundation of your success is how you look then, regardless of the part played by talent and the reassurance found in money and adulation, the root of your success is the very definition of superficial. It is, surely, hard to reconcile that with feeling in any way deserving.

None of that would have mattered were it not for one simple fact: Kate showed every sign of *wanting* to feel deserving. She needed to be more than 'just' a model – a career with which she had long had a love/hate/boredom relationship. It is the recurrent theme of her working life, the snag in the fabric of her reality. And it is perhaps why a sense of real satisfaction, of feeling complete and fulfilled, continued to elude her when she sought it in romance.

Kate was free to date openly once more. She and Jefferson were no longer together and the couple had negotiated the prickly subject of a routine of care for Lila. Both Kate's mother and Jefferson's parents were keen to be involved grandparents and willing to help as much as needs be. Kate had a full-time nanny, and Lila and her nanny would continue to live with her. There was never any question that Jefferson would be there for his daughter. As he and Kate had never married, he could not be compelled to stick around, but he wanted to. The flipside of course was that if Jefferson's relationship with Kate soured, she would hold the ultimate trump card: access to Lila. To their credit, however they might squabble, like any other parents, over what was best for their daughter, the point was always just that: what was *best* for Lila. It was a motivation to which they would stay true in the years ahead, when Kate's life took a dark turn.

In the spring of 2004 Kate reportedly embarked on a brief romance with actor Daniel Craig. 'Friends' spoke of how desperately in love they were and how marriage to the quietly rugged Craig was a real possibility, even though he had little interest in being cool and, heaven forfend, wore corduroy trousers. It was all so much breathless chatter and within four months the couple had split. When Kate and Craig called it a day, she was oblivious to the existence of the next most significant man in her life, though he was already known to some of her close friends and had already begun to edge into the public consciousness. For Kate, meeting Pete Doherty was only a handful of months away. Had he been less erratic in his habits and more reliable in turning up for social events, they might well have met sooner. Many of Kate's friends, and family members, would be very relieved that they did not.

The world around Kate had changed since she had first em-barked on life as a model. Relationships had been made, broken and made once more. Children had been born. Marriages had ended. Fortunes had been made. Scandals ridden out. The Britpop culture with which she and her peers had risen had bubbled up from the underground and was now so mainstream it was all but over. As Noel Gallagher put it, 'the squares' had got into his music. It had made Oasis a fortune – in one week alone, he once boasted, the band's record sales made Noel a million four times over – but it had changed something exciting into something mainstream and that left a gap in the market. The wild, exciting days had been Liam and Patsy and Noel and Meg, living it up on Primrose Hill in a storm of cocaine, cigarettes and alcohol. It was thrilling, but it was a thing of the past.

Kate had been 'bang into' that scene, but she, more than anyone perhaps, was always on the lookout for the next big thing. The next big thing in music came in the form of John Hassall, Gary Powell, Carl Barat, Pete Doherty and their band The Libertines. The Britpop scene had become so successful, with its protagonists moving from the clubs of Manchester to mansions in the Home Counties, that music had to be reinvented if it was to have any relevance to the next generation of fans. What emerged in place of that now overblown scene was far more gritty and dangerous and it would appeal to Kate's hunger for sensation and excitement and the part of her that was turned on by what she regarded as passion and talent in others.

Noel Gallagher perhaps best summed up the nature of the new scene that began bubbling up in the early 2000s and boiled over into Kate's world at the beginning of 2005. 'There was a void after Oasis,' he said. 'The Oasis generation kind of moved on and the new one popped up and they were even more fucking mental than we were. Our kind of going out – cigarettes and alcohol, a bit of fucking coke, some pills and fucking having it till seven o'clock in the morning – turned into heroin and crack and self-harm.'

The Libertines had been signed to Rough Trade record label in December 2001 and Carl and Pete rented a flat together in Bethnal Green. They called it The Albion Rooms and gave impromptu gigs there, much to the neighbours' increasing annoyance. Pearl Lowe and Danny Goffey went to see them play one night in Notting Hill in 2002. They hung out with them afterwards and Pete and Carl were so charming, so spirited and so evidently talented that they rapidly became close. At the beginning of 2004, The Libertines were voted Best New Band at the NME Awards for their album, recorded the previous year. It saw them take another step towards Kate, as her friend Mick Jones, former guitarist and singer with The Clash, was called in to record and produce their first album, *Up the Bracket*. They did so at the RAK studios in St John's Wood, just round the corner from Kate. It was Doherty's working relationship with Mick Jones that endured and which would, ultimately, lead him to Kate.

By the time she first caught sight of the doe-eyed, boyishly skinny figure of Pete Doherty, The Libertines had imploded and Doherty's reputation had acquired the dark lustre of a celebrated, troubled youth. His friendship with Barat did not survive the impact of his drug-riddled excesses and Barat had gone his own way, establishing another band, Dirty Pretty Things, while Doherty started Babyshambles.

Draw up a list of habits and character traits that no mother would want to find in her daughter's boyfriend and Doherty would tick every box. No amount of charm, intelligence and native talent would cancel out the negatives. Pete was five years younger than Kate. By the time she met him, he had fathered an eighteen-month-old son, Astile – born to Lisa Moorish, former flatmate of Meg Mathews and mother to a child by Liam Gallagher. He had spent four weeks of a six-month sentence in prison for burglary. He was addicted to heroin, with three failed attempts at rehabilitation to his name. His drug use made his behaviour unpredictable and his moods violently changeable. He had little to recommend him as a partner. She fell for him instantly.

17

There had been a moment, somewhere between Lila's conception and birth, when it looked as though Kate might have found a certain permanence and stability in her life. While she danced her way through her thirtieth birthday there were still some close to her who were inclined to look at Jefferson and Lila and conclude that, save for the occasional wild day and night, that time of stability was glimmering on the horizon.

Twelve months on it was pretty clear that any such light had been a false dawn. Life, fashion, trends . . . they may be cyclical but as 2004 gave way to 2005, it was becoming clear that part of Kate's gift – and curse – was that she wasn't part of those shifting loops; they revolved around her. Increasingly, the only permanent thing about Kate's world was her centrality to it. Some of those around about her would find that, when it came to their place in Kate's affections, the most solid ground could turn to quicksand in a heartbeat. It made being with Kate a peculiarly thrilling and stressful experience: a disconcerting mixture of the familial and the almost feral.

On 18 November, Kate completed on the purchase of her long-dreamed-of country house. A romantic rambling farmhouse, built in Cotswold stone, it came complete with water rights for the animal troughs that ran along the side of a separate barn. Kate paid over £2 million for it, taking occupation the following month, once all the requisite paperwork was in place.

She filled the house with her trademark mixture of country kitchen gentility – Wedgwood crockery, hand-painted egg cups and the like – and rock'n'roll artwork and objets: candlesticks shaped like upturned revolvers, prints of Sid Vicious and, above the living-room mantelpiece, a work by American poet and artist Rene Ricard, in which the words 'in the half-life of a drug' are scrawled in yellow paint across a rural scene straight out of Constable and mounted in a heavy gilt frame. Christmas 2004 was spent here with Jefferson and Lila. It was probably the first Christmas of which Lila was likely to have any awareness or recollection, and it mattered to both her parents that they should spend it as a family.

New Year was a different story; this time Jefferson was not invited. Kate flew to Edinburgh. From there she drove south for an hour or so to the Borders town of Innerleithen, Peebleshire, and the secluded comfort of Glen House, where she would see in 2005 with a large group of friends. The house may have been stuck in 5,000 acres of Scottish landscape but it was not so remote as to be off the fashion map – far from it. Glen House, with all its 19th-century castellated grandeur, is home to the Tennant family, and it was here that model Stella Tennant spent many summers and, long before Kate and co. descended on it, Mario Testino was sent there by Burberry to shoot a heavily pregnant Stella for one of their campaigns. The place had literary heritage too. Oscar Wilde was among the more illustrious of the Tennant family's guests over the years.

Kate arrived to a rousing welcome from the friends already gathered. Lila was there, excitable and happy, as was her nanny. Lila was not the only child present; several of the group –

which included Davinia, Annabel Nielson, Bobby Gillespie and Katy England, Pearl Lowe and Danny Goffey, Mick Jones and his wife Miranda, James Brown and Rhys Ifans – had brought their offspring (and nannies, of course). They drank, smoked, played parlour games, indulged themselves, argued, sang and generally did whatever the hell they wanted as privileged members of Kate's court. And why not?

They had a whale of a time, with Kate on energetic and playful form, surrounded by a cluster of people she genuinely liked and trusted. But however enjoyable their time in the castle, shut away from 'real' life, one inescapable fact remained. Kate was alone. She knew the adolescent thrill of having a crush and who would have blamed her for wanting that again? Who could blame her for needing somebody to challenge and excite her?

Being one of the most beautiful and desirable women in the world had undoubtedly also made her one of the least approachable as far as many men were concerned. And the Kate Moss who appeared on billboards and advertising campaigns across the globe was a 2D imagining of the real girl/woman who lounged around in her Scottish castle, playing the chatelaine with teenage enthusiasm and wishing to meet her Prince Charming – or some punk version of him. She was used to getting what she wanted, but as 2004 came to a close, it seemed she was still waiting for the heart-thumping exhilaration of lust at first sight. So she did what any girl would do in her position: she let her friends suggest a likely lad. The name that popped up was certainly not one her friends met with universal approval.

Pete was already on Kate's radar – after all, their worlds and her interest in music had already overlapped – but so far he has only registered a blip on the outer fringes. In December

Babyshambles had been in the line-up alongside Ronnie Wood and the Charlatans at a charity gig at Shepherd's Bush Empire. It was something of a family affair for the Woods – Jo, Leah and youngest son Tyrone were all there – and Kate, Samantha (Morton), Sadie, Fran Cutler, Davinia . . . the whole gang turned up to cheer Ronnie on. Kate was taken by the rawness of the aptly named Babyshambles even then, but probably hadn't considered him a real romantic prospect. Maybe his name was mentioned at that New Year house party and she started to think again.

When they got back to London, in the first week of the New Year, Mick Jones was due back in the studio to continue working with Pete Doherty and Babyshambles. Kate was invited along to watch them perform, meet the band and see in full flow this young, exciting man who was searing through the music industry with such heat. When Doherty played, he did so as though it was the last hour of his life. It was death or glory. Kate had her hit.

They spoke briefly on that first day. Doherty was lightly witty and engaging, but he certainly didn't appear overwhelmed or even particularly excited by the presence of a supermodel in his recording studio. That degree of nonchalance – one that was later enhanced to the point of rudeness by the cocoon of drugs that left him untouched by and uninterested in reality – appealed to Kate. In common with many famous faces, she probably wasn't immune to the uncertainty as to whether somebody was interested in her for being 'Kate Moss' or for being Kate. Kate and Pete saw each other again a couple of times before the event at which their relationship was consummated, but it was already clear to her friends that Kate was smitten.

She was girlish and giggly in his presence. Nervously she

asked her friends to bring Pete over to where she sat one night when she spotted him across the crowded bar at Electric House, the private members' club that's part of the Soho House Group. Some might interpret her actions as a high-handed summoning, but possibly the opposite was true. She may have been simply uncertain of his response and that made her reluctant to approach him herself. Still, she wasn't backward in coming forward when she insisted that Doherty be part of the 'super-group' playing at her thirty-first birthday party that year.

Nobody in Doherty's circle, or from the very early days Kate, was under any illusion about his drug use, though it would be one thing *knowing* about it and quite another *living* with it. Pete had progressed from smoking to injecting heroin the previous year, but Kate had yet to witness the results as his family had done only days before she met him, when he had suffered the agonies of withdrawal over Christmas.

He had spent the festive season with his family in Dorset – having been posted all over the world, his army major father, Peter, and mother, Jackie (a nurse), had been back in Britain for four months. He has two sisters, Emily and Amy Jo, and for all of them that Christmas, Pete's suffering was as difficult to witness as his addiction was to comprehend. He was shaking, sweating, unable to stand, needing to use the bathroom often and gripped by appalling cramps. He was so ill that he couldn't go to church with his family on Christmas Day as they had always done. After five painful days his parents drove him back to London. He had gigs to play, appointments to keep and an album to begin. 'Straight' Pete was always full of the best intentions.

On the day that Pete was due to travel to Kate's house in the country – the location of her birthday party that year – he moved into a newly built apartment in London with the help of his parents. For all his rock'n'roll lifestyle, he was the son of two caring middle-class parents, who were both beside themselves with worry at the path their son's life was evidently taking. He was in good spirits, looking forward no doubt to the night ahead. Peter and Jackie Doherty left similarly buoyant. They would return the following week with kitchen utensils, tea towels, books and so on, but by then Pete's life would have lurched into a different realm. Suddenly he would be one half of a very famous couple indeed, and he and Kate would have embarked on a violent, passionate and destructive affair.

The theme for Kate's thirty-first birthday was taken from the Rolling Stones film *Rock and Roll Circus*. The film was of an event put together by the Stones on 11 December 1968, though it wasn't released until 1996. The original *Rock and Roll Circus* consisted of two concerts on a circus stage, and Kate's thirty-first would bring back memories for more than one guest. Back in 1968, as well as a gig by the Stones, there was Eric Clapton, The Who, Taj Mahal, Marianne Faithfull and Jethro Tull. John Lennon and Yoko Ono performed as part of a supergroup called The Dirty Mac, along with Eric Clapton, Mitch Mitchell – the drummer from The Jimi Hendrix Experience – and Keith Richards. Close to four decades on, Kate recreated the dark carnival vibe.

Posters in the style of the Stones's original artwork, heralding the presence of the 'Rock and Roll Circus' were hung on the barn walls. Inside a circus stage had been erected and the rafters draped with red, white and black reels of fabric, giving the impression of a vast big top. A glitter ball hung in the centre of the ceiling, bathing the barn in myriad reflections of light. Kate had her own supergroup, though they had very nearly split up following an argument in rehearsals before their one and only performance. The group included Paul Simonon and Mick Jones of The Clash, performing together again for the first time in fifteen years, with vocals from Bobby Gillespie and Pete Doherty.

Glaswegian Bobby had known Kate many years. He was very much in love with his girlfriend Katy England and would marry her two years later, but as with many of the men in Kate's life, she inspired a protective instinct in him. For all his wildness and rock-star habits, Bobby didn't appear impressed by this latest addition to Kate's circle, or the extent to which she was so obviously taken by him. Still, when the night arrived, the band played without incident. The guests had started arriving early in the evening, and once again the night would be split into several all but separate parties, though this time the lines were drawn according to stamina and proclivities rather than geographic location.

In a decidedly polite and pragmatic gesture, Kate had invited several of her neighbours to the evening, to which fancy dress was compulsory. So local farmers and well-heeled villagers found themselves mingling in the living area and kitchen of Kate's country home with urban guests such as Jay Jopling, Sam Taylor-Wood and the like. Kate's mother and brother were there, James Brown, Samantha Morton, Jefferson, Travis singer Fran Healy, Sadie and Jackson Scott, REM singer Michael Stipe, whom Kate had met two years previously at a party for Jefferson's magazine *Dazed & Confused*. Marianne Faithfull was there, of course, suffering no doubt from a distinct sense of déjà vu, as was Anita Pallenberg. It was all the old gang and a few new additions.

As ringmaster of the evening, Kate wore a gold tailcoat and top hat. She sang with Trish Simonon (Paul's glamorous then-wife) and Pearl Lowe, and James Brown took to the stage for a rousing version of 'Leader of the Pack', sung, of course, in

Kate's honour. As the evening wore on, three distinct 'sets' were established. In the barn were the guests who wanted to dance, whoop and holler while Shane MacGowan of The Pogues DJed. Downstairs in the living areas of the house there was a slightly quieter, though no less enjoyable vibe, as music was confined to the background and people drank, smoke and chatted amiably. Upstairs in the bedrooms, however, the scene was altogether more hardcore.

In such a large rambling house it was quite possible for guests in one section not to be aware of what was going on in another. Lila was tucked up safely in bed, her nanny on hand, away from where Pete was relapsing, along with a small group of friends. Earlier he had given Kate her birthday present, the lyrics to his song 'What Katie Did', handwritten and framed. The song was not about Kate but the girlfriend from whom Pete had recently separated, Katie Moriarty, but it didn't seem to matter. By the end of the evening Pete and Kate were very much together. There was little doubt in anybody's mind that they were now a couple. The party rumbled on until dawn, when some guests drifted away. The majority had, of course, left many hours earlier, braving the explosion of paparazzi flashbulbs from the cars camped at the gates at the end of the farm's long driveway. Others stayed on as the birthday girl's big day turned, with some predictability, into two or three days.

It was not long before Kate and Pete's relationship fell, publicly at least, into the pattern it was to follow for close to three years. It was a pattern that would alarm Kate's family and many of her friends though, revealingly, few would have the gumption to voice their concerns publicly. Kate wasn't ignorant of Pete's obvious failings, but in the classic mantra of the put-upon female – a role into which few would expect Kate to fall – she tolerated a great deal 'because she loved him'.

And so the routine began: Pete would appear splashed across the redtops in some drug-related tale of compromise or impropriety and hot on its heels would come word that Kate was 'having second thoughts', 'issuing ultimatums' and so on. Yet for all the speculation – and there was plenty of it – there was never any physical evidence of Kate's supposed uncertainty. She had fallen for Pete, and for a long, long time he could do no wrong – no matter how much wrong he did.

Barely two weeks after their relationship began, on 30 January, pictures of Pete chasing the dragon were published in a Sunday tabloid newspaper. Kate was in New York working when the photographs appeared. She was back, though not present, three days later when Pete was arrested and charged with robbery and blackmailing the man who had taken and sold the pictures – documentary-maker Max Carlish – at the Rookery Hotel in Islington. Carlish was reportedly taken to hospital with two black eyes and a broken nose after allegedly coming to blows with Pete and his then manager James Mullord. Mullord was not arrested in relation to the incident and the charges against Pete were swiftly dropped.

It was a messy affair with neither man emerging in a favourable light. Carlish had filmed Pete taking drugs during a failed attempt to make a documentary about Pete and his band Babyshambles. The programme featured both Carlish's footage and his antics in trying to get that footage, which the producers recognized was the real story. Entitled *Stalking Pete Doherty*, the programme was broadcast on Channel 4 that May. The programme suggested that somewhere along the way Carlish had crossed the line between documentary-maker and stalker. He appeared to have lost perspective and gave the impression he had come to believe that he was some sort of rock star by proxy, describing himself as a sort of 'posh Bez' of Babyshambles playing idiot savant to the band.

The programme highlighted two of the singer's character traits that would be cause for concern with Kate's friends and advisers. Even before meeting Kate, Pete's circle of friends had expanded from a trustworthy group of longstanding allies to encompass a hotch-potch of 'friends' and associates banded together with the fickle camaraderie of junkies. As the summer of Carlish's filming drew on – the footage was filmed in 2004 – the extent of Pete's drug-taking was threatening to split his latest band. Yet the access Carlish had to Pete's comings and goings, at least at the beginning of his attempted rockumentary, was extraordinary.

Pete was an open book and a tabloid front page waiting to happen. That was bound to sound alarm bells in Kate's camp. And even if Pete erred on the side of discretion at times, what of some of the people around him? What might they say or sell or do for money to buy another hit? Especially now that Pete's media value had rocketed thanks to his relationship with Kate. Carlish's images had been all but worthless before Pete started dating Kate – Channel 4 had already told him they wouldn't be taking his programme, though the decision was swiftly reversed once Kate was in the equation.

The second point of concern was that though Pete presented himself as a gentle, amiable creature, the Rookery debacle raised the spectre of violence. If pushed or desperate, what was Doherty capable of? The previous summer he had narrowly escaped prison when arrested in possession of a flick knife, and that February he spent six days in Pentonville prison, after which he was released on bail and given a house curfew between the hours of 10p.m. and 7a.m.

But while 'insiders' leaked tales of Kate's concern over her new amour's latest scandal, Pete confidently asserted that he would be going into rehab, that he and Kate would marry and that he was happy. 'Who wouldn't be? I want to make it work,' he said. 'The drugs have got to stop or I'll lose her. I owe it to her. I owe it to everyone.' And no doubt Pete meant it when he vowed he to get clean and stay clean; no doubt he meant it each of the many times he said it. In that he was no different from any other addict.

February 2005 was Pete's rehab number five and this time he decided to have a naltrexone implant. The effects of this procedure would last between six and twelve weeks. A small incision in his lower abdomen would be made under local anaesthetic and the implant inserted. Naltrexone blocks the receptor sites in the brain, making a heroin high impossible and causing rapid and intense withdrawal from any opiate lingering in the system. It was the first time Pete had undergone this process and it was testament to his genuine desire to get clean. Sadly it would not be his last. Barely a month later, when his mother visited the London apartment into which she and her husband had helped Pete move in the New Year, she found evidence of the chaos in which Pete existed. It was March and Pete's twenty-sixth birthday, and his mother had brought flowers, champagne and vain hopes. 'My hope at this time,' she admits, 'was that the implant he'd had would work. And he'd done it voluntarily, which I felt was a positive step. Still, I thought, how on earth did it get to this?'

In the months ahead there would be many of Kate's friends and family who would ponder that same question as Pete and

Kate bounced through the newspapers and celebrity gossip magazines. Each time Pete was hauled before a magistrate or pictured with a groupie with his eyes rolling back in his head, high on crack or smack, a new and intense focus was placed on Kate's love life. And increasingly the question was asked, 'What does she see in him?' But there was not, for the time being, any question of intervention on Sarah Doukas's part. As an agent, however close, she had always maintained that there were certain questions she did not ask and a line she would not cross. Kate's relationship with Pete seemed to be behind that line.

Perhaps it would have been easier for Sarah to raise issues with Kate if the money had stopped rolling in, but in the early months – and further down the line too – Kate's association with Pete did not harm her career one jot. Quite the opposite. Kate had moved towards brand endorsements, and each time her face was in the paper, regardless of the reason, it kept her in the public consciousness and her stock at a premium. It maintained her cool factor too. Kate was moving seamlessly from supermodel to rock model.

Part of the reason Britpop had imploded was because its heroes, who had begun their life on the fringes of mainstream culture, had become mainstream multi-millionaires, utterly out of touch with their fans and beyond any reality they could comprehend. The same had happened with the supermodels. But just as music had been reinvented with The Libertines – a band now credited with inspiring a whole new musical scene populated by bands like the Kaiser Chiefs, Franz Ferdinand and so on – Kate too had been reinvented, albeit by association.

In April, Kate was featured on the cover of *i-D* magazine and across sixteen pages in a picture story entitled 'I love rock'n'roll'. Had the images been of another girl, it could have been flicked through and written off as the styling conceit it was, but Kate had the sort of credibility not easily ignored. She may have been the face of Dior and Coco Mademoiselle, but she was Rimmel's gal too, and now that she was on the arm of an obviously down-at-heel rebel, she seemed as much Pete's fan as his object of desire.

Of course this cut both ways and left her open to looking rather foolish and adolescent – not a good look for a mother in her thirties – but for the time being it worked. She was both rock chick and groupie; icon and girl next door. The fact that she seemed smitten by the sort of man your mother – never mind *her* mother – would blanch at gave her an approachable vulnerability that great wealth and celebrity might otherwise have blotted out. There was no escaping the fact that, whatever Pete's talents and virtues when straight, Kate had fallen for a man who was in the process of making one big mistake. But the reality of her romance with him seemed far removed from the lurching speculations and rumours that, from the very beginning, filled the magazines and newspapers on an almost daily basis.

Some of Kate's friends expressed concerns over Pete's suitability. He was a charming guy, they cautioned, that much was clear, but he was a hopeless addict with a string of arrests and rehab attempts behind him and little to indicate an ability to change. Some found themselves cut off for their efforts, leaving others to worry that, though this relationship could only end badly, there was nothing they could do but watch as it ran its course. From the very beginning Kate's affair with Pete played to the most dangerous and childish side of her personality. The more people criticized or cautioned, the more the pair cast themselves as the outlaws they imagined they were: they were

Bonnie and Clyde, Sid and Nancy, F. Scott and Zelda Fitzgerald all rolled into one. The fact that none of these grand passions ended with anything other than disaster only added to the appeal.

As for the drugs? Pete always thought of his heroin habit in terms of the opium drinking and smoking of the Romantic poets and writers. He thought he was Thomas De Quincey or Coleridge with the wit of Oscar Wilde and the darkness of his most famous character Dorian Gray – a book that Kate had long listed as one of her favourites. There was something of Depp's wildness in Pete, but where Depp was constantly seeking out new heroes and inspirations, Pete's notion of heroic was stuck in schoolboy English lessons. He had dropped out of his English course at Queen Mary, part of the University of London, after the first year. Pete had got famous, or at least got noticed for his native talent, so rapidly and enthusiastically that, just like Kate, something inside seemed to have stopped developing. He then compounded the arrested development that accompanies youthful fame by engulfing himself in a miasma of drugs, and he lacked the depth of life experience to see his error.

Pete and Kate's own writings give a real flavour of the intensity of their relationship and of the Romantic roles in which they cast each other. They provide a far clearer under-standing of the passion that existed between the two than the 'on-off' version of events as chronicled through the daily news. Lying next to Kate in bed in her house in the country in the early spring of 2005 Pete wrote, 'In the birdsong lullaby of a summer morning and lull I tiptoe to the window around which is wound a noble tangle of leaves and – oh glorious – red, white and blue roses . . . You lay sleeping under bear-cat, the softest of soft fur white polar silky bed covers . . . I kiss your sleepy head and shoulders and I'd kiss your shadow 2 [sic] your shadow's reflection . . . although if you're still vampiring it up you'll not have a reflection my sweet. I reach for your hand and amidst your stirring and regular breathing your arm is lifeless and your fingers have no grasp for you *are* asleep though even as I write this you stretch and scratch and wiggle now and settle again. I kiss your face, shoulders and neckle [*sic*] with many sweet salty tasting kisses.

'I would betray my fate,' he carried on. 'Before I would my heart in fact I'd betray the whole world and all in it before betraying my heart . . . I mean to say you have my heart although you are kicking me in your sleep and so you don't love me . . . oh but you do. Say, "I love you so," and my senses are ransacked, raised to cinders . . .'

As for Kate, all her passion and all her frustration at how helpless it left her was laid bare when she wrote, 'You have touched my heart and soul, little fucker. I wish you wouldn't ring my door now go. I could kiss you again and float away. You make me high, my sweet, my skin shivers and longs be held by you [*sic*].'

Cut off from the outside world both Pete and Kate seemed convinced that they had somehow discovered the true versions of themselves that nobody else could ever see, never mind understand. Friends saw a junkie who let Kate down, who would leave her waiting for him to turn up at her home or at the pub and simply never show. They saw a man with filthy fingernails, an East End flat in disarray and a musical talent that seemed to be stalling before it began. They saw a string of court appearances and failed attempts at rehab. They saw a young man wasting so much but wasting it nevertheless. They saw Kate, her hair unwashed and unkempt, her face free of make-up because Pete like to see 'the true' Kate. They saw the adverse headlines and the rumbling concerns over Lila's welfare.

Considering the dynamic between them, Kate's longtime friend David Tang says, 'I've met all her boyfriends. Pete has this contrary behaviour that you wouldn't expect a diva to tolerate. They're living on the edge, and that's what they want. It's in defiance of something. I don't understand it, but they find it incredibly romantic. Like Bonnie and Clyde.' Marianne Faithfull certainly had little patience with the notion that drugs were in any way inspirational or Romantic. She had made that mistake herself. 'Maybe it worked for De Quincey and Cocteau, and it sounds good when you're fifteen, but ultimately I think it's incredibly immature. It's practically *infantile*. If you're a working artist you haven't got time for that shit . . . It doesn't create anything. It's a supreme form of narcissism.

'As far as I'm concerned,' she says, 'those overheated Romantic visions of the world are done! I don't want to see things as romantic and doomed and beautiful. In real life, people go through problems and deal with them. These young kids in bands who are attracted to smack and crack cocaine and shit are dazzled by images of glamorous decadence. A lot of them, let's face it, really bought into that fascination with the lower depths, what they now call the Old Rock Star's Manual. Where it all ends up . . . is with Brando in the cave [this is a reference to *Apocalypse Now* and the end of Brando's character's descent into madness] with a copy of *The Romantic Agony* . . . he has never let himself say no to anything. He's simply indulged every urge, every whim. He's not a grand character. He's horrible; he's a monster! That's what happens when you take the Romantic agony or the Romantic ecstasy to its illogical conclusion . . . It's akin to being a child or reviving childhood. You can see how those two things mesh – childlike invention and childish self-indulgence – but at some point you have to say, I can't live like that any more.'

Truth be told, Pete said that many times over, but he seemed to lack the will to stick it. Ultimately it would be Kate who made the break, by which time she had tolerated far more than anybody would have believed possible.

On 11 April 2005 the Crown Prosecution Service dropped all charges against Pete in relation to the February fracas with documentary-maker Max Carlish. The case was dropped on the grounds of insubstantial evidence. There will always be two versions of what happened at the Rookery Hotel that night. Pete, according to one report, claimed that he had been in a Jacuzzi waiting for Kate's arrival when Carlish charged into his room brandishing a sword and started taking swipes. Carlish claimed that he had gone to see Pete in an attempt to finish his abortive documentary and that Pete had asked him for money. Carlish assumed it would be for drugs and refused, sending Pete into a rage, during which he punched the film-maker in the face twice. Hard. Carlish claimed that the attack was both ferocious and frighteningly accurate. There was unlikely to be any doubt over which version Kate chose to believe.

That month Pete moved his belongings into the farm, stacking his Tony Hancock memorabilia – both he and his father were fans and once members of the Tony Hancock Appreciation Society – his books, his music and painting in the farm outbuilding he referred to as the potting shed. Throughout this time Pete was trying to establish Babyshambles as a worthy successor to The Libertines, which involved touring and gigging all over the place. Kate too was often working and shooting overseas. Pete complained, 'How can I throw myself into her when she's off so often?'

In the midst of all this, Jefferson and his parents continued to try to provide Lila with some sort of balance to the frenetic lifestyle her mother and Pete had. This is not to suggest that Kate was neglectful of her daughter. She would take Lila to ballet classes and tuck her into bed and read her a bedtime story when work allowed. They would bake cakes together in the kitchen of her country home, they would dress up and so on and in Linda Lila had a very involved grandmother who was willing to help out when necessary. But there was no avoiding the extraordinary nature of Kate's life, and however much Douglas and Teresa Hack trusted Kate, Pete was an anxiety-inducing and unpredictable presence. Jefferson assured his parents that Lila was always safe and that he would not stand idly by if he feared anything to the contrary, but it simply wasn't an issue. Still, they worried, of course they did. Who would not? Kate's life seemed to be heading in a new, and worryingly old, direction with Pete. It had not made her happy before – this 'vampiring it up' – it had ended in rehab and damage limitation.

But with Pete it seemed that hedonism and chaos was all part of the tortuous appeal. He was convinced that it was part of his creative persona – certainly there were enough people round him feeding that notion. Kate seemed to feel more confident in her own creative bent by proxy. She wrote in his journal. She wrote poetry and started tentatively beginning to sing with him. Pete, with his 'welcome-all-comers' approach to music and life, was happy to go along with this development. At the time he was working on new material for Babyshambles' first album, which was still in progress and still being produced by Mick Jones.

Out in the potting shed in the Cotswolds or high up in her attic at the top of the farmhouse, Pete and Kate would drink and smoke and sing. Kate had turned the space in the house's eaves into a vast dressing, or dressing-up, room. There were mirrors and wardrobes and a swinging basket chair hanging from the ceiling. As they noodled away on bits of lyrics and melodies, the tune that appealed to Kate most was 'La Belle et La Bête'. It appealed to the artistic pretentions of both. The title was taken from Cocteau's 1946 reworking of *The Beauty and The Beast* fairytale. And it appealed to a more basic instinct. After all, it was pretty obvious who was being cast in which role.

The song would become bound up in Pete and Kate's story, but it wasn't written with her involvement, nor was it written as a comment on their relationship. Pete had worked on it before meeting Kate and the writing credits go to him, Robert Chevalley and poet Peter 'Wolfman' Wolfe (no stranger to drink issues and cocaine). In fact, though Kate did not know it at the time, if there had been a 'beauty' inspiring the song at all, it was the model Irina Lazareanu. Coincidentally, the dark-haired Romanian-born model, eight years Kate's junior, appeared briefly in Max Carlish's film, sitting in a bath with Pete and two others. She was tucked up against him wearing only a bra and knickers while he wore white Y-fronts.

Realizing the role Irina had in Pete's life, Kate took the model under her wing, going as far as to request her for certain jobs, most notably the launch of her first design collection. Kate befriended the model and promoted her. Had Kate felt threatened by Irina's youth and Pete's evident affection for her, she could hardly have played a cleverer game. Kate had always possessed an uncanny capacity to draw people's attention towards her and away from anything else. And for a while Irina certainly seemed in awe of Kate and, perhaps just as importantly, under her watchful eye. After Pete and Kate split, it was another matter; he and Irina dated and were even briefly engaged.

With hindsight the whole saga would lend a certain piquancy to the lyrics sung by Kate on 'La Belle et La Bête', in which she repeatedly asks, 'Is she more beautiful than me? Is she more beautiful?' For as much as being in love with Pete made Kate feel creative and alive, it came at a price. With Pete came drugs, unreliable behaviour and flirtations with groupies, broken promises, worry and heartache. When Kate wrote, 'You love them more than you love me,' she was as likely to be talking about Pete's drug use as the groupies who tailed him or any more corporeal rival for his affections. And yet, with the corrosive illogic of an addict, Kate was hooked: the lows of being with Pete were worth it for the highs.

18

It must have been a long time since Kate had felt such nerves. There were a couple of times that may have borne comparison: Paris, 1990, when the runway at John Galliano's fashion week show must have seemed to stretch like an eternity before her; Milan, 1999, her post-Priory comeback for Versace, when she walked the runway sober for the first time in a decade. But even then, both of these experiences were part of the fashion world, a realm she understood and in which she was revered. This was different.

It was three o'clock in the morning. Three hours into Saturday, 14 May 2005 and two hours away from the end of Trinity College Dublin's ball. It was cold, but that didn't account for the way Kate visibly shivered. Babyshambles was one of the acts booked for Trinity College's May Ball, which, though students wore black tie and ball gowns, bore more resemblance to a mini music festival than the sort of genteel evening one might usually associate with such an event. There were three stages erected in tents of various sizes, two dance tents and several bars. The university's vast cobbled courtyard was given over to the night. The Irish Garda patrolled the grounds to ensure the safety and reasonable behaviour of the thousands of students who had each bought a ticket and queued for several hours at the university gates on College Green to be there.

It wasn't the promise of Babyshambles that drew the majority of them, not really. The band wasn't headlining, though it was later reported that they were. The main attraction that night, or certainly the main performer on the main stage, was Dizzee Rascal. Babyshambles had yet to release their first album, and in spite of their strong student following it was really the lustre of The Libertines that drew the 400 or so students to the tent where they were playing.

Kate and Pete had spent a large swathe of the previous day drinking in the bar of the Clarence Hotel – the sleek boutique hotel across the River Liffey which is owned by U2 bandmates Bono and The Edge. It had an appropriately rock'n'roll pedigree for the couple and their drinking partners had been of a similar persuasion as friend Shane MacGowan and his long-suffering partner Victoria joined them at the bar. Still, Pete appeared remarkably sober when he finally took to the stage. The lateness of the hour was no reflection on his timekeeping, it was simply taken for granted that the ball would go on until dawn and so, in turn, would the entertainment.

Babyshambles had been on stage for close to an hour by the time a stumble of drunken recognition began to weave its way through the well-refreshed students. Kate was in the crowd, smiling, singing along and enjoying her anonymity. Once it was lost, security guards helped her towards the front and side of the stage, where she stood, beer can in one hand, cigarette in the other, watching Pete perform. He was in good form, throwing the microphone out to the crowd and asking what song they wanted. Once they had exhausted Babyshambles' limited repertoire, the calls came for Libertines songs and

Pete happily played along. Then he turned to Kate and gestured for her to come on, don't be shy.

Nobody had heard 'La Belle et La Bête' – it would not be released for another six months – and certainly nobody expected Kate to sing. It was the first time she had ever done so for anyone other than her friends. As she took her place centre stage it was clear that she was utterly petrified. She sang her lines, rooted to the spot while Pete moved around energetically, willing her on and encouraging her with warm gestures and glances.

Most of the crowd were so tired and out of it that many missed the fact that she'd been on stage at all. Pete was well known for letting fans get up on stage, with him, so perhaps in their drunken stupor some assumed that this had happened again. But two things struck those who were aware of what was going on: Kate's nervousness and her beauty. When Pete sang the lines 'She's La Belle et la Bête at the ball. You know she could have us all' there was a roar of approval from those at the front. Kate wore a fur shrug, jeans and moccasin boots. Her voice was sweet enough, though it wavered with nerves and she was obviously relieved when the song was over and she could return to the edge of the stage to jig around in the background. There were few things in life that saw Kate challenge herself and, for all his flaws, there were few people who, like Pete, would push and nudge her on to do so. His influence, however, was not always so positive.

Later that month Pete joined Kate in Cannes, where she was staying for the film festival. There was a party atmosphere – Bobby Gillespie was there with Katy England. Kate spoilt Pete who was, by his own admission, 'totally skint' at the time. It did not seem to bother her, though; she was devoted to him.

As proof of that devotion they each had a tattoo on their bum: a K in a love heart on his, a P on hers. Kate seemed to like to look after him and she liked to indulge him. That spring in Cannes they had a riot – almost literally.

Towards the end of their stay festivities or, as Pete later described it, 'derangement of the senses', led to some serious carnage taking place in Kate's hotel room. Mirrors were smashed and Pete, Kate and the room ended up gory with the Bloody Mary that was thrown around the place. The following day Pete, Bobby and Katy wrote some explanatory notes to the hotel manager. None sounded particularly sorry for the mess or the trouble. The only thing any of them seemed concerned with was that Kate should not look bad or take the blame. The same thought had no doubt occurred to Kate.

'Dear Sir,' Pete wrote. 'Soz about the carnage, but don't get the hump with Kate, it was her mate Katy – Bobby's girl – who really went loopy and trashed the joint. Love Peter Doherty.' Katy added an understandable 'PS. Dear Sir – in fact I was the innocent amongst the group of drunkenness. Things got out of hand, please forgive their extravagant behaviour. It's an extravagant place.'

As for Bobby, he was rather more robust in his words: 'DEAR SIR, WE HAD A FUCKING RIOT IN YOUR BEAUTIFUL HOTEL. IT WAS A BLAST, THANKS FOR THE UPGRADE TO THE OPULENT MANSION. SOME COCAINE ON ROOM SERVICE WOULDN'T GO AMISS AND COULD SAVE YOU A FEW MIRRORS ETC. YOURS B. Gillespie.'

It was all getting worryingly reckless and their behaviour showed an alarming miscalculation. When you rampage through hotel rooms, leaving a 'sorry' scrawled on scrap paper, and fly back home without any comeback, it's easy to feel untouchable. When friends err on the side of caution for fear of offending, it's easy to believe that any disapproval has evaporated. And when the jobs keep rolling in, as they did for Kate, it's easy to think that what you do behind closed doors doesn't matter. What people don't know, or what people in the industry are prepared to turn a blind eye to, can't hurt. But the mistake that Kate seemed to make was in thinking that her censors, should there be any, would be found in the industry in which she worked, or the people who signed her cheques.

Kate was not untouchable, not entirely, because she, or at least her image, had long been a commodity, and a commodity is only worth what people will pay for it. It's a harsh sentiment when applied to a person, but true nevertheless. The danger with Doherty was not *what* he was doing, or how often or how much, it was how recklessly and indiscreetly. The people who would be Kate's censors – in less time than anyone could imagine – the people to whom she would have to pay lip service, were not fashion industry insiders or the press. The people who really held sway were the buying public, people who had bought into a two-dimensional image of Kate and needed to see it preserved.

For Kate's family and friends it was painful to watch her being treated really rather badly by Pete at times. For her advisers, whatever their concern for Kate personally, they must also have worried about how much her fans were starting to see. And yet they seemed effectively to have to stand by, unable perhaps to cross that line and voice alarm at the possible impact of Kate's personal life on everything else.

That same month Kate was cast as the new face of celebrated jeweller H. Stern and in June she, the brand and photographer Rankin teamed up to produce what was intended to be a commemorative campaign. Hans Stern had become famous in the Fifties for using coloured Brazilian gemstones at a time when they were far from fashionable. He had fled to Brazil from his hometown in Essen, Germany, on the outbreak of World War II and became known as 'Brazil's King of Coloured Gems'. The brand was now an international success, with stores in twenty-six countries, and Stern wanted to celebrate its sixtieth anniversary in style. Kate was chosen because, according to a spokesman for the brand, 'She is the best representation of the H. Stern woman: someone who has a confirmed taste and uses jewellery to complement her personality, not as a status symbol. Kate [has a] unique standing in the worlds of fashion and design and her role as style icon and opinion leader.' It was a standing that had just seen her honoured in New York, where she was awarded a Fashion Influence Award by the Council of Fashion Designers of America.

The concept behind the shoot was simple. Rankin's images would 'showcase Kate's sparkling golden skin as if she were a jewel herself'. The campaign represented a £1.5 million investment on H. Stern's part. Its scope would be international and it would launch in magazines in America in November 2005, rolling on to feature in fifty of the worlds's most elite fashion and lifestyle magazines. Additional shots of Kate would be included in a limited-edition hardcover book. But it never happened. By the time the volte-face was performed it would be too late to withdraw the advertisements already bought and booked in magazines hitting the shelves in November and December 2005. But all those other plans were scrapped because, by then, as far as H. Stern was concerned, Kate's 'sparkling skin' had lost its lustre.

Kate returned home from the H. Stern shoot that June, unaware of how limited its distribution would be. As far as she knew, it was simply another job successfully completed. She also worked with Nick Knight, a photographer who had shot her many times and who had been commissioned to do a cover shoot with Kate for the September edition of *Vogue*. The image showed Kate styled in Bardotesque chic. She wore pale lipstick and heavy eyeliner, while her glossy hair was held up and back. She wore a pencil skirt, cinched in with a wide belt and paired with a pale blue chiffon blouse. It was a coolly beautiful version of Kate, and though it wasn't destined to be the image of her that generated the most publicity that September, it marked something of an anniversary for both model and photographer. It was Knight's tenth cover and Kate's twentieth in what was turning out to be a busy summer, both personally and professionally.

Kate met Pete's mother at Glastonbury where Pete was performing once again. They were late, having got stuck in traffic on the drive south from London, so there was little time for pleasantries before Pete and the band had to go on stage. Kate listened and sang along in the wings. It would be two years before she summoned up the courage to join Pete on stage in front of an audience of that size to sing a few lines or the couple's signature song, 'La Belle et La Bête'. Her Dublin experience may have been fun, but in this if in little else that summer, Kate showed restraint. Kate was something of a veteran festival-goer, having gone to them as a teenager with Corinne Day. Then, as their worlds shifted and their lives went in different directions, Kate's circle included so many musicians that it would have been impossible not to be a regular festival-goer.

For Pete's mother, Jackie, the brief encounter with her son that June afternoon was one she looked back on with mixed feelings. Of course she was thrilled to see him, but festivals weren't really her bag, particularly given the fact that it poured that year, turning the Somerset fields into a vast muddy quagmire, while the summer air was filled with the unmistakable stench of chemical toilets. But it was her emotional discomfort that was more pertinent. Jackie was aware that Pete's latest naltrexone implant was in its penultimate month, though even with it his behaviour was nothing if not unpredictable. As for Kate and Pete's grand passion, in true Romantic style it would sometimes find expression with undertones of violence.

On 5 July, designer Hedi Slimane celebrated his birthday and the launch of Dior Homme Spring/Summer collection 2006. There was nothing surprising about Kate's invitation to such an event, but it would be wrong to assume that Pete was there only as Kate's 'plus one'. Slimane had worked with Pete on more than one occasion as art director of a couple of magazine articles looking at rock's young bloods. The pieces – one in *Interview*, the other in French magazine *Liberation* – both featured Babyshambles, though it was Pete alone who was pictured in full stage-sweaty, bare-chested form. Coincidentally, the *Liberation* picture story included a look at American vocalist Alison Mosshart, who was part of a little-known band called The Kills, along with her partner Jamie Hince. Alison would go on to date Jefferson Hack, who in turn would introduce a then single Kate to Jamie. And so the mish-mash of interlinked relationships that had characterized the heady days of 'Primrose Hell' lived on.

Jefferson was at Hedi Slimane's birthday party in Montmartre that night, and he and Kate chatted and danced together. Sir Elton John and his partner David Furnish were also among the guests. Pete had performed with Sir Elton on the London stage of the summer's Live8 concert. His rendition of Mark Bolan's 'Children of the Revolution' was roundly mocked as a shambling disaster, but looking back on the footage, the criticism seems unfair – indicative more perhaps of a gathering disapproval of Pete, who had by then established himself as the most famous heroin addict of the time.

He was what middle-class parents feared: he had, after all, been one of their sons, and now their kids were listening to and looking at him. He was proof positive that nothing they could provide – neither education, love, nor opportunity – could bulletproof their kids against temptation and addiction. Still, Sir Elton seemed perfectly happy to see and spend time with Pete, regardless of his critics. Slimane had provided his guests from London with first-class return tickets on the Eurostar. Both Pete and Kate had to be back the next day, so on 6 July they boarded the train.

It was clear from the start that there were tensions between them, and soon those tensions bubbled over into a full-scale bust-up. Pete recalled that journey: 'Kate and I fucking fighting all the way on the Eurostar until finally blood runs down my palm and up my head and before I leg it to oblivion leaving her at the station calling me a this that and the other and a so-and-so (accompanied by hand gestures) and the dramatic exit just on queue [*sic*] as my deranged senses all aflame moving away from the flashion [*sic*] of bulbs of the ninja papperazi's [*sic*] and dear old Jimmy Mullord sticking a left hook right in the mush of one of the photographers – "smack!" he caught him a good 'un I will say so meself.' Pete went on to admit that his drug use was as rampant and unapologetic as ever, and that he had been 'shameless . . . scene after scene, piping, pinned and powdering notes on planes . . . debauching it at the airports all over Europe . . .' Perhaps there was a hint of romanticizing in Pete's description of a relationship that spilled over into violence – the notion seemed to be that theirs was a passion so forceful it could not be kept within conventional bounds. But even if the darker elements of what passed between Kate and Pete was only verbal in form, most people would wince.

This was getting out of hand and it was about to threaten every plan, project and contract secured by Kate, who, remarkably, was still somehow holding her professional life together against this torrid backdrop.

One particularly exciting project arose in August, when editor Carine Roitfeld and creative director Fabien Baron invited Kate to guest-edit the December edition of French *Vogue*. Kate embraced the offer enthusiastically. She had loved being a stylist on a shoot because she'd found her suggestions were taken on board in a way that they were not when she was on the other side of the camera. With an invitation to guest-edit she could do so much more. The magazine would be both a homage to Kate on *Vogue*'s part and also a chance for Kate to turn the lens back on the industry and the people working in it that she found exciting. To an extent, the magazine would become a sort of year book for Kate and her friends. She and Pete planned to record 'La Belle et La Bête' and give a copy away with each edition, and there would be a small feature on Babyshambles inside. They were hardly the sort of band who would normally make it into the pages of French *Vogue*, but with Kate the tone was dark, rocky, glamorous and decadent. She had started out part of a movement that shook up rather staid notions of beauty, and seventeen years on she was still at it.

Every aspect of her style would be another insight into her friends and her life. There would be pages on Alexander McQueen, John Galliano, Burberry, Louis Vuitton, Stella McCartney, Jade Jagger – with whom she had re-established a friendship post-Dan Macmillan – and Vivienne Westwood. But this would not only be about fashion, she would have features on artists too – four pages were devoted to the work of Jake and Dinos Chapman – as well as picking out books she loved. One such book was photographer Eve Arnold's work *Marilyn Monroe*. Arnold met Marilyn on a photoshoot for *Esquire* magazine in 1952, and the bond that developed between the two women lasted a decade. The book that Kate chose chronicled that friendship through the hundred or so photographs Arnold took of Marilyn during six extended photography sessions, one of which lasted two months. Perhaps there were echoes of Kate's experiences with Corinne Day in this scenario. Perhaps it was a simple fascination with Marilyn – a woman she'd always wanted to meet to ask the simple question, 'Was it worth it?' – that inspired Kate's choice. Another was a book of the paintings of Lucian Freud. And of course there would be pictures of Kate and four alternate covers by Craig McDean, Mario Testino, David Sims and Mario Sorrenti.

It would not turn out quite as Kate, Carine and Fabien had hoped, but still, that single edition of French *Vogue* would prove arguably more illuminating of Kate's success, character, style, influences and interests than the thousands of words of coverage that would flood the newstands and momentarily jeopardize its realization.

On 6 September Kate went to Metropolis Studios in Chiswick, where Babyshambles were working on material for their album. It was late at night, the atmosphere was relaxed and members of the band milled around. Kate chatted with Mick Jones, teased Pete and wanted to work on 'La Belle et La Bête'. The session went on into the early hours of the morning. A few days later, Kate and Pete flew to New York. It was the beginning of the city's fashion week and she had a shoot with

Mario Sorrenti for *W* magazine. On 11 September they both
went to the launch party of Jefferson's latest publication,
Another Magazine.

With so many people in town for fashion week, it was fun
for Kate, who worked and buzzed around the town she loved
and which had long been a second home to her. She urged
Pete to get up and out of their hotel room and join her, to
leave the full ashtrays, the clutter of room service plates and
cutlery and dirty towels, which were accumulating by the day,
and enjoy New York with her. But most of the time Pete
simply wanted to cool his heels indoors. He didn't feel great –
the wound from his naltrexone implant had become infected.
'My body is spitting out naltrexone bullets,' he wrote as he
counted the days until it would be entirely used up. 'Five
down, twenty-five to go.' They stayed where Kate always stayed,
room 606 of the Mercer Hotel. The room held many fond
memories for Kate, but it was about to acquire an altogether
less favourable slot in her personal history. She had barely
fallen asleep when, early in the morning of 15 September, the
telephone rang. It was Sarah with news that she had hoped
never to have to break, but which, as it would transpire, had
been rather a long time coming . . . certainly for the journalist
who had been working on the story for weeks.

Somebody had secretly filmed Kate's visit to Metropolis
studios earlier that month and sold the footage to the *Daily
Mirror*. The pictures were grainy, but they would nevertheless
be impossible to explain away. There was Kate, perched on the
edge of a leather sofa, casual in a sleeveless T-shirt, knee-high
boots and a tiny denim mini, her hair dishevelled and tucked
behind one ear so she could focus on the business in hand.
Balanced rather precariously to her right was a CD cover, on
which she meticulously chopped and crushed up a block of

white powder. She used a credit card, carefully sharing the powder into equal, generous lines, then she took a rolled-up banknote and snorted one. She handed it around; Mick Jones followed suit and others in the studio were welcome to partake.

The film also showed Kate smoking heavily throughout, drinking shots of vodka and whisky, pouring herself a large glass of wine and having a beer. The story was printed over five pages. Sarah read it to Kate over the phone, from the scream of the front page – 'COCAINE KATE' – to the turn-page headline: 'HIGH AS A KATE'. It claimed that Kate racked up the lines of cocaine from a 'mammoth stash, which she kept safely in her handbag'. Kate was, Sarah recalled, 'gutted. Absolutely devastated.'

For perhaps the first time in a very long time she didn't know what to do. Nobody seemed to. Of course, a great deal of the burden of damage limitation and rehabilitation would fall on Sarah's shoulders. Some of the emails and telephone calls that surged into the offices of Storm were supportive, but a great many were abusive, so much so that Sarah's IT man forbade her to look at her laptop until he had edited the contents of her inbox.

As for Kate, she was stranded in the place where she had always felt comfortable and at home. Her upset must have turned to anger at the betrayal and back again. She needed to talk to her mother. She needed to talk to Jefferson. He was shocked, of course, by the furore that had engulfed him and his family, but he wasn't angry with Kate. He felt sorry for her. She seemed broken and vulnerable. She called him repeatedly in the hours after the story broke and in the days that followed, always with one question: 'What shall I do?'

He was with Lila at his parents' in Ramsgate – the visit had been planned long before the scandal. He handed the telephone to Lila so Kate could speak to her. The first thing Lila said was, 'Love you, Mummy.' Kate had planned to take Lila to Disney World in Florida for her third birthday, but that seemed impossible now. Jefferson's parents hoped that the story would provide Kate with a 'wake-up call'. They hoped that she would learn from it and that, in time, it would turn out to be the best thing that ever happened to her. In a way it did, but not in the way they imagined.

The night the story broke, advertising guru David Lipman went to Kate's hotel suite, hugged her and told her, 'Kate, this is going to be a storm. You are going to need to stand strong and stand tough. This is not going to go away. Whatever you do . . . don't think you owe anybody anything but yourself. When you make that decision, do me one favour, see Lila Grace in your eyes.' At this Kate dissolved into tears. Friends telephoned with their support, among them Tracey Emin, Sam Taylor-Wood, Bella Freud and, significantly, Fabien Baron. Johnny Depp telephoned too, and wished Kate well. Publicly he noted that it was sad that she seemed no longer 'allowed to be human'.

Four days after the scandal hit, Pete flew back to Britain as Babyshambles had a gig on the twentieth. A week later he was arrested, following a performance in Shrewsbury, on suspicion of drug possession. Although charges were eventually dropped, it was hardly the sort of publicity Kate needed as she and her advisers embarked on the business of damage limitation. Kate had meetings with her agent in New York and her legal advisers. She had friends to call on, of course, but ever since the story had broken the paparazzi attention had reached an unbearable peak. Kate was used to the press and paparazzi, but this was different. Now they hungrily seethed and jostled outside her hotel. One step out of the front door was enough to send them into a frenzy of activity: flashbulbs popped, questions were yelled and allegations hollered. It must have been physically frightening, infuriating and intimidating. Kate was pushed – at times literally – for a response and goaded into giving some reaction. When it came it was an unambiguous instruction to 'Fuck off, just fuck off!'

Mario Sorrenti, who met Kate for lunch at Omen in Soho and witnessed the 'pack' at work, compared the swarming paps to 'rats over garbage' – an unfortunate analogy in some respects, but expressive nevertheless. Days earlier Kate was being courted by Swedish high-street chain H&M, who wanted her to design a line of clothing for them. She had already signed a deal to advertise her friend Stella McCartney's H&M range, but Kate found both offers withdrawn. The store issued a statement explaining, 'We thought we were going to go in one direction. After looking at it more closely, the management team in Sweden took time over the weekend to analyse the situation and decided after a meeting that it was better to cancel the campaign at this point.'

Kate's contract as the face of Coco Mademoiselle was due to expire in October and they decided they would not be renewing it. Burberry, who did not have an exclusive contract with Kate but had worked with her on nine of their previous fifteen advertising campaigns, were scheduled to shoot a new campaign with Kate that autumn. Fabien Baron spoke to Burberry's CEO, Rose Marie Bravo, suggesting they stand by their choice. He knew that Bravo had 'always adored Moss'. His efforts were in vain, but he told Kate not to worry. 'They will bring you back,' he told her. In due course Burberry did, but it was not 'they' to whom Baron was referring, but the British press.

Kate's initial instinct after the shock of discovering her predicament seemed to be to say nothing other than telling the world, or rather those trying to report events to it, exactly where to go. But as more and more brands held summit meetings and seemed set to snatch away another lucrative deal, Kate was advised to take a more humble approach. She was, after all, in America, the land of public confession and redemption. Kate said, 'I'm sorry.'

On Thursday 22 November, one week after the scandal broke, Storm issued a written statement from Kate that went around the world. It read, 'I take full responsibility for my actions. I also accept that there are various personal issues that I need to address and have starting taking the difficult, yet necessary, steps to resolve them. I want to apologise to all of the people I have let down because of my behaviour, which has reflected badly on my family, friends, co-workers, business associates and others. I am trying to be positive, and the support and love I have received are invaluable.'

It was hardly an emotional outpouring, but it had been carefully scripted by Sarah and checked over by lawyers to ensure that a delicate balance was struck: this should be an acknowledgement of error, not an admission of guilt. Such self-explanation may have been anathema to Kate – though her seven-day silence was probably held in panic as much as defiance – but it worked. The very next day Rimmel announced that 'in light of this statement and Kate's determination to address these issues' their relationship with Kate would continue. When H&M, Burberry and Chanel effectively dropped Kate, it seemed inevitable that this was just the beginning, that Kate would be haemorrhaging contracts before the month was out. Now things looked less bleak. Kate's statement was as clever as it was timely and had neatly avoided detailing any specifics when it came to the 'behaviour' for which she was apologizing.

When those grainy images first appeared in the newspapers the matter had become more than a scandal, it was also the subject of a police inquiry. But this was not the open-and-shut case that many might have thought the inevitable outcome of such supposed photographic 'evidence'. In fact, it was the beginning of a seven-month Scotland Yard inquiry that cost an estimated £250,000. The investigation was supervised closely by one of the force's most senior officers, Commissioner Sir Ian Blair.

Within days of the story breaking, he made it known that the police wanted to talk to Kate about the newspaper allegations just as soon as she returned to Britain. Within days of issuing her apology, Kate made it equally clear that helping police with their inquiries was not top of her list of priorities. She flew from New York to Arizona, drove high into the Sonoran desert and surrendered herself to the tender mercies of The Meadows, a rehabilitation clinic and licensed psychiatric acute hospital. Her treatment would last thirty days. The centre specializes in family therapy sessions and, however 'healing' such a process might be, it is not something likely to be easy for anybody to contemplate. There would be cynical suggestions that Kate's rehabilitation was more to do with effecting a career, rather than personal, recovery. But if there was an element of pragmatism about it there was certainly no proof that Kate and those close to her did anything but take this phase in her life seriously. Her mother flew across the Atlantic to be near her and Jefferson flew Lila to see Kate.

Jefferson's parents were divided over the wisdom of this particular supportive gesture, but Kate must have been desperate to see her little girl. She had missed her third birthday and, looking through the pictures that Jefferson showed Kate of Lila on the day of her party, dressed as a little fairy with sparkly pink wings, must have been a bittersweet experience. Kate had made Lila a card and sent her a heart necklace, but she must have been pining for her. But Douglas Hack wondered aloud just who stood to benefit from flying Lila 'halfway round the world to see her mother, then endure a heartbreaking meeting before having to be dragged away to fly back home'. His wife, however, thought it could only speed Kate's recovery and remind her just how important that recovery was. Had she known that Kate was still very much in touch with Pete and showing no signs of wanting to cut him out of her life, as many friends now openly asked her to do, she might have been less inclined towards that standpoint.

While Kate was addressing her issues, Pete was giving interviews talking about how much they missed each other. He said, 'She's doing really well. I shouldn't say really. I just miss her. She says she just wants to be with me. She says she doesn't know why I love her, I don't know why she loves me, but that's just the way it is.'

After she had completed her thirty-day stint at The Meadows, Kate wanted Pete to go through the same pro- gramme, but he wondered whether she just wanted him to have to go through what she had. It probably didn't ocurr to him that she might have wanted him to do so as an act of support or dawning realization that if one of them were to fully address what she referred to as 'issues' and stand any chance of doing so permanently, then they would both have to. The problem was that Pete didn't believe that life without drugs was necessarily better; being with Kate might have been a strong motivating factor, but still that doubt lingered. 'I think some people's lives would be ruined with drugs,' he once explained. 'And some would be dramatically improved.'

Out in the 'real' world, Sarah continued to firefight on Kate's behalf and had found some powerful allies. French *Vogue* did not ditch their plans to have Kate as guest editor and cover girl for the December 2005/January 2006 edition. The truth was that the 'bad-girl thing', as UK *Vogue* editor Alexandra Schulman described it, was what 'everybody knew they were buying into' when they bought into Kate. And so Carine Roitfeld and Fabien Baron made a shrewd decision and decided not to gloss over her dangerous allure but embrace it. Across a picture of Kate ran the words, 'Kate Moss, Scandaleuse Beauté'.

There would have to be adjustments, of course. The four covers by four photographers idea had to be ditched as Kate disappeared into rehab having only completed the shoot with Craig McDean. He had taken *La Belle et La Bête* as a theme, and given the circumstances it could hardly have been more appropriate. As social commentators and marketing executives tried to decide into which category Kate fell, McDean's images showed her as both exquisite 'bête' and monstrous 'belle'. Plans to feature Kate in several fashion stories had to be rethought too, but unable to be there in person, Kate had selected the models that would feature in her stead. She chose Irina Lazareneau and, in the process handed the then little-known model the first of two big breaks.

There was a hint of feisty defiance in the pages of *Vogue* that month that sat rather well with its guest editrice, however unfortunate the root of it all. Alexander McQueen was always going to be featured in the edition, but now he would be pictured walking down the catwalk wearing a T-shirt with the message of support 'We love you, Kate' written across the front. As for Carine Roitfeld, in her letter from the editor she positively celebrated Kate's appeal: 'Despite the discretion that characterizes her, you can hear echoes of a private life peppered with broken loves, stupefying excess, sleepless nights spent with rock circles . . . this young English girl could have come straight out of a novel by Bret Easton Ellis . . . For all these reasons we decided, before the summer, to honour Kate Moss this Christmas. The media storm which is now raging about her has never shaken this desire. She is the top model of the century and, though perhaps not a model daughter, for women and designers alike she is, nevertheless, the most inspirational icon and muse.'

Such unstinting praise would go a long way towards ensuring that, however much the storm raged – and it would do so for many months more – Kate need no longer worry about being treated as a fashion pariah. Next off the blocks was Pirelli, who released a picture of Kate looking incredibly sexy as a prelude to their 2006 calendar, in which she would feature.

Richard Branson, a friend and supporter of both Sarah and Kate, did his bit to be supportive, too, and in December Virgin Mobile announced that they would be filming an advertisement featuring Kate. The film would be launched online on 20 December and would be broadcast on television for the first time on Christmas Eve. It showed Kate padding around a bright, airy flat, making a cup of tea and listening with increasing interest to a telephone call from her supposed agent, Kyle. 'I just got you the mother of all contracts,' he boasts. 'Trust me, this is exactly what we've been looking for and they want you. We're back on top, hon . . . don't call it a comeback . . . I'm going to get the paperwork done and I will call you back, kitten.' The shot then pans back to reveal the New York skyline against which Kyle is filmed to be a cardboard display in a Virgin Mobile shop where a gormless assistant enquires, 'Does she want a case with that then?' The tagline was the *coup de grâce*, 'Virgin Mobile. One contract worth keeping.'

The advert hit just the right note: the humour was light and enough time had passed for it to be appropriate. If Kate had suffered from anything following the 'Cocaine Kate' debacle it was of seeming too aloof and angry – the only voice the public could hear at first was of her shouting, 'Just fuck off!' at paparazzi in New York. Now they had an altogether more relaxed, appealing Kate at the forefront of their minds. It was far more difficult to be judgemental and disapproving of 'nice Kate' than of the dishevelled version, as she had appeared in those grainy pictures in the papers. People started to warm to her again. Suddenly she seemed less villain, more victim. Just three months after the storm blew up, the tide had turned. It was extraordinary.

But when it came to her relationship with Pete – and his with drugs – things were not looking so healthy. He had checked into The Meadows as promised on 28 November, but nine days later he checked out again. Kate had little choice but to distance herself from him. She clearly had to think about Lila, her family, her friends, her work and herself. Leaving Pete was the logical thing to do, but the trouble with logical solutions to illogical problems is that they rarely, if ever, stick.

19

One hundred and forty two days after she received that devastating telephone call from Sarah, Kate returned to Britain. It was not a lengthy stay. She landed, headed to Scotland Yard headquarters, where she was interviewed under caution, then she, Linda and Lila drove to Heathrow and boarded a flight to Miami. Kate may not have been able to take Lila to Florida and Disney World for her birthday, but she seemed determined not to let her daughter down now. By the time they returned it was a full five months since the scandal had broken and something remarkable was about to happen: Kate's cocaine 'bounce'.

For all the mouth-clasping gasps of shock with which the notion of a model doing drugs had been met the previous year, the truth was that nobody cared, not really. In fact, as if to prove that no publicity is bad publicity, the whole affair gave Kate's career – post-apology, post-rehab, post-Doherty (for the time being at least) – a welcome shot in the arm. By the close of the year, Kate would not only have effected a monumental comeback, she would be crowned British Model of the Year – the year in question being the most publicly torrid of her career.

French *Vogue*'s support had gone a long way towards instilling confidence in any brands that may have wavered towards the end of the previous year, and in April Fabien Baron, who had been so disappointed by Burberry's decision to drop Kate from that season's advertising, saw another opportunity to support her by reuniting Kate with Calvin Klein. 'Kate and the Calvin Klein brand have a long history together and it felt natural to reunite them for this new jeans campaign,' he explained. It would, he continued, 'inevitably re-ignite that spark and highlight the sexy, cool essence of Kate and Calvin Klein'. Kate was paid £500,000 for the campaign that would feature her alongside Jamie Dornan, a young model who was then dating Keira Knightley. The vote of confidence was priceless. Three days after the Klein deal was announced came news that Kate was the new face of Nikon's Coolpix S6. The Japanese company signed her for £1.5 million with Bill Oberlander, the advertising executive who cast her, describing her as 'the icon for fashion and sophistication'.

Already Kate was making more money than she had lost through the decisions of Chanel, H&M and, temporarily, Burberry. Bulgari jewellery signed Kate for £1 million while the brand's perfume paid another £700,000; Longchamps signed her for £1.1 million; Roberto Cavalli, who would later use Pete as a model too, stumped up £800,000; the Virgin Mobile deal had brought in £1.2 million; Stella McCartney paid £1 million and Rimmel renewed their commitment with a £3 million, three-year contract.

By the end of the spring the police inquiry that had begun with the publication of those infamous stills from secretly filmed footage was over and what little material it had generated had been handed over to the Crown Prosecution Service. The CPS did not take long to conclude that the video footage, although an 'absolutely clear indication' that Kate had been taking controlled drugs, was not enough to guarantee a successful prosecution. Whatever common sense might dictate, there was no way of proving in a court of law that the powder Kate was sniffing was cocaine or indeed any other Class-A drug. All the while the contracts kept rolling in as Kate added Burberry, Versace, Belstaff, Louis Vuitton, Yurman jewellery, Dior and Agent Provocateur to her already blooming workbook. The last of that list was as much a reciprocal act of friendship as a money-driven deal. Then husband and wife – they have since split – the founders of the sexy underwear store, Serena Rees and Paul Corre, had been friends of Kate for a long time, and besides, the project that they had in mind was intriguing.

It would take the form of four films, directed by Mike Figgis, which would be drip fed to the public via the Internet and ultimately in a DVD set over several months. The first would appear in May, the second in November, the third in January 2007 and the final one that March. Kate would play Miss X, and these would be her erotic fantasies, acted out in a deserted townhouse in London, filmed at night and featuring, of course, Agent Provacateur undies. When the first of the films was launched on the Internet it crashed the site. That which had not killed Kate's career had only made it richer. In 2005 her annual earnings were estimated at £11 million. One year on from the scandal, she was on track for £30 million.

Her relationship with Pete seemed similarly impervious to public opprobrium. The previous December Kate had been pictured on the slopes of Aspen with a young model called Jamie Burke, but the flirtation had not been proof that she was over Pete as many had speculated. Pete's failure to last the course at The Meadows had been a profound disappointment to all who knew and loved him, Lisa Moorish, the mother of his child, Astile, Kate and his own mother Jackie among them.

But that failure and disappointment did not mean that what existed between Kate and Pete had evaporated. When Pete said that Kate had told him she didn't know why he loved her, it showed a side of her that few would ever see and without which their relationship made no sense. There were a great many people who would agree that Kate didn't deserve Pete, but not in the way that her helpless words implied. If Kate didn't know why Pete loved her, then she didn't seem to know her own worth. It was a sorry state of affairs for a woman who, on paper, was valued at three times more than she had been the previous year, and it was not likely to be rectified by a continuing relationship with a man who at times, Kate herself seemed to feel, loved drugs more than he loved her. He had not cleared up his act; far from it.

In April pictures were published of Pete apparently injecting an unconscious girl as she lay on a kitchen floor. It was later claimed that he was drawing blood, not injecting 'a noxious substance', and that the purpose of the exercise was 'art'. Whatever the details, the overall impression was one of squalor, and yet, by May 2006, Pete and Kate were back together. In most ways they had never really been apart. Life carried on and increasingly Kate found herself happiest in the country. Buzzing round country lanes in her little blue MG sports car, with Pete holding on to his hat in the passenger seat; having lunch at the nearby pub; hanging out by the swimming pool in her grounds; baking cakes with Lila and her friends; drinking, smoking and singing with Pete in the dressing room/attic.

But while their relationship drifted along much as before, Sarah, who had been instrumental in resuscitating Kate's career when it briefly arrested the previous year, was aware that Kate remained restless and hungry for more. One of the most devastating aspects of the scandal for Kate had been the cessation of talks with H&M to design her own clothing line for them. Kate was thirty-two years old and she was more in demand than ever, but no model goes on forever. Kate had always assumed that something other than modelling would present itself, but increasingly the time was coming to actively seek that something out. She needed the right partner if she were to move into design and more obvious 'Kate branding', and she was about to find him.

Every successful business story has a certain amount of myth surrounding it. Kate's collaboration with Sir Philip Green to create her own collections for Topshop would be no different. On 15 May, Kate was among guests at a charity auction hosted by Bella Freud, in aid of the Hoping Foundation for Palestinian refugee children. The auction was held at Annabel's nightclub, and among the many items Kate had donated, one – a kiss – went to Sir Philip Green, who paid £60,000 for the privilege and then donated it to the person he outbid, Jemima Khan. Perhaps it was an indication of his generous spirit; perhaps it was because he was at the event with his wife, Tina. The kiss, which many present assumed would be a chaste peck on the cheek, was a sixty-second, lingering smooch, with Kate sweeping Jemima's hair back from her face and clutching her neck. Nervous laughter ensued.

A fortnight after that kiss, Kate bumped into Sir Philip at China Tang, David Tang's restaurant in the Dorchester Hotel. She was arriving as he was just leaving. 'That was a bit of fun wasn't it?' Kate said. 'I suppose it all depends on your idea of fun,' he replied. Kate and Sir Philip had only met a couple of times and he had an early start the next day, so was in no mood to chat. As he was about to move on, though, Kate said, 'I'm a girl from Croydon, you're a boy from Croydon, why don't we do something together?' This vague flirtation piqued Sir Philip's interest. 'What do you have in mind?' he said. 'I've always wanted to do my own clothing collection,' Kate admitted, to which Sir Philip simply replied, 'Call me,' handing over his private number and leaving, unconvinced that he would hear from her. The rest, according to the myth, would be smooth-flowing history. Well, not quite.

A few days later, Kate's PA *did* call Sir Philip and said that Kate wanted to come in for lunch the following day, would that be all right. A meeting was agreed, and much to Sir Philip's surprise, Kate turned up at his Arcadia Group Headquarters in Oxford Street – from where he runs Topshop, Topman, Burton, Wallis, Miss Selfridge and Dorothy Perkins – without an entourage. And so the fifth richest man in Britain, worth £4.9 billion, and the most famous model and style icon in the world, sat down for a chat. They were joined for the most part by Jane Shepherdson, then brand director of the Topshop chain, and together they discussed what Kate could do. Sir Philip warmed to Kate's charm; she was impressive on this face-to-face meeting.

They talked for two hours, but when she left Sir Philip remained unconvinced. He did not truly believe that Kate had the desire, drive and potential to build a long-term brand, and he wasn't interested in the sort of one-hit wonder H&M had embarked on with some of their celebrity lines. He didn't care for a few thousand items and a day-long scrum of shoppers before normal business resumed. When Kate left that day, he simply wasn't sure that, for all her energy, enthusiasm and charm, she had the staying power or understood what would be required should they embark on a working relationship. Nevertheless, he asked Kate to come into his offices again, and this time to bring Sarah Doukas.

Another meeting was arranged, at which Sir Philip wasn't interested in girlish enthusiasm so much as straight answers. He grilled Sarah. 'Has Kate been speaking to other retailers about this? Is she serious? Does she have the time?' He wanted her to know that the project under discussion was not some three-hour photoshoot to publicize a handbag. This was a far more intense meeting than Kate's previous encounter and Sarah was silent for some time. After eighteen years representing Kate she knew her flaws and foibles, but she also knew Kate's creativity and how much she needed something to fulfil that aspect of her personality. She informed Sir Philip that Kate had wanted to do this for a long time and that she had simply never found the right partner for the endeavour. Notoriously gruff, Sir Philip nodded in response. He would get back to them 'in a week or so'. The meeting was over. He wanted to think about it. He did so and was inclined to forge ahead. The agreement was drawn up in July, but again he felt a tug of uncertainty and backed off. He said he wanted to sleep on it, which he did throughout all of August as he holidayed in the Mediterranean.

Topshop and Topman generated £100 million of profit on sales of £700 million – that's a lot of business to protect. When Sir Philip returned from his holiday the deal was still very much on the table but far from signed and sealed. He had serious reservations. It must have been a frustrating but refreshing experience for Kate. In her love life she had always been intrigued by men who didn't fawn and fall at her feet. Now in business this power play in which simply being Kate Moss was not enough to guarantee a signed deal must have proved invigorating.

Sir Philip called Kate into his office once more and told

her bluntly that if they were to go ahead she would have to convince him of her commitment. She would have to look him in the eye and tell him that she would make herself available to his designers, that she would do interviews to promote the brand, that she would be committed to making the venture a success – whatever that took. Kate gave him her word and asked if, finally, they were going to sign off the deal. Sir Philip's response was like a bucket of cold water down the back of her neck: 'No.'

There was one more thing. Sir Philip, ever the showman, wanted Kate to come to Topshop's fashion show. The show, held the day before London Fashion Week, was viewed disparagingly by certain fashionistas, who saw the timing as a cheap way to piggyback on Fashion Week proper. The show would start at 3.30p.m. Kate said she couldn't go as she had a birthday party to attend in Gloucesteshire in the morning. For Sir Philip this was non-negotiable. He would put a helicopter in the fields behind her country home at 1.30p.m.

It was 17 September and Kate and Sir Philip had been negotiating for more than three months. When photographs of the two side by side at the Topshop fashion show that year appeared in newspapers the following day, as Sir Philip can have been in little doubt they would, it was speculated that Kate would be announced as the face of Topshop's spring campaign. She was, after all, 'just a model'. But as they shared a private joke in the front row of the show, both Kate and Sir Philip had something far more ambitious in mind.

Always a visionary, Sir Philip recognized that, if successful, signing Kate could be the entré into the international market that he'd been looking for. He wanted to 'crack' America and make Topshop a truly global brand, while Kate wanted to prove, if only to herself, that she was more than an exquisitely pretty face. Three days later the full ambition, and risk, of the venture was made public as Sir Philip and Kate announced the launch of the Kate Moss Topshop collection.

The terms of the deal had been carefully worked out, giving Kate a financial as well as creative incentive to ensure her line's success. There was a £3 million downpayment, backed up by a structured deal that would give Kate a healthy percentage of royalties: the more Topshop sold, the more Kate earned. This was her first experience of a financially incentivized sales-driven role in fashion. That night, Kate and Sir Philip went back to China Tang, where it all started, and celebrated in style. They drank Cristal and ate exquisite food, and when they came out Sir Philip would get his first intoxicating taste of what life with Kate could be like as the flashbulbs exploded.

They started work on the collection the very next day. Kate had wanted to come into the offices at 2p.m. Sir Philip said 1.30p.m. She turned up at 1.10p.m. and called to inform him she was early. It was a delicate dance. Both Sir Philip and Kate were used to being in charge. He found making decisions by committee tiresome, while Kate insisted on signing off each and every piece personally. He provided her with six designers, buyers and merchandisers. She brought her own team, including stylist Katy England and hairdresser James Brown. When, in October, Jane Shepherdson resigned her position, it was assumed that she left because she had clashed with Sir Philip over Kate. He would always insist that her support of Kate had been wholehearted and that, had it not been, he would never have forged on with the deal. Still, the departure served to underline the risk Sir Philip had taken.

Kate was nothing if not controversial, and it seemed no coincidence that, as his relationship with Kate strengthened,

Sir Philip made certain that it never extended to meeting Pete. If anything was likely to taint a brand that relied heavily on the spending power of teenage girls and their parents, it was glad-handing one of the country's most notorious drug addicts.

Pete's behaviour was starting to try even Kate's patience as the destructive cycle continued with tiresome predictability. Kate had once complained that being a model was like Groundhog Day; being with Pete must have felt strikingly similar. Drugs, arrest, court appearances, bail conditions, let-downs, naltrexone implants, romantic promises and gestures; moments of light, frustration, despair; Sid and Nancy flights of fancy – it simply went round and round. Again and again Pete would ruin moments of sheer enjoyment for Kate. He would frequently fail to turn up at her home or whatever pub they had arranged to meet, leaving her punching his number into her mobile phone, helplessly pursuing him and trying to track him down. Yet again and again she would let his behaviour go, forgive him and take him back.

In December Kate announced that Irina Lazareneau would be modelling her first Topshop collection alongside her. It was the only evidence of Pete's indirect influence in the process and Sir Philip was probably at pains to keep it that way. Had there ever been any possibility of his and others' stance softening, then Pete's outlandish behaviour that New Year would probably have put paid to it.

It should have been a wonderful celebration – certainly Kate had much to look forward to in the coming year and much to be glad to leave behind in the previous one. Kate and Pete had travelled to Phuket, Thailand, and the Amanpuri Hotel, where they were two of the guests of David Tang and his wife Lucy. It was an odd assembly of celebrities, business tycoons and royalty. Sarah Ferguson was there – she and Kate had met a few years earlier at Sketch in London, when the Duchess of York had been out celebrating her forty-fifth birthday party. Kate's daughter was there, as were Princesses Beatrice and Eugenie, who were delighted by Lila, who earnestly enquired why, if they were real princesses, they weren't wearing pink dresses and tiaras. There was a party during the day, followed by a more raucous celebration that took Kate, Pete and co. into 2007 in buoyant mood. Then Pete ruined it all.

A few days after New Year Kate and Pete had a furious argument, which ended with Pete storming out of their hotel room. What happened next is predictably blurry, but what is certain is that Pete ended up injecting cocaine in a nearby hostel, having been spotted by two female tourists buying syringes and needles at a local chemist. He was filmed and the pictures once more made their way into the national press. He then compounded his misdemeanour with an altercation with a local taxi driver, which led to Thai police questioning him. He claimed he was attacked 'for no reason', but his inability to pay his fare having flounced out with little but the clothes on his back seems to offer some motivation. Kate must have been understandably furious. This was getting tiresome. Pete returned to Britain. Kate stayed on in Thailand.

Back in Britain at the farm, Kate's anger had not abated. Drug addicts lie, steal and cheat, and as long as Pete was a drug addict, theirs would be a relationship where trust was not built but undermined. This surely could not go on forever. Kate must have known it and Pete probably knew it too. His behaviour over New Year had marked an 'all time low', and he worried, 'Kate will not tolerate this shite.'

On 29 January at three o'clock in the afternoon Pete began a detox programme at the Charter Nightingale Hospital in

Lisson Grove. It was where Pearl Lowe had been treated for post-natal depression and heroin addiction and it was near Kate's London home, allowing her to visit and support Pete as much as was possible. As the treatment drew to a close, Pete scrawled in the pages of his ever-present journal: 'Saturday morning at the latest will see me once more in my love's loving arms. We have been close this time past and with me smack and needle free we shall marry in the summer and I become ten times happier than any given smackhead. Huzzah!'

They would do nothing of the sort. As Pete tried for the umpteenth time to kick the habits by which he was increasingly defined, Kate was getting on with her life. Pete was still part of it, and would be for some months to come, but it seemed an almost imperceptible change was taking place. It was clear to many that she continued to be intoxicated by his presence, but the vintage diamond ring she had once worn as proof of their intention to marry was no longer permanently on her finger. That, it seemed, had become an 'on/off' affair. Kate must have been tiring of the disappointments and of the female groupies who persistently texted and called their idol. Images of Kate and Pete would still appear in the newspapers and magazines redolent of the shambolicly, rock'n'roll facet of them both. She would be pictured, cigarette in hand, leaning backwards out of a window backstage at the Hackney Empire, roaring with laughter and seemingly on the cusp of disaster, or wandering down Oxford Street with him as dawn broke, bottle in hand, cigarette in mouth. And people would suck air through their teeth, shake their heads and say it could only end badly. Certainly there had been a time when Kate was so head over heels for Pete that she would have risked everything for him. In fact, arguably she already had.

But despite his continued place in her heart, that time

looked like it had passed, and proof of the subtle shift seemed to come on 30 April 2007 with the launch of Kate's Topshop collection. True to her word, Kate had committed time and effort as well as her face and name to the collection. She had given interviews; she had turned up on drizzly, grey London mornings for photoshoots; she had pored over the design ideas at a series of meetings and fittings.

The derivative nature of that first collection was the subject of some criticism. Kate had not, it was fair to say, designed the clothes so much as selected them from her own wardrobe – in the sense that the designs were inspired by some of her favourite items. It was something that seemed to offend many a fashion purist, but for the shoppers – and when it came down to it, their opinion mattered above all others – it would prove an intrinsic part of the appeal, since it offered an unexpected insight into Kate. She had, after all, trawled through her own wardrobe, distilling her influences and form-ative fashion experiences, which as any young woman knows are inextricably linked with formative moments in her life. And in the version of her style – herself – that she offered up, a startling and poignant truth was visible for those who cared to look.

There amid the floral dresses, waistcoats and hotpants she had favoured in recent years was a simple dress. It was a replica of the dress she had worn more than a decade earlier on the night that her book, *Kate*, launched in New York. Much had happened since she had revelled in the self-consciously cool venue of the Danziger Gallery with Johnny Depp by her side, laughing wildly, calling for a ban on all things French. But those New York nights with Depp had not faded into the background – quite the reverse. Twelve years on that was still a time by which Kate in many ways seemed to define herself.

It resonated through the years. More intimate still, the dress that she was wearing on the evening she and Depp met, a vintage number in eau de Nil with a fine lace overlay, would find its way into the second Topshop collection as inspiration for a piece in it.

Kate's first collection was limited to ninety pieces, though many more had been made up, toyed with and dismissed along the way. Prices would range from £12 to £200 – historically steep for a Topshop buy. Ideologically, 'selling Kate' would prove no trouble, but logistically it proved a colossal feat of organization. 200,000 items would be shipped to Topshop's 227 UK outlets in time for a specially early 7a.m. opening on 1 May, but at 8p.m. on 30 April there would be a preview at the chain's flagship Oxford Street store.

Sir Philip Green asked Kate if she wanted him to have Oxford Street closed for the occasion. She reacted with horror at the thought, though when it came to it and the street seethed with a crowd of thousands, her decision may have seemed rash. The store had closed at 5.30p.m. with some theatricality as curtains were drawn over its windows with the promise of opening again at 8p.m. to reveal Kate's collection. Kate would briefly join the shop mannequins in the window. The evening would be run with military precision – it was the only way to guarantee any sort of crowd control. Batches of shoppers would be allowed into the shop for twenty minutes during the four-hour launch evening and purchases would be limited to five items, while shoppers could try on a maximum of eight garments – the idea being to avoid bulk buying and reselling on eBay.

There were skinny jeans embroidered with the letter K and the stars, swallows and sweethearts that were inked onto her own body. There were vests, waistcoats and asymmetric prom dresses. When eight o'clock came, Kate prowled fleetingly into the window wearing a red satin sheath dress, cut on the bias and skimming over her barely there curves. Friends and family got a first glimpse of the shop and were visible in the background, drinking champagne as they perched on displays and enthused that the whole thing was just 'gorge'.

Linda was there, together with Fran, Sadie, Davinia – all the usual crowd – but one person notable by his absence was Pete. Sir Philip had apparently made it clear that Pete was not to be part of the official launch. There would be no pictures of Kate and Pete taken that night to link Sir Philip's brand of fashion with Pete's brand of living. Pete had, in fact, already appeared with Kate in a photoshoot in which Kate wore her collection. The shoot, at her country home, had run in *Dazed & Confused* – not the sort of magazine in which one would expect to see high-street fashions, but with Kate came universal appeal. The issue bore the headline THE INDEPENDENT STATE OF KATE, in what seemed a rather defiant celebration of the model, but there seemed to be no such defiance from Kate when it came to the business of selling her clothes in Sir Philip's shops. If he did not want Pete there, which seemed the case, Kate would respect that. When it came to the 'independent state of Kate', it seemed Pete's citizenship was no longer guaranteed.

That night David Tang hosted a party for Kate, appropriately held at China Tang in the Dorchester. Among the throng of friends who joined Kate and Sir Philip to celebrate was Fran, Sadie, James Brown, Danny Goffey, David Walliams, Natalie Imbruglia, Kate's PA Fiona and, fleetingly, Sir Philip's sixteen-year-old daughter Chloe. They dined in a private room before those who wanted to continue the revels moved to the hotel's private bar. Kate was giggling and girlish. She sat on Sir Philip's knee and playfully stroked his hair. They drank champagne, shots of tequila and vodka. It was fun. They bantered and chatted. Kate danced when a favourite tune came on. She seemed relieved and elated.

It was just after one o'clock in the morning when the party wound down. Kate left and Sir Philip picked up the drinks tab – the collection, and Kate, would be worth every penny of his investment. Within one week of its launch, Kate's Topshop collection had generated sales in excess of £3 million. The publicity alone had been worth an additional £2–3 million. Work on Kate's next collection began immediately, and this time her increasing confidence in her design ideas would shine through.

For the time being, the success of Kate's first Topshop collection was a powerful affirmation of just how influential the girl from Croydon had become. She had moved from high-fashion icon to high-street brand without diminishing her stock at either end of the spectrum. Kate's impact could be measured in the 10 per cent rise in Topshop sales that followed hot on the heels of her first collection and her popularity could be gauged in the thousands of people who crowded into Oxford Street to witness the launch, or queued in shops around the country for their chance to wear Kate Moss.

The demographic was vast; a rough estimate would put the age group to which she appealed anywhere between fifteen and fifty. In short, pretty much everybody with a pound in their pocket and the desire to spend it. And in the very month when her commercial worth was being so palpably demon-strated, the extent to which she could claim cultural as well as financial currency was also on display.

There has long been a debate over the place of fashion photography in the galleries of art, and there will always be those that say the whole argument is specious as there *is* no place for it. But at the beginning of 2007, Corinne Day was invited to photograph Kate for the National Portrait Gallery's permanent collection. So, as shoppers rushed into Topshop, gallery visitors lingered over images of Kate in a series of headshots taken by Day at Kate's north London home that formed part of the 'Faces of Fashion' exhibition. Kate wore no make-up, although her eyelashes were curled. Corinne engaged her in conversation, then chronicled her changing faces. Drinking, laughing, frowning ... the nine pictures ultimately selected by Corinne presented Kate as the changing, unchanging standard by which contemporary beauty had come to be judged. Kate the brand co-existed seamlessly with Kate the muse.

Some months later there would be a further insight into a facet of Kate for which she personally wanted recognition with the October release of *Shotters Nation*, the second Babyshamble's album. Kate's name would appear in the writing credits of four of the songs. This was not about money – she had no intention of taking any of the song royalties – it was about personal validation. Kate had written some of the lyrics with Pete as they lay in bed together in her country home and she wanted her contribution to be known. But by the time Kate had added songwriter – or at least co-writer – to her list of achievements, she and Pete were no longer together and this time it looked permanent.

Pete had left a London nightclub in the small hours of one June morning and stumbled into the back of a car with a little-known model. It was not the first infidelity on Pete's part, but it was the most crashingly public. Kate reportedly had Pete's belongings removed from her London home while she went to Ibiza for a few days with Sadie, Davinia and Lila. Pete begged for her forgiveness just as publicly as he had incurred her wrath, through the pages of a tabloid newspaper. Surprisingly, Kate seemed to find his attempts to woo her back faintly amusing, even sweet. She might have wavered, even taken him back, were it not for her resolve stiffening in the company of her friends Sadie and Davinia. As it was, Kate finally seemed to see the folly of continuing this Groundhog Day relationship cycle. But it still must have hurt.

On her return to Britain Kate spent very little time in her home in Melina Place, staying instead with Davinia and her husband. Maybe the house held too many memories of her time with Pete, but both practically and emotionally Kate looked to have outgrown the place. And outgrown Pete. It was time to move on. She would remain in touch with Pete and must be fond of him – they had shared too much for that to be erased – but they would no longer be together. When Kate's second, more assured and wide-ranging Topshop collection was launched with a party hosted by Sir Philip at Annabel's, The Kills singer Jamie Hince was by her side. Both the collection and relationship seemed more mature than Kate's previous offerings and former love affair.

The collection was, fashion writers agreed, more 'fashion-focused'. It was less about recreating outfits Kate had worn and garments she loved and more about providing raw ingredients for shoppers to pull together their own take on Kate's 'style ID'. It was an eclectic mix: pleated baby-doll dresses hung next to long striped college scarves; preppy cashmere-mix vests were sold alongside super sexy wet-look maxi dresses. There wasn't quite the furore that met the first collection, but what had taken its place was, for Sir Philip, a reassuringly constant enthusiasm. Within two days of the second collection going on sale on 7 September, Topshop's online webstore had seen its market share increase six-fold.

On the night of the launch, while Kate happily took to the dance floor in Annabel's, spinning around and showing off the flared black satin catsuit that, of all the items in her second collection, was probably the least wearable for most women, Jamie Hince was content to encourage her from the sidelines. Their relationship was only a few weeks old and Hince was unused to the voltage of attention that accompanied Kate. It was something with which he seemed destined to struggle as their affair carried on in the weeks and months that followed. 'I don't want to be part of lowering cultural standards,' he complained with no visible irony. 'If somebody like me, who is basically a nobody, is reported on for going to a bar, then what have we become?' He had a point.

Friends who watched them together breathed a unified sigh of relief at this new presence in Kate's life. Hince was a decent bloke and Kate seemed once more girlish and giggly and loving being in lust, if not in love quite yet. Linda for one must have welcomed anyone whose presence cast a shadow over Pete. The more clear water that existed between Kate and him the better, and if Hince could eclipse Pete and push that part of Kate's life further into the past then that was all well and good.

Kate had Jefferson to thank for making the introductions. He was dating Jamie's bandmate, flatmate and onetime lover Alison Mosshart. Given the intensity of the relationship between Jamie and Alison and between Jefferson and Kate, it might have seemed natural to assume some awkwardness, but while Alison regarded Kate with a certain wariness initially – she wouldn't be the first to feel threatened by Kate's presence – it turned out to be a remarkably amicable and uncontroversial 'swap'.

There was a lot about Jamie that appealed to Kate, a lot that was, in the light of her previous romances, predictable. First there was his love of rock and punk. Born in Buckinghamshire, Hince had grown up listening to the Velvet Underground – he even looked a bit like Lou Reed. His musical influences – bands like Captain Beefheart and the Magic Band, the Ramones and the New York Dolls – chimed with Kate's own fascination with and knowledge of music. The month after the Topshop launch, Kate appeared on a night out wearing a T-shirt with the print of a man's face visible beneath her partially buttoned blouse. Reports ran that it was a picture of Hince and that the choice of wardrobe was intended as a gesture of adoration for her new man. It was nothing of the sort, though it revealed something far more intimate between the two. The man on her chest was Richard Hell, the American front man of Seventies punk band Richard Hell & The Voidoids, an idol of Hince's and the man credited with originating the punk fashion look. This was real fringe stuff and when it was publicly misinterpreted the confusion must have turned it into a pleasing in-joke for the pair.

Then there was Hince's slightly self-conscious sense of himself as an artist. His relationship with Kate may have put him in the public eye, but he and Alison has been thumping away just left of centre of the music scene for nearly a decade by then. He had earned the nickname 'Hotel' from all the dumps they'd stayed in along the road, furthering their music, though their enthusiasm for their oeuvre had yet to find a match in the public. In 'downtimes' Hince would sketch, noodle away on his guitar or smoke one of an endless stream of cigarettes.

There was also a whiff of counter-culture about him, of the punk/art school sensibility also found in Depp, Jefferson – the only one who really *was* a former art school student – and Pete. Hince was nearing his thirty-ninth birthday when he and

Kate met. He was hardly a choirboy – though his veganism would somehow be equated with clean living in some corners of the press – but he was a grown-up to Pete's feckless child and a far more acceptable face of rock'n'roll. His presence at Kate's side at her second Topshop launch was proof of that.

In reality, on that particular night, it didn't matter to many whether Hince's place in her life would be permanent or fleeting. What *did* matter to most of the public was that Kate had finally ditched Pete when his behaviour had, many felt, conspired to publicly humiliate her. Enough was enough: Kate had not survived at the top of her game for twenty years without developing a shard of ice in her heart that meant she could move on and move up, however strong the bonds that threatened to hold her back and tie her down.

It is two decades since Sarah Doukas first caught that tantalizing glimpse of Kate in JFK airport. Nobody could have anticipated that, two decades on, Kate's success would be so great or so enduring. In December 2007, Sir Philip Green was listed number one in the fashion industry's bible, *Drapers'* 'Power 100'. He was praised for his influence, innovation, spending power, industry knowledge and star quality. He was praised, in the main, for signing Kate – a move that paved the way for a full-blown Topshop launch in America in 2008. Marks & Spencer chief executive Stuart Rose was number three on the list. Kate was number six. She was, according to *Drapers*, now 'more brand than model'.

In the months that followed her Topshop collaboration, Kate would launch her own perfume – the fragrance that, she said, encompassed everything she felt about being 'feminine, a bit rock'n'roll, a bit edgy, a bit light, a bit dark' was an instant UK bestseller – and invest both money and face-time in her friend James Brown's line of hair products. She would begin her twentieth year in the business with inclusion in the 2008 edition of *Who's Who* – news that would be met with much huffing and puffing by society's self-appointed moral guardians, who wince at the notion that highbrow and plucked-brow cultures could ever be anything but mutually exclusive. They are not.

Kate's cultural influence is profound, far-reaching and hard won. Certainly she works to maintain her physical allure. As the years have rolled on, she has added more beauty treatments to a once barely there regime of facials and massages. And while she may have been blessed with good bone structure, she has acquired, kept and listened to good accountants, management and legal advisers.

Many people have tried to define just what it is about Kate that is so compelling and enduring. Photographer David Bailey said that what made Kate so appealing was her 'democratic look. She's the kind of girl you wished lived next door, but she's never going to. She's almost in reach, but she's not in reach'.

It is the 'almost' which is compelling. In that 'almost' all the success, wealth, drama and beauty coexist with something altogether more familiar but, like a word lost on the tip of your tongue, elusive. After twenty years Kate has become an icon. After twenty years she has remained 'almost in reach'. And, after twenty years in an industry that works by the season, to have achieved one whilst retaining the other is no mean feat.

BIBLIOGRAPHY

Lila Says by Anonymous
Pete Doherty: My Prodigal Son by Jacqueline Doherty
The Books of Albion: The Collected Writings of Pete Doherty
Faithfull: An Autobiography by Marianne Faithfull with
    David Dalton
Memories, Dreams and Reflections by Marianne Faithfull
All That Glitters by Pearl Lowe
Kate by Kate Moss, with a foreword by Liz Tilberis
Archive editions of *Vogue, Dazed & Confused, Select,
    The Face, Elle, Harper's Bazaar, i-D* and *Q*

Index

Index

Index

Index

Index